The 1933 New York Giants

ALSO BY LOU HERNÁNDEZ
AND FROM MCFARLAND

*Manager of Giants: The Tactics, Temper
and True Record of John McGraw* (2017)

*Chronology of Latin Americans
in Baseball, 1871–2015* (2016)

*Baseball's Great Hispanic Pitchers: Seventeen Aces
from the Major, Negro and Latin American Leagues* (2015)

*Memories of Winter Ball:
Interviews with Players in the Latin American
Winter Leagues of the 1950s* (2013)

*The Rise of the Latin American Baseball Leagues, 1947–1961:
Cuba, the Dominican Republic, Mexico,
Nicaragua, Panama, Puerto Rico and Venezuela* (2011)

The 1933 New York Giants
Bill Terry's Unexpected World Champions

Lou Hernández

McFarland & Company, Inc., Publishers
Jefferson, North Carolina

Unless otherwise noted photographs and illustrations are from the author's collection.

LIBRARY OF CONGRESS CATALOGUING-IN-PUBLICATION DATA

Names: Hernández, Lou, 1958– author.
Title: The 1933 New York Giants : Bill Terry's unexpected world champions / Lou Hernández.
Description: Jefferson, North Carolina : McFarland & Company, Inc., Publishers, 2017. | Includes bibliographical references and index.
Identifiers: LCCN 2017011900 | ISBN 9781476664033 (softcover : acid free paper) ∞
Subjects: LCSH: New York Giants (Baseball team)—History. | Terry, Bill, 1898–1989. | Baseball managers—United States—Biography.
Classification: LCC GV875.N42 H47 2017 | DDC 796.357/64097471—dc23
LC record available at https://lccn.loc.gov/2017011900

BRITISH LIBRARY CATALOGUING DATA ARE AVAILABLE

ISBN (print) 978-1-4766-6403-3
ISBN (ebook) 978-1-4766-2461-7

© 2017 Lou Hernández. All rights reserved

No part of this book may be reproduced or transmitted in any form or by any means, electronic or mechanical, including photocopying or recording, or by any information storage and retrieval system, without permission in writing from the publisher.

Front cover: The 1933 New York Giants (courtesy of the National Pastime Museum, www.TheNationalPastimeMuseum.com)

McFarland & Company, Inc., Publishers
  Box 611, Jefferson, North Carolina 28640
  www.mcfarlandpub.com

Para Milagros,
un oasis en una tierra desolada, un espíritu indomable
al frente de la adversidad y privación.

(For Milagros,
an oasis in a desolate land, an indomitable spirit
in the face of hardship and privation.)

Acknowledgments

The newspaper search engine newspapers.com proved to be an invaluable wealth of information. It brought to my computer screen a broad range of period newspapers from across the country, from which I culled the lion's share of quotations used within. Other indispensable online sources were the statistically-based retrosheet.org and baseball-reference.com.

Source for the "true outcome" references in the "Introduction" is *Clubhouse Confidential*, which aired February 14, 2013, on the MLB Network. The November 10, 2016, *Clubhouse Confidential* provided the 2016 strikeout figures.

The book *Wins, Losses & Empty Seats: How Baseball Outlasted The Great Depression* provided helpful and informative numerical data, pertaining not only to baseball but to the population at large. Its author, David George Surdam, accessed the financial records of the major league teams of this era, which were presented years later during the congressional hearings investigating organized baseball in 1951.

Outstanding individual biographies written about star Giants players helped immensely in the understanding and development of some of the more iconic personalities detailed in this project. Those literary works are listed in the bibliography. My personal thanks, as well, to those SABR colleagues who dedicated a "Bioproject" to those players who happened to play for the championship team chosen by this writer to explore. They are duly mentioned in the appropriate reference section at the back of the book.

Table of Contents

Acknowledgments	vii
Preface	1
Introduction	3
1. The Infield Led by "Memphis Bill"	7
2. The Outfield Headed by "Master Melvin"	38
3. The Pitching Staff Sustained by "The Meal Ticket"	53
4. The Bullpen Stabilized by "The Pride of Havana"	89
5. The Championship Season—First Half	115
6. "The Game of the Century"	137
7. The Championship Season—Second Half	144
8. The World Series: The Terryman versus the Croninites	172
Postscript	199
Appendix: New York Giants 1933 Team Statistics	201
Chapter Notes	211
Bibliography	219
Index	221

Preface

I was drawn to this particular New York Giants team by one man—Adolfo Luque, who won the clinching game of the World Series at an age few athletes have been able to compete competitively. Luque was a remarkable international player and manager. I have used portions of other books to chronicle his accomplishments and am glad to be able to further supplement his persona with sections from this work.

The 1933 New York Giants became the first New York National League team to win the World Series in 11 years and the first without John McGraw as its manager. The club was populated with a few extremely talented players and a fine and interesting cross-section of members that reflected the general composition of all major league clubs at the time.

The champion Giants were led by one William H. Terry, their player-manager, who was in his first full season at the helm. After taking over the team the prior June, Terry made wholesale changes in a short period of time and quickly molded the club into surprising winners. Terry, like McGraw before him, had all-encompassing trade authority. In an era where there were few front office executives compared to today, and no scouting departments to speak of, managers, working along with club owners, greatly influenced a team's trading and purchasing of players.

For me, Bill Terry turned out to be the most fascinating New York Giant. As an individual, Terry had two defining characteristics: courage and fearlessness. He had the fortitude to go out on his own at a young age and to face the future without trepidation. Terry might have been a captain of industry had he not been athletically sidetracked as the captain steering the New York Giants. As it was, Terry became, far and away, the most diversely successful New York Giants graduate. Terry's biographer, Joe Williams, wrote that, at his death, the former Giants player was worth $30 million. While in uniform, though, Terry never developed a great affinity toward the national press corps, and as usual in such cases, the feeling was mutual. But that friction only served to make his job as manager a little less enjoyable. It never detracted from his greatness on the field. One detrimental result of the strained relations was Terry's delayed induction into the Hall of Fame.

An early example of Terry's fearlessness was his plunge into holy matrimony before he turned 18. He met a local girl, eventually followed her to Memphis and married her, and stayed married for 68 years until death did part them. In much of these sentimental regards, Terry was like many of the men in our story. At least a dozen of the married players on the team tied the knot with their high school or hometown sweethearts and maintained long, enduring marriages.

Because of volume concerns, I could not present the post–1933 lives of our illustrious team's members, as I originally intended. Sixty-year-old John McGraw succumbed to uremic poisoning less than two years after giving up the reins of his beloved team. Main protagonist Terry outlived his wife by a few years and died in 1989 at the age of 90. Mel Ott, as many baseball fans know, died prior to his 50th birthday, following a tragic automobile accident in his home state of Louisiana. Carl Hubbell, who had been a close friend of Ott, passed away on the 30th anniversary of Ott's death, November 21, 1988. He was 85. Adolfo Luque suffered a fatal heart seizure on July 3, 1957, while in a Havana hospital, where he was recovering from a prior cardiac incident. He was a month shy of turning 67. Luque's bullpen cohort, Hi Bell, had the misfortune of being the first and youngest championship team member to pass on. He was only 51 when he died after a heart attack in June of 1949. Reserve outfielder Howard Peel attained the distinction of being the longest living 1933 Giants alumni. Peel lived to the ripe old age of 94. Ten and one-half years after Peel's 1994 death, the last surviving member of the 1933 world champions, third-string catcher Harry Danning died on November 29, 2004. He was 93.

Introduction

Baseball and America were very different in 1933 from today. One might expect that in both cases. One striking difference in the former is that the game in 1933 had more action than today. The "true outcomes"—strikeout, walk and home run—accounted for 16.8 percent of results in a game. Eighty years later, entering the 2013 season, it was 30.3 percent and climbing. (The fourth "true outcome"—HBP—was not a computed factor.) The advent of harder-throwing pitchers and free-swinging, undisciplined hitters is diminishing the number of balls hit into play and reducing the engagement of the fielders, consequently depriving fans of more excitement. At the end of 2016, the strikeout rate alone rose to 21.1 percent.

The estimated population of the United States in 1933 was 125,690,000. As a leading economic indicator, the Dow Jones Industrial Average commenced the same Depression year at 59.93 and closed at the exceedingly higher level of 99.90 on the last day of trading in December. As of 2016, the national population was around 324,000,000. The same, but exponentially bigger, stock market index topped 21,000 in early 2017. Because the DJIA is driven by "forward looking" components, the higher trading values in 1933 did not translate into immediate relief for the downtrodden. Similarly, the great economic morass into which the industrialized world had been sunk, triggered by Black Tuesday in October 1929, did not materialize the next day, or even the next year.

The Gross National Product was measured in billions eight decades ago; today the total value of goods and services and overseas investments generated by our nation is calculated in the trillions. GNP cratered to 55.6 billion in 1933, down from 103.1 billion in 1929. The average worker's annual salary in 1933 was $1,045, for those fortunate to have a steady means of income. It was spirit-crushing year for the "average Joe" in America. A time for many bread lines and soup kitchens in major cities throughout the country. An estimated 15 million laborers trudged along without jobs. Unemployment peaked at the Depression-high of nearly 25 percent—skyrocketing from 3.2 percent in 1929.

Construction of the Golden Gate Bridge began over the first days of January 1933. Nearly five months later, May 24, the grand dame of America's bridges, in Brooklyn, celebrated her 50th anniversary. In the spring of 1933, gasoline was 18 cents a gallon. It costs three cents to mail a first class letter. For indulgence in ground coffee, a homemaker budgeted 26 cents per pound. A fashionable pair of ladies shoes would set the wearer back $2.00. A luxury item like a six-tube radio console could be had for $69.50.

In the world of entertainment, a ticket to the flickers brought the best bang for one's hard-earned buck—excluding possibly a bleacher seat at a big league doubleheader. For 25–30 cents, a moviegoer was treated to iconic films such as "Cavalcade," "Bombshell," "The Invisible Man," "I'm No Angel," "Dinner at Eight" and "Duck Soup." There were *three* Busby Berkeley musical spectaculars released within a seven-month time frame: "42nd Street," "Footlight Parade" and "Gold Diggers of 1933." And there was *King Kong,* which opened in New York in March to packed theatres.

The classic fantasy thriller may have been one of the few box office exception during the year, however. A passage from David George Surdam's 2011 book *Wins, Losses & Empty Seats: How Baseball Outlasted the Great Depression* stated that "motion pictures initially saw an increase in nominal consumer spending between 1929 and 1930 and held steady in 1931. The industry then experienced a sharp drop that reached bottom in 1933."[1]

Included in the price of most movie tickets, current event trailers and cartoons accompanied the feature films, whether or not they were well attended. In one such short that year, *Popeye the Sailor* made his first animated appearance.

Also making his debut, over on the radio, *The Lone Ranger* burst into parlors, fronted by the rousing refrains of the *William Tell Overture.* Versatile song-and-dance man Eddie Cantor owned the most popular radio program, while former vaudevillian Jack Benny, who celebrated his *actual* 39th birthday in February, kept building his wireless audience. *Newsweek* hit the weekly presses for the first time.

Beginning in April, the populace could legally whet their whistle with their favorite barley and hops suds-derivative for the first time since 1920. To celebrate, Anheuser-Busch sent President Roosevelt two cases of beer. In September, the company unveiled a new advertising campaign, dubbing its Budweiser brand "king of beers."

After the World Series, an opportunistic and now-repellent broadsheet cigarette advertisement made the rounds, touting "21 out of 23 New York Giants players smoke Camels," including all of the team's stars. Earlier in the baseball season, Lou Gehrig established a new record for playing in consecutive games, bettering Everett Scott's previous longevity record. In July, a month before Gehrig set his new mark, an 18-year-old Joe DiMaggio concluded a 61-game hitting streak in the Pacific Coast League. The first East-West All-Star Game, the Negro Leagues' answer to their white peers' "Game of the Century," was initiated to the delight of black baseball fans in September.

On the non-baseball sports front, the NFL incorporated two big new rule changes, moving the goal posts from the back of the end zone to the goal line and legalizing the forward pass from anywhere behind the line of scrimmage. A new indoor mile record was set by Greg Cunningham of the U.S. in 4:09:08. The New York Rangers won Lord Stanley's Cup. Italian Primo Carnera became heavyweight champion of the world after knocking out Jack Sharkey. In December, the Chicago Bears were crowned first NFL champions, defeating the New York Giants, 23–21, at Wrigley Field.

The same month, tennis champion Helen Jacobs was named "Female Athlete of the Year," one day after her male counterpart was crowned. That masculine equivalent was Carl Hubbell of the New York Giants.

1

The Infield Led by "Memphis Bill"

"'I'll take it,"[1] answered Bill Terry.

He had been asked by John McGraw if he was interested in succeeding him as manager of the New York Giants. Terry was stunned, as all of baseball would be, by the news McGraw had just given him: that he had decided to quit his post effective immediately. McGraw had called Terry into his office in the Polo Grounds clubhouse. As had all the Giants players that day (June 2), Terry changed into uniform and was on the field, anticipating the scheduled Thursday doubleheader against the Philadelphia Phillies.

The first baseman had not known what to expect when he was summoned. He and McGraw had not been on normal speaking terms for quite some time. After the initial shock passed, Terry insisted that, if he accepted, he had to be the *only* manager, the sole person in charge of the club. "I told him," said Terry, in one of his first interviews as the new skipper, "'if I'm going to be manager of the Giants, I want to be boss. I don't want anybody second-guessing me.' Mac was fine about it. 'I'll never call you, Bill,' he said. 'If you want to ask me anything, you send for me.'"[2]

When he was satisfied with the assurances from McGraw, Terry accepted the position right on the spot. McGraw urged him to take some time to consider the decision. Terry said he did not require any. His former boss suggested that Terry shower and change and meet him upstairs in Charles Stoneham's office. Terry did so, and in front of McGraw and two other front office men, the 33-year-old formally accepted the position from Stoneham in the owner's upper-floor enclave. All parties shook hands. "McGraw acted like a man who was glad to get a great weight off his back,"[3] Terry told a reporter afterward.

The Giants canceled their twin bill that day simply because of McGraw's decision. The Dodgers played two games in Brooklyn against the Boston Braves on the same afternoon. Stoneham was prepared to bypass the receipts from two games in deference to McGraw's declaration. It was not much of a sacrifice, considering how much money McGraw had made for the Giants over the years. Stoneham and his front office team must have also felt a need to prepare for the ground-shaking event and aftershocks that the news would generate.

"Like a bolt of lightning from a clear sky, came the news that John Joseph McGraw had resigned the management of the Giants,"[4] proclaimed the *New York Sun's* Joe Vila. If there had been a baseball Richter scale, this announcement would have delivered a record magnitude. "The Leaning Tower of Pisa had fallen and the Seven Hills of Rome were in dust,"[5] Grantland Rice described the startling news event. "[McGraw] is the man who typifies the spirit of baseball," another news outlet expressed. "His name is as synonymous to baseball as Rockefeller is to Standard Oil and Ford is tied to the automobile."[6]

One out-of-town writer offered a more grounded take on the surprising news. "Stomach trouble and sinus disorders have made life miserable for the most dominant figure in the game," wrote Quentin Reynolds, "and baseball to him had become a drudgery instead of the exhilarating battle it had once been."[7]

The selection of Terry as manager was nearly as big a surprise as McGraw's resignation. Dave Bancroft, former Giants shortstop under McGraw and now first base coach, had figured to be McGraw's managerial successor. Bancroft was not a "Terry man," however. McGraw's departure and Terry's appointment prompted the coach to hang up his uniform. The official announcement had Bancroft staying on in the Giants organization as an administrative assistant to McGraw. Unofficially, Bancroft was not thought to be "hard-boiled" enough to succeed McGraw.

Many years later, Terry revealed that McGraw would have preferred outfielder Freddie Lindstrom take over the team. The decision to put him in charge of the Giants came from Stoneham. If there was any preferred status on McGraw's Giants, among position players, Terry, outfielder Mel Ott and Lindstrom were the individuals most likely to have earned it. These were players whom, because of their talent, McGraw would or could not berate as he openly did other team members. Terry and Lindstrom were also known not to hold their tongues at any harsh talking from McGraw that they perceived as unfair. After the current 1932 season, Lindstrom, feeling he had been betrayed, or at least misled into thinking the prime appointment would be his, expressed his desire to be traded.

The Giants, indisputably, made the right choice with Terry. The new manager retained third base coach Ivy Olson and said he would take over along the first base coaching or assign another older player to the post. "I'm going to let them [team] relax and see what they can do toward getting out of last place,"⁸ Terry said before he managed his first game. He also relaxed conduct codes for his players that were in place under the prior chieftain. "They won't have to report to the park at 10 in the morning or get to bed at any certain hour. All I'm going to do is ask that they play good ball and if they don't do that for me then they're out."⁹

The day after McGraw stepped down, June 3, Lou Gehrig slugged four home runs in a game at Shibe Park. With few exceptions, the story of McGraw's resignation was still monopolizing the sports headlines in the country's newspapers and relegated Gehrig's gargantuan feat to reduced column space. Gehrig's manager was asked his thoughts on the bigger news. "McGraw must have been pretty sick," said Joe McCarthy, "for he is not the kind to give up baseball without a reason."¹⁰ Baseball's other long-tenured manager, Connie Mack, said: "The whole baseball fraternity will feel keenly the passing of such a man from active participation in it. To lose his brilliant mind is a blow to the game."¹¹

The Giants released a multi-paragraph, prepared statement by McGraw, which made clear that he was stepping down because of health reasons—"doctor's orders"—the result of his deteriorating sinus condition. Many newspapers published the prepared statement in its entirety.

Again, claiming the threat of rain, the New York club canceled two scheduled games with the Phillies on June 3 at the Polo Grounds. (The Dodgers played their scheduled contest against Boston in Brooklyn.) The local press caught up with Terry later in the day at his hotel suite on the Upper West Side of Manhattan. Terry was described by one writer as being "a symphony in brown, with his dark hair parted exactly in the middle slicked down, his face tanned by infield suns, and wearing his modish brown suit."¹²

Terry confessed,

> I haven't had a chance to get my feet under me yet. We're going to start fresh from the foot of the ladder and work up. We've got to win. In a couple of weeks, I'll have to be down to 23 players, won't I? We've got a good ball club. It is up to me now. I'm going to work with the players and I'm going to give them a chance to work with me. I told 'em all that in the clubhouse at the Polo Grounds this forenoon before they called off the games with the Phillies.
>
> The newspaper boys all had me down as not hitting it off so hot with the Giants club. But I never had any trouble with McGraw or Mr. Stoneham except in the spring when I wanted more money.¹³

Terry had been one of the last players to sign his contract for 1932. He had been rightly angered over receiving a 40 percent pay cut offer from his reported $23,000 salary in 1931. This after hitting .349 and barely losing out on the NL batting title to the Cardinals' Chick Hafey. He led the league in triples with 20 and runs scored with 121. The owners had the players over a barrel as the ruinous financial freefall that had devastated the U.S.—and world—continued to spiral to impoverishing levels never before seen. Players everywhere had to accept salary slashes or seem like ingrates in the eyes of the working class who struggled to maintain a roof over their heads. Commissioner Landis self-imposed a $15,000 cut in pay on his $65,000 annual compensation. Not even Babe Ruth was spared, having to stage a spring holdout to mitigate his reduction to only $52,000 from the $80,000 paycheck he received in 1931. No one was Babe Ruth, of course, but Terry, having hit .401 just two seasons earlier, seemed to be getting the exceptionally short end of the respect stick from his bosses.

On his way to spring camp in Los Angeles, John McGraw stopped over in New Orleans to meet with his disgruntled star. McGraw and Terry had not engaged in civil conversation for a year and a half, since a 1930 disagreement. McGraw's business sense always overrode any personal animosity he harbored at times with people. A closed-door morning session on February 19, in McGraw's hotel suite, did not break the stalemate, but following a second private meeting in the afternoon, a new deal was announced. "We have come to terms and we are both satisfied,"[14] declared McGraw, adding there would be no salary figures released. (The most often speculated compromise was in the $20,000 range.)

Facing the press alongside McGraw, Terry's initial response to the obvious question did not come across as very resounding. "Well, I guess so," he said. "Yes, quote me as saying I am satisfied."[15]

Seven months later, Terry was given a two-year contract extension, reflecting his dual capacity as player and diamond strategist. Though the Giants limped to the finish line in next-to-last place (72–82, and 55–59 under Terry), management was obviously pleased with the way the new man was running things. The top brass could not have found much to criticize about Terry's season with the bat, either. He hit .350 (second in the league again), racking up 225 hits, with 28 home runs among them.

The offensive numbers reinforced a months-old response Terry had given a reporter who had inquired whether the newly-appointed Giants field commander thought he could handle the extra burden of managing, while maintaining his customary high level of play at first base. Terry, who participated in all 154 of the Giants' games on the season, had replied, "Don't make me laugh."[16]

William Harold Terry was a focused, driven and intrepid man. These self-determining qualities eventually made him a multimillionaire—with his

1. The Infield Led by "Memphis Bill"

baseball salaries amounting to the smallest portion of his wealth. Bill Terry was, first and foremost, however, a family man, and his triumphs in life—on and off the baseball diamond—can be traced to his desire to provide for his family.

The only child of Atlantans William T. Terry and Bertha Blackman, Terry came into the world on October 30, 1898. As a youth, he spent many an afternoon watching Atlanta Crackers games with his friends. Unable to scrounge up the price of admission, Terry and his cohorts relied on scaling the trees beyond the wooden outfield fences at Ponce de Leon Park to watch the Southern Association games. His affinity for the game burgeoned during these lazy Georgian summer afternoons.

The youthful Terry did not have a stable home life—his bickering parents were constantly uprooting him during his pre-teen years, moving from house to house, new neighborhood to new neighborhood. The outings to watch the Crackers may have been the only pleasant consistency during Terry's young life. With his parents' marriage on the rocks, Terry went to work as a laborer before he turned 13. Apparently not close to either parent, Terry, with this act, exhibited the first strains of self-determination that would lead him to multi-level successes in his life.

His parents could not make their marriage work, and by 1915 had split up. Young Bill, who looked older than his years, had left home before the breakup and had already worked at jobs loading trucks and hauling heavy flour bags. (Terry would grow to 6'2" and tip the scales at over 200 pounds.) It was around this time when two eventful occurrences happened upon Terry. He met his future wife through a mutual acquaintance and started playing baseball professionally.

The ballplaying began in 1915 with the Dothan club of the Florida-Alabama-Georgia-League (FLAG)—as a pitcher. The 16-year-old Terry pitched two poor games for Dothan and was released to the Newnan Cowetas of the Georgia-Alabama League. He pitched much better for Newnan and returned to the club the following season. The same summer of 1916, his girlfriend Elvena Sneed's father was transferred to Memphis, Tennessee, by the manufacturing company that employed him. The Sneed family relocated with him. Terry was crushed.

Terry was sold by Newnan, after the club played out its schedule, to Shreveport of the Texas League, and Terry's pitching helped Shreveport nearly capture the pennant. Not yet 18, Terry married Elvena that 1916 off-season and honeymooned in New Orleans. Terry's parents did not attend their son's wedding in Memphis, where he settled with his new wife.

After a mediocre 1917 season with Shreveport, and with his teenage bride pregnant, Terry left baseball completely for a higher-paying job with a battery-making company. After the birth of his first son, Bill Jr., he landed a position with Standard Oil Company in Memphis—an association Terry would maintain within different levels of the company for more than 20 years. Standard Oil fielded a corporate baseball team that played once or twice on weekends, and Terry returned to the sport he was born to play. It was with the Standard Oil Polarines that Terry first started to play first base, a position at which he placed himself as the appointed manager of the team. He was still only 20 years old. He also continued to pitch. As a non-professional team, none of the players were paid.

In 1918, Norman "Kid" Elberfeld, manager of the Class A Little Rock Travelers, bought Terry's contract from Shreveport. Terry's decision to change careers left Elberfeld without a player. Three years later, in 1921, Terry brushed into Elberfeld's domain with his traveling performances with the Polarines, and rekindled the Southern Association pilot's interest. Kid Elberfeld was a turn-of-the-century player cut from the same coarse baseball cloth as John McGraw. It was hardly surprising that he and McGraw were friends. Elberfeld alerted McGraw about his former prospect and arranged with Terry to meet the famous manager.

The meeting took place April 1, 1922, at the Peabody Hotel in Memphis, during a spring exhibition stopover by the New York Giants to play the Memphis Chicks. Terry visited McGraw's suite. Anybody as young as Terry would have been awestruck by McGraw. And very few, indeed, would not have jumped at the opportunity to play within his organization. After all, McGraw's name was perhaps the most celebrated in the modern game. He led the most recognized baseball team in the world, and his club had won the most recently played World Series.

Unfazed, the 23-year-old Terry set a price for his services that would make him rededicate himself to baseball and continue to provide a comfortable life for his fledging family. But McGraw told Terry the $800 monthly wage he was seeking was too much. The uncompromising family man politely left the suite and headed back to his salesman job and part-time baseball playing at Standard Oil, without a single misgiving. A month later, a Giants executive contacted Terry. McGraw was willing to meet Terry's price. The transplanted Tennessean joined the Giants in New York, worked out for McGraw and made a good impression. McGraw, who, until then, had not seen Terry play and was guided strictly by Elberfeld's recommendation, paid Elberfeld $750 for Terry. As a favor to his former catcher, Roger Bresnahan, McGraw placed Terry with the Bresnahan-owned Toledo Mud Hens in 1922.

It was with the Mud Hens that Terry made his permanent transition from the mound to first base. Terry himself facilitated the move with stellar hitting and not-so-stellar pitching. The following season, 1923, the strapping player hit .377 for the Mud Hens and took over as manager of the team on August 1. In September, the first baseman was called up by the Giants. He played three games for the World Series-bound club. He obtained his first hit—a single off Boston Braves pitcher Jesse Barnes—in his first big league start on September 30. It was his only hit in seven at-bats for the big league club.

In 1924, three future Hall of Famers would make the Giants team as rookies out of spring training: Terry, Freddie Lindstrom and Hack Wilson. Terry caught the very early eye of Brooklyn sportswriter Ernest J. Lanigan, who "introduced" the new Giants prospect to readers in January of 1924.

> William H. Terry of 204 S. Willett Street, Memphis, Tenn. is the athlete of whom the Little Napoleon expects quite a lot ... and he may become as famous as the other William H. Terry, first a star with the Brooklyn Bridegrooms back in the 1880s. William H. Terry No. 2, who might just as well be nicknamed now "Memphis Bill," started out to be a pitcher and might be a pitcher yet only that John J. McGraw, who has owned him for a couple of seasons, told magnate Roger Bresnahan of Toledo to keep Memphis Bill out of the box and play him at first.[17]

It strongly appears that Lanigan may have been responsible for providing Terry's nickname.

Terry would later refute that McGraw had been responsible for making him a first baseman. He had already been playing first base with his corporate team before joining the Mud Hens. New York Giants historian Peter Williams speculated that it was more than likely a group decision reached by Terry, Mud Hens manager George "Possum" Whitted, and owner Bresnahan.

That spring Terry won a spot as back-up to first baseman George "High Pockets" Kelly—also an eventual Cooperstown inductee. A left-handed hitter, Terry smashed the first of his 154 lifetime home runs on May 16 at Cubs Park off Rip Wheeler. Terry socked two home runs on the day in a 16–12, Giants slugfest win. Terry hit .239 in 77 games as a rookie member of a fourth straight Giants pennant-winning team. He saw action in five games in the World Series against the Washington Senators and hit .429 (6-for-14) with a solo home run. The Giants were beaten in a tense, 12-inning Game Seven by the Senators. Terry started the final game but was taken out in the sixth inning, after the Senators had switched starters (two batters into the game) to a left-handed pitcher. In light of the extra innings that followed, McGraw is sometimes criticized for a premature removal of Terry. But the manager made the pinch-hitting move for Terry with right-handed hitter Irish Meusel, after the Giants put two men on base with no one out. Terry had been 0-for-2. The

Giants scored their complement of runs in the game—three—in the inning Terry was removed (6th).

In the off-season, failing to recognize the young player's potential or feeling a paramount need to improve his starting staff, McGraw was willing to deal Terry to Cincinnati for either of two pitchers—until the transaction was derailed in the final hours. "Memphis Bill Terry, the clouting first baseman of the Giants, is not going to play in Cincinnati next season," alerted one newsprint notice.

> The deal McGraw had pending with the Reds for the last few days failed yesterday when [manager] Jack Hendricks refused to give up Pete Donohue or Eppa Rixey, the southpaw, for Terry. Hendricks was perfectly willing to part with Adolfo Luque, but McGraw refused to add the Cuban pitcher to the Giants ... and the deal was called off. Hendricks will now endeavor to buy Jack Neun from the Detroit Tigers to play first base for the Reds next year.[18]

(The Reds' starting first baseman, Jake Daubert, had tragically passed away at the end of the season, following a debilitating illness.)

In 1925, the Giants fell considerably short of capturing a fifth consecutive pennant, lagging 8½ games, in second place, behind the Pittsburgh Pirates. Terry hit .319 as the regular first baseman in 133 games. An injury to second sacker Frankie Frisch forced McGraw to use Kelly at second base that season. Over the winter, the sophomore player was again one of the names McGraw presented to the Cincinnati Reds in a multi-player trade offer. The Philadelphia Phillies were also said to have offered versatile catcher/outfielder Butch Henline for the young Terry and veteran Ross Youngs, a proposal which McGraw immediately squashed. (It was well known around the league that McGraw wanted and needed an experienced backstop.) Pitcher Burleigh Grimes was dangled by Brooklyn in a deal involving Terry, but McGraw likely turned it down because of the salary Grimes commanded. By the time McGraw declared late in December that he would not be making any trades, it appeared Terry had wisely been removed as bargaining leverage. "John McGraw's announcement," read the wire report, "that he declined to trade George Kelly and [rookie] Fred Fitzsimmons for Edd Roush and Adolfo Luque was regarded by baseball men that McGraw intends to stand pat with his Giants for 1926."[19]

Why did it seem McGraw was so willing to part ways with Terry? Did the manager still carry a chip on his shoulder over Terry not agreeing to sign right off the bat with the Giants in their initial hotel meeting? The second-year player had brazenly held out for more money at the start of the 1925 season, which annoyed McGraw and may have been a contributing factor in McGraw trying to send the young player (and the rest of the team) a message over self-importance. (Marjorie, Terry's second child, had been born prior to the

1925 season. Given Terry's displayed conviction to provide for his family, the holdout probably developed from this blessed event.) Earlier in the summer of 1925, a rumor had circulated in several daily papers that Cincinnati Reds owner August "Garry" Herrmann had offered $50,000 to McGraw for the green Terry. The amount was probably not exaggerated, given Cincinnati's prior interest and needs.

McGraw possibly recognized Terry as an unpolished gem. He had said as much during the hot stove league the prior year, when his current, aging first baseman's name had also been bandied about in trade speculations. "Why should I give players like Terry and Kelly away?" demanded McGraw. "You can't pick that kind up every day in the week. They're too hard to get, and I don't notice any clubs offering to give me their equivalent."[20] Regardless of the praise, McGraw would have traded Terry if his price had been met, and the Giants would have been left with a gaping hole.

As McGraw was indicating not to expect any deals during the winter of 1925–1926, he also revealed his intentions of putting Kelly back at first base and returning a healthy Frankie Frisch to his normal spot at second for the upcoming campaign. This left Terry the odd man out, and the first baseman saw his playing time cut to 98 games and only 225 at-bats in 1926. He hit .289—the last time he would hit below .310. He did not elevate his standing when he held out again for a higher salary, which caused him to miss the first two weeks of the 1926 season. "McGraw has made no attempt to conceal the fact that he is far from pleased with a man who played two years as a substitute, yet demands a two year contract at $10,000 [per year]," apprised one spring report on the matter. "There isn't a doubt that he will trade Terry if he can get what he wants for him."[21] Flaunting the leverage he had in the contract impasse, McGraw was quoted as saying, "Let him [Terry] stay where he is. We don't need him."[22]

The Giants slipped badly in 1926, forging only a 74–77 record. The club dropped into the second division for the first time in 11 years. Somewhat lost in the disappointing year was the debut of 17-year-old Melvin Ott.

The following season, Terry emerged as a star, hitting .326 with 20 home runs and 121 runs batted in. He participated in 150 games. Clearing the way for the star's emergence, High Pockets Kelly was traded to Cincinnati for Edd Roush in February.

The newly installed first stringer made a resounding mark on Opening Day, April 12, 1927. At the Baker Bowl, Terry clubbed a grand slam and drove in six runs as the Giants cranked out 17 hits in 15–7 slugfest win. The first baseman had two other hits and scored three times. On June 16, Terry became only the second left-handed hitter to hit a home run over the left-center field wall at Sportsman's Park. (Babe Ruth was the first.) Terry collected three hits and four RBI in the Giants' 10–5 win. Also clocking a home run, and driving in four runs, was Terry's new teammate, Rogers Hornsby, who banged out four hits. Hornsby overshadowed Terry—and everyone else on the team—during the year. The previous December, McGraw had landed the superstar from the St. Louis Cardinals in a sensational swap for the dynamic but unrepentant truant, Frankie Frisch, and pitcher Jimmy Ring.

The Giants improved dramatically in 1927 with a 92–62 mark, a scant two games off the pennant-winning pace of the Pittsburgh Pirates. Battling erysipelas, a skin infection possibly related to his sinus condition, McGraw was forced to relinquish managing the team to Hornsby with the Giants 2½ games from first place on September 3. During the year, Hornsby clashed with the manager as a player, clashed with teammates as a manager, and had a bitter disagreement with traveling secretary James Tierney, who openly criticized a Hornsby-inspired play initiated by Travis Jackson. Hornsby, who hit .361, was traded in the off-season (practically given away) to the Boston Braves, in a transaction made by Charles Stoneham in defense of Tierney.

Without Hornsby in 1928, the 93–61 Giants also finished two games behind the league's first place team—Hornsby's former team, the St. Louis Cardinals. Of added significance, rookie pitcher Carl Hubbell joined the Giants near the end of July.

Terry duplicated his .326 batting average from 1927, playing in 149 games. He hit for the cycle on May 29 at Ebbets Field. He collected six RBI as part of the four-hit day. The Giants, behind Freddie Fitzsimmons, comfortably defeated the Robins, 12–5. On September 18, Terry hit his first walk-off home run. It was a tenth-inning belt that provided the Giants with a 3–2 win over Pittsburgh. The Pirates' Joe Dawson threw the fateful pitch.

During the same year, the Terrys welcomed their third child, a second son named Kenn.

The now-30-year-old Terry came back and punished the baseball at a .372 clip in 1929. He hit 14 home runs, drove home 117 runs, and accumulated 226 hits, including two five-hit games. The first came June 18 in the first game of an Ebbets Field doubleheader. Terry banged out four singles and a three-run home run. The long ball came against starter Dazzy Vance, who did not last the third inning. Scoring early and late helped Brooklyn nose out an 8–7 decision, however. In the second game, the Giants' initial sacker lashed out four more hits in five at-bats, but Babe Herman delighted a large crowd of 25,000 with a ninth-inning home run and a 7–6 walk-off win. The nine hits on the day boosted Terry's average to a league-leading .402.

The batting average had leveled off to .365 before Terry's second five-hit game two weeks later. Terry's output accounted for a quarter of his team's safeties at Braves Field on July 3, as the Giants overwhelmed Boston, 11–3. A home run and double by the slugging first baseman were six of the 34 total bases racked up by New York hitters. The Giants were four games behind the league-leading Chicago Cubs, but things went south from that point. Though winning a respectable 84 games, McGraw's club placed two slots and 13½ games behind the pennant-winning Cubs.

Ten days after the Cubs lost to the Philadelphia Athletics in the 1929 World Series, the stock market shuddered, in a prelude to the industrialized world's greatest economic downturn of the 20th century. Because equity trading was something far removed from the average citizen in the 1920s, the Wall Street collapse that followed a few days later did not resonate immediately with the catastrophic consequences that would follow. The sensational newspaper headlines notwithstanding, the public at large remained detached from the terrible financial event and could not sympathize to any great degree with the stories of fortunes lost overnight by previously wealthy speculators.

Reflecting the temporary social disconnect with the pending economic doom, baseball attendance in 1930 was significantly higher than in 1929. Fans flocked to the ballparks in both leagues, as there was an even sharper spike in offense within the already escalated hitting in the Live Ball Era. If 1968 was the "Year of the Pitcher," then 1930 was the "Year of the Hitter"—and the greatest "pure" hitter that year was the National League's William H. Terry, first baseman of the New York Giants.

In 1930, Terry reached the transcendent height of his craft with a batting average of .401. Terry did not miss a game on the campaign. He accumulated a whopping 254 hits, 139 runs, 39 doubles, 15 triples, 23 homers and 129 RBI. All the more extraordinary, he walked only 57 times.

Terry came out of the gate with two hits on Opening Day and hit safely in 26 of his first 27 games. Over the first five weeks of the season, Terry hit .427 and slugged .726. In mid–June, his average dropped below .400. In today's statistically attuned age of baseball, where players' agents petition major league baseball to have official scorer's decisions changed to benefit their clients for more favorable contract negotiation purposes, it is refreshing to note a scoring incident after a game involving Terry, which gave a glimpse into his character. "For a slant on the kind of fellow Terry is," one privied writer reported, "the first inning error charged to Lindstrom was transferred to Terry, at Bill's own request. Terry came into the press box and said it was unfair to give Lindstrom the error. 'Freddie's throw on [Ira] Flagstead's grounder was good, but I juggled it and deserved the error,'[23] said Terry." The play transpired on June 11 and had no effect on the Giants' 9–2 victory.

Eleven days afterward, McGraw moved Terry down a peg in the order to fourth, placing Freddie Lindstrom in the third position in the lineup. Terry hit cleanup for the rest of the season. Terry collected 80 multi-hit games on the year, including two five-hit games. Both of them came against crosstown rival Brooklyn, on August 5 and 30. In the former contest, the Giants faced Robins pitcher Adolfo Luque, who held McGraw's men at bay for as close to an entire baseball game as possible. "With two outs in the ninth inning Luque led, 6 to 1," wrote Tommy Holmes. "He had two strikes on the next batter. And then within half a dozen pitched balls, the sewed up ball game burst its stitches and scattered all over the premises."[24] After two men reached base, Luque permitted consecutive RBI singles to Freddy Leach and Freddie Lindstrom, before Terry followed with a clutch, game-tying, three-run home run. After retiring the Robins in the bottom of the inning, the inspired Giants scored twice in the tenth, but first place Brooklyn rallied with three runs in the same inning for a wild and exciting 9–8 victory. Terry concluded the game with a batting average of .407. Reliever Ray Phelps was the winning Robins pitcher.

Brooklyn had relinquished first place to the Chicago Cubs by the time of Terry's next hit-barrage against them. The second five-hit caper took place at the Polo Grounds. Four singles and a triple, as he drove in a run and scored once. The Giants carried the day, 7–4. The Memphis Mauler raised his average from .403 to .409.

As the season was winding down, baseball correspondents, as they usually did, began offering their selections for the best players, by position, in baseball—what amounted to a de facto all-star team. Someone polled John McGraw. His selections were: Terry, first base; George Grantham, second base; Lindstrom, third base; Travis Jackson, shortstop; Chuck Klein, Al Simmons and Hack Wilson, outfield; Mickey Cochrane, catcher; Lefty Grove and Wes Ferrell, left- and right-handed pitchers.

Babe Ruth, who was surprisingly slighted by McGraw's list, was also asked to weigh in. He modestly omitted himself from his top selectees. He chose Terry over teammate Lou Gehrig and did not differ from McGraw otherwise, except for two American League-leaning instances: Charlie Gehringer, second base, and Joe Cronin, shortstop.

Terry experienced just two hitless spells of three games in a row all season, and three other two-game droughts. He registered at least one hit in 129 of the 154 games in which he played. The first baseman racked up the highest on base (.452) and slugging (.619) marks of his career. Defensively, Terry led all NL first basemen in assists (128) and putouts (1,538).

Analyzing his season with 21st-century statistics, Terry posted the league's highest WAR rating at 7.6. Although his offensive Wins Above

Replacement mark of 6.9 trailed Hack Wilson (8.3) and Babe Herman (7.6) and Chuck Klein (7.0), the bump Terry gained on defense and the defensive deductions the others received, elevated the Giants' first baseman over everyone. Terry was a standout in the field. His Range Factor (assists + putouts/games played) of 10.82 was second only to former teammate High Pockets Kelly, who played only 89 games at first base with Cincinnati and Chicago in 1930 and pulled in an 11.06 rating. A left-handed fielder, Terry led the National League in Range Factor in all but two (1930 and 1931) of his ten full seasons manning first base. He is ranked tenth all-time in Range Factor among first baseman. A testament to Terry's outstanding glove work was published in a year-end *Sporting News* issue. The story included a begrudging-sounding compliment from Terry's manager and read:

> During the late season at the Polo Grounds, Terry not only batted with tremendous power but fielded his position magnificently. He executed difficult plays that reminded veteran fans of the days of Hal Chase, who had always been called the king of first basemen. "Chase was faster in making plays and in using his head," said McGraw. "But Terry today is making plays that put Chase in the limelight and is hitting the ball with far greater results. In my opinion, Terry is the best first baseman that ever played on my teams. At that time, Chase had lost some of his speed and he wasn't the smart hitter he used to be in the American League. Yes, I would say, all things considered, Terry is Chase's equal, if not his superior."[25]

Terry's average never dipped below .375 during the season. On August 4, the Giants' leading hitter cracked .400 for the first time since June 11. Heading into September, he was hitting .405. On the second day of the month, Terry pulled in a career high in RBI with seven. A home run, double and a pair of singles generated the mark as the Giants were 18–5 victors at the Baker Bowl. The next day, the splendid first baseman reached a late-season peak of .414 after recording three hits in the first game of a doubleheader at Boston. He then weathered his longest hitting drought (0-for-16), from his last at-bat in the first game of a DH, September 3, to his final at-bat in game one of a DH, September 6. His average dipped to .398 on September 19, following an 0-for-4 collar against two Cincinnati pitchers.

But Terry boosted his average to .402 by collecting six hits in a doubleheader the next day against the same Ohio club. A week later, Terry was batting .404, entering the final series of the season against the Philadelphia Phillies. It was a two-game set, September 27–28, at the Polo Grounds. The eliminated-from-contention Giants were six games behind the St. Louis Cardinals; the national newspapers were more focused on whether Terry would win the batting title than whether he would hit .400, an accomplishment reached several times by other players in the prior decade. Terry was battling it out with Babe Herman. With two games left for Terry and three for Brooklyn's Herman, the outcome seemed a foregone conclusion, measured by Terry's .404 average and Herman's .393 mark.

Terry went 1-for-4 against the Phillies, a single which drove in a run in the Giants' 5–3 win. Again, the primary focus was on something other than his batting average. "Bill Terry got a single in the fifth inning," read part of the game story in the *Brooklyn Daily Eagle*, "which scored Lindstrom and also tied the National League record of 254 hits, which was made by last season by Lefty O'Doul."[26] Herman collected three hits in eight at-bats in his doubleheader, and both men lost a point on their averages. The next day, Terry failed to register a hit in four trips to the plate, which included a walk. He lost two points and finished at .401. With a 2-for-5 game, Herman boosted his average by a point to .393. Securing the batting title—and not the .400 level—was the main thrust of the headlines that followed. Incidentally, Terry hit over .400 in every National League park but Sportsman's Park and Braves Field.

Some observers have implied that Terry benefitted from the "hitting curve" of 1930 batting averages. (The National League hit .303.) But simply put, no one else in baseball hit .400. Playing in every game of the season, Terry recorded 633 at-bats. Ted Williams, hitting .406 in 1941, received 147 bases on balls (compared to Terry's 57) and registered 456 at-bats. It was much more incumbent on Terry to remain productive with the multitude of balls he put in play, in comparison to Williams. Had he been more selective at the plate and walked more, it could be argued that Terry would have hit for a *significantly* higher average.

In the days before writers sought out players after the game for commentary, it is not widely known what Terry's immediate reaction was to the end of his monumental season. It would not be off base to say that he maintained his practical and unassuming character, that he said goodbye to his teammates, wishing them well in the off-season and, without fanfare, left the Giants' clubhouse. "If Terry had the colorful qualities of Ruth or some of the other widely advertised sluggers," recounted Joe Vila, "he would be hailed as one of the greatest players of all-time. But he is a modest chap, always minding his business, yet playing the game for all it is worth."[27] Terry could also have hung around and packed up his traveling trunk for shipment back to Memphis—or he may have already done so. More than likely he would have left without acknowledging the man who had written out the lineup cards for so many years—if the *man* had been there. McGraw had been missing from the team for two months due to his health concerns. In whatever state of mind Bill Terry left the Polo Grounds on September 28, a silhouette sketched with personal satisfaction was surely his companion. Not because he had become the first Giants player to win a batting title in 15 years (since Larry Doyle), or had hit .401, but because the best season of his career was sure to give him bargaining power in contract talks for 1931.

Not that Terry was scuffling for money. Things were going well for him with his off-season position with Standard Oil. The company, more and more, took advantage of Terry's increasing fame by utilizing him promotionally in the public relations end of the business. On the side, Terry was more than dabbling in Memphis real estate by this point. He had begun purchasing rundown dwellings, restoring them and converting the homes into rental properties. That same winter of 1930, he won a low five-figure settlement from a nationally known bus company after being run off the highway by one of the company's buses. Terry was traveling with his wife and three children. No one was injured.

The business-keen Terry, aware of the large crowds he had played in front of in 1930, asked the Giants for a multi-year deal. Not surprisingly, that was not well received by management, and this led to another holdout by the premier player. The Giants, for their part, were not willing to reward Terry at all for his stupendous season. "Although Terry is recognized generally as the best first baseman, if not the best infielder in all of baseball," asserted one report, "the Giants flatly rejected his salary demand. Terry was offered a one-year agreement of $18,000, the same salary he received in 1930."[28]

As the standoff broached the second week of March, Terry indicated a willingness to compromise. "Big Bill Terry today, the New York Giants' stubborn first baseman," read an *Associated Press* report out of Memphis, "slashed his holdout demands from $30,000 a year for three years to $25,000 for one. 'We don't want him, nor does any other club at $25,000,' replied Giants president Charles Stoneham, who had presented $22,000 as a final offer."[29] Stoneham also threatened to trade Terry.

Terry stood firm. "It will be $25,000 or nothing," he said. "I'll stay out of baseball all year before I weaken. I am in a position to stay out. I'm just as stubborn as Stoneham. Baseball writers say my trading price is $150,000. Do you think the Giants would want to discard a piece of material worth that much over $3,000?"[30]

The Terry-McGraw feud that had eliminated civil dialogue between the two was apparently put aside, as the company man and holdout began conversing for several days over the phone, with McGraw making the long distance calls to Memphis from San Antonio, where the Giants were training. Whether he felt a pressing obligation to his Giants fans, received a nudging acceptance from his wife, or could not resist the draw of the game—or perhaps a combination of all three—Terry acquiesced the most and agreed to terms on March 12.

"McGraw and I agreed not to disclose terms," he said from Memphis, as he prepaid to depart for San Antonio. "But the salary I will get is a nice one and I am satisfied."[31] Terry's desired $25,000 figure had been derived from the salary agreed to by holdout Lou Gehrig, who had recently come to terms with the Yankees. Gehrig had originally asked Jacob Ruppert for a three-year deal at $30,000 per annum. Terry withdrew his original multi-year demand when Gehrig settled for a one-year contract. Terry contended that he was Gehrig's overall equal, inclusive of his defense and what he meant to the ball club. Truth was, Terry was still the Giants' best player and biggest drawing card. In the end, the exceptional hitter accepted $23,000. Among a notable list of unsigned players around the same late time were: Al Simmons, Chuck Klein, Dazzy Vance, Babe Herman, and Frankie Frisch.

Frisch's 1931 Cardinals began pulling away from the National League pack in mid–July and never looked back. The 87–65 Giants concluded the season a distant second, 13 games behind. Terry had another stellar campaign. Playing in every game again, he hit .349 and led the league in runs with 121 and triples with 20. He stroked 42 doubles, hit only nine home runs, but drove in 112 runs.

Terry was apparently not seduced by the Polo Grounds' short right field bleachers, preferring, or content with, other long hits that did not leave the yard. In only three seasons did he hit at least 20 home runs. Terry said after he retired that when he first came up, McGraw convinced him to concentrate on hitting the ball up the middle. A man of his size and talent certainly could have hit more home runs than he did if he wanted, but perhaps he felt his average would have suffered as a consequence.

An example of this hit-to-all-fields mentality came on August 24, 1931. Terry ended the second game of a doubleheader at the Polo Grounds with a long hit to left field that sailed over the head of the Cubs' Danny Taylor, who fell down in a stumbling attempt to catch the ball, which skipped all the way to the bullpen in deep left-center. Terry circled the bases to hand Freddie Fitzsimmons a 2–1 win and a split of the day's games against Chicago. (Thirteen of Terry's 16 lifetime inside-the-park home runs were hit at the Polo Grounds. By comparison, the pull-hitting Mel Ott's only two IPHRs came in his home park, both early in his career.)

In the National League's closest race for a batting title since 1892, Terry's .3486 average fell fractionally short of Chick Hafey's .3489. Hafey's Cardinals teammate Jim Bottomley also hit .3482.

The next season, 1932, Terry and 23-year-old Mel Ott provided the top offensive production on the team. But with Carl Hubbell the only regular starting pitcher to pull his weight, the Giants regressed badly. Terry was again the model of consistent brilliance. Not once absent from the lineup, the star first baseman hit .350, with 42 doubles and 11 triples, knocked home 117 runs and hit a career-high 28 home runs. Four of them stayed within the Polo Grounds' outfield expanses. One exceptionally long drive was hit on June 22. Terry had plenty of time to circle the bases following the long wallop "that bounced off the Captain Eddie Grant monument 483 feet from home plate."[32] A hometown newspaperman added, "The ball never touched grass at any part of its flight. It landed on the cinders in the distant centerfield alcove that splits the bleachers."[33]

Later in the summer, on August 13, Terry took the more conventional circuit jog with three home runs in one game for the only time in his career. All three long balls were clouted against Brooklyn pitcher Sloppy Thurston. Hurling in the first game of a doubleheader in which all pitchers were treated like second-class citizens, Thurston's ineffectiveness did not cost him, as his mates bombarded six Giants pitchers for three home runs of their own—and 18 runs. Thurston, who had four of Brooklyn's 24 hits, pitched an 18-9, complete game win. The Dodgers also won the nightcap, by a more respectable 5-4 count.

Before his long-ball flexing, the veteran first baseman had jumped off to a hot start, hitting .397 in 13 April games. On the last day of the Giants' first homestand, April 19, the Memphis slugger homered twice, the second blast a three-run shot in the bottom of the ninth inning that tied the contest against the Boston Braves. The visitors wrested away a 13-inning win, 8-7, spoiling a six-RBI day by Terry.

At the end of May, Terry had slipped to .310. On June 1, he single-handedly produced the Giants' first run, in the team's 4-2 loss to the Philadelphia Phillies, with an inside-the-park four-bagger. Terry had to pound the Polo Grounds' pillows furiously to reach home plate ahead of the relay throw after his deep drive. Mel Ott followed Terry's exciting, second-inning hit with a more conventional circuit slam. With the loss, the Giants, 17-23, fell back into last place, eight games behind the league-leading Cubs. On sick leave, John McGraw had made a cameo appearance before the game, hoping to instill some life into his stumbling team.

The next day, Terry reported for work, as usual, in Upper Manhattan. After a pre-game warm-up on the field and notification that the Giants had postponed the scheduled contests with the visiting Phillies because of a threat of rain, he was called from the clubhouse into John McGraw's office.

Terry entered the office. He was instructed by McGraw to keep the door open. Terry would later admit that he thought he was going to be told that he had been traded.

While Terry and the Giants were engaged in their caustic contact squabble of 1931, John McGraw had already decided to move third baseman Freddie Lindstrom to the outfield and place rookie Johnny Vergez at Lindstrom's former position for the upcoming season.

"It's not quite clear why the Giants need another third baseman with Freddie Lindstrom one of the best in the business," wondered syndicated columnist Alan Gould, as did many Giants fans. "But they have acquired one of the Pacific Coast League aces in Johnny Vergez, a star for two years with Oakland."[34]

Vergez was coming off a standout year in 1930 with the Oakland Oaks, hitting .309 with 211 hits and 29 homers in 188 games. The PCL player did not shake McGraw's faith in him, beating out Urbane Pickering and Eddie Marshall for the job. A native of Oakland, California, Vergez had reached his hometown club after playing the 1927 season and part of 1928 with the Ogden Gunners of the Utah-Idaho League. He began his professional career in 1926, as a 19-year-old third baseman with the Class D Terrell Terrors. McGraw was said to have paid $35,000 to the Oaks' management for the five-foot, eight-inch, 165-pound player of French descent. Christened Jean Louis, and born July 9, 1906, to Gabriel and Theresa Vergez (Bordenave), Vergez was an only child. "Johnny's" certificate of marriage to Helen Fay Porterfield stated the groom's parents were both born in France. Vergez married Helen, a local girl and one year his junior, on November 13, 1930.

Vergez had quite a productive first season in 1931 for the Giants, knocking 13 balls out of the park and driving in 81 runs. He hit a respectable .278, though he slumped over the final two-and-a-half months. He played in 152 games, all of them at the hot corner. He was considered the top rookie in the majors at his position. Even though his team was a consistent winner on the season, Vergez and others could only watch helplessly as the 102-win Cardinals outclassed the league.

During the winter, Vergez was already looking forward to his second big league season, indicating an expected physical improvement.

> From the day I reported to the Giants camp at San Antonio the first of March, I started working at top speed believing I had to work my head off to make the team. As I figure it, the nervous strain I was under during these days and the early month of the season, took more out of me than from the regulars. Along September I was completely worn out. I do not expect to have to undergo this strain [again] and therefore I will have more strength and vitality to carry me through the summer.[35]

Little did Vergez know that his strength and vitality would be drained in a very different and much more painful manner in the new year. A few games into the 1932 season, Vergez helped lift the Giants to their first victory with a grand slam on April 17. The Giants were victorious, 6–0, over the Boston Braves, behind Hal Schumacher's two-hit shutout. Vergez had also homered on Opening Day, five days earlier. The two long balls accounted for one-third of his home run total for the season. The reduced power numbers reflected a similar decline in his batting average. Hitting in the low .240s in late July, Vergez was benched by new manager Terry. The right-handed-hitting third sacker regained his starting job on August 31 and closed out the season batting .261 in 118 games.

However, a more valid excuse for being "off one's game" was rarely had than by Vergez in 1932. On March 26, while the Giants were playing the Oakland Oaks in an exhibition contest, the second-year player twisted his ankle sliding into home plate. He had to be carried off the field by teammates. The injury turned out to be only a mild sprain. The same day, the player received news that his infant son had been stricken with infantile paralysis. On the evening of April 3, the Giants boarded a train to take them east in preparation for the new season. Vergez sent word to the departing club that his baby had died. (The child was named John Louis.)

Overcoming a family tragedy, third baseman Johnny Vergez contributed with an outstanding year at the plate in 1933 for the Giants.

The bereaved father rejoined the team in time to sock his Opening Day homer. For much of the season, though, he not only had his own grief with which to contend, but also the assumed responsibility of his wife's fragile health. She was said to be on the verge of a nervous breakdown over the loss of her only child. Johnny relocated Helen to New York and offered all the support he could to her.

On May 12, the Giants were in Pittsburgh when the terrible news of the discovery of Charles Lindbergh, Jr.'s body was broadcast. The announced death of the 20-month-old child may have been more personally felt by the Vergezes, with their recent loss, than most sympathetic parents.

After he became manager, Terry took Vergez aside. "Take it easy, kid," Terry said to him. "Don't worry. No matter what happens you'll be with us next year."[36] Terry was true to his word.

Someone who did not have to worry about a job on the club was Travis Jackson. A product of Waldo, Arkansas, Jackson had established himself as an elite shortstop since 1924, his second full year with the Giants. In 1922, Jackson debuted for New York, five weeks shy of his 19th birthday and with a handful of games left on the Giants' schedule. He appeared in three contests and was hitless in eight trips to the plate. Two months into the 1923 season, Jackson replaced starting shortstop Dave Bancroft, who was stricken with a case of influenza. The young player also filled in at third base, at times, for the ailing Heinie Groh, McGraw's overpriced trade purchase of two years earlier. "Jackson is the most remarkable young player developed in the majors this year,"[37] gushed Giants coach Hughie Jennings.

Travis Calvin Jackson showed he was a talented ball player at a young age. He was born November 2, 1903, and named after William Barrett Travis, the commanding officer during the battle of the Alamo. Jackson entered the minor league baseball ranks as a 17-year-old infielder in 1921 with the Little Rock Travelers, managed by Kid Elberfeld. A short time after recommending Bill Terry to John McGraw, Elberfeld tried to sell his famous baseball friend on another prospect, and succeeded. McGraw purchased the young Jackson's contract from Little Rock in June 1922, permitting Jackson to finish out the full minor league season. (With the Travelers that season, Travis committed a *Bad News Bears*–type error total of 73. Many of the miscues came on wild throws to first base, unleashed by his strong arm's erratic aim.)

In 1923, the Arkansan rookie collected four hits in a game three times for the Giants. The third time came on August 4, when, with two singles, a double and home run, he knocked in a career-high eight runs. The first-place Giants pasted the Cincinnati Reds, 14–4, at Redland Field. The win was the first of a surprising five-game sweep over a contending Reds squad. The Giants, in the process, hit the league's best pitcher, Adolfo Luque, very hard in two of the games, including this one.

After playing in 91 games at shortstop and third base in 1923, and hitting .275, Jackson became the Giants' regular shortstop in 1924. The move was facilitated by the off-season trading of Bancroft to the Boston Braves in a five player deal. One of the two most productive hitters for the Giants in the recently concluded World Series, Casey Stengel, was also sent packing by

McGraw in the transaction. "He is a great player right now," stated McGraw about the 20-year-old Jackson, following the trade. "A wonder boy, clean cut with steady habits and good sense. I am counting on him. He is a second Frisch."[38]

The Giants nosed out the Brooklyn Dodgers for the pennant by a game and a half in 1924. Jackson anchored the shortstop position for the flag wavers, who were no doubt anxious to avenge their 1923 World Series loss to the New York Yankees. His 151 games played were the most of any Giants player. In 596 at-bats, Jackson hit .302, with 11 home runs and 76 RBI. He committed a league-topping 58 errors.

Despite the defensive shortcomings, at season's end McGraw singled out Jackson as the main reason for the team's success. "This was the toughest pennant we ever won—and Travis Jackson is the man who did most to win it," praised the Giants' bossman. "He made many hits and many runs and was effective all the time in the field. Youngs had a great year and Kelly, too— but if you had to pin me down to one man, it's Jackson."[39] Six of McGraw's eight regulars hit over .300, with Kelly leading the league in RBI with 136 and Frisch scoring the most runs with 121. Outfielder Ross Youngs hit .356.

The Giants lost a heartbreaking World Series in 1924. The man who had played so well for the club during the regular season had a difficult time of it under the autumn limelight. Jackson hit an anemic .074, with two hits in 27 at-bats. He played every inning of the seven-game Series, which included two 12-inning affairs. He committed three errors.

The Giants infielder would have to wait nine years to play in another World Series. In between, Jackson's play propagated his standing throughout the league as a premier shortstop, though for the next three seasons he was hampered by injuries or illness that significantly cut down on his playing time. A knee injury in 1925 limited Jackson to 110 games in the field. A New York-based report pointed to the Jackson injury as a cause for the Giants' failure to win an unprecedented fifth straight pennant. "Travis Jackson, best short fielder in the league outside Glenn Wright," read the season-ending summary, "pulled a tendon in his leg, and without him the Polo Grounders couldn't quite make the grade."[40] The Giants were in first place by one game over the Pittsburgh Pirates at the time of Jackson's July 16 injury. The Pirates, who had been playing well all year, went 46–26 in their final 72 games to steam past New York and claim the pennant. The 8½-game margin by which the Pirates won places strong doubt on any one player's ability to have altered the outcome. Jackson hit .285 with nine home runs.

The following season, the shortstop reinjured his repaired knee when he caught a spike sliding into home plate in a game against the pennant-bound St. Louis Cardinals on May 14. He was lost to the Giants as a fielder until the third week of June. Jackson came on strong with the bat over the second half of the season. He raised his lethargic average from .242 early in July to .327, in 385 at-bats, by the end of the campaign.

On August 21, 1926, Jackson's double play partner, Frankie Frisch, temporarily took his leave of the Giants. Frisch deserted the club in St. Louis after enduring a berating from John McGraw the day before, in front of the team, for missing a sign during a critical point in a game. (Billy Southworth had tried McGraw's patience similarly on the field, prompting McGraw to trade the reserve outfielder to St. Louis in mid–June.) The Frisch-less Giants lost that day to the Cardinals and dropped 8½ games behind the first-place Pittsburgh Pirates. Frisch did not return to the team until September 8 when McGraw's 62–67 team had fallen 14½ games behind St. Louis. The Giants went through the motions for the remainder of the campaign and ended up in the second division for the first time in more than a decade.

In 1927, Jackson missed the first 22 games of the campaign due to an appendix operation. He made a gradual return to the lineup, playing a few games at third base before moving into his old spot. Upon his return to shortstop, he encountered a new double play man in Rogers Hornsby. In the batter's box, Jackson otherwise maintained the hitting form of the past season. His primary offensive numbers were a .318 average, 14 home runs and an impressive 98 RBI. Despite playing only 122 games at shortstop, Jackson's 444 assists were the most among his peers. The Pittsburgh Pirates gained the National League's seat of prominence in a close, hard-fought battle over the Cardinals and Giants.

In 1928 and 1929, Jackson, listed at 5'10½" and 160 pounds, led the league in games played at shortstop (149 and 149) and topped all short fielders in assists (547 and 552). In both campaigns, his average dipped below .300— considerably so in 1928, to .270.

Jackson's 1928 calendar year began with an upgrade to his personal life. The infielder's family had relocated to Memphis, Tennessee, during his younger years, and this announcement from the Bluff City, on January 24, delivered the enhancing circumstances: "Travis Jackson, New York Giants' shortstop, and Miss Mary Blackman of Waldo, Ark., were married at the Claridge Hotel here today. The couple left for a motor trip to Florida. Jackson's hometown is also in Waldo; he was raised directly across the street from his bride's home and the two have known each other since childhood."[41]

Jackson accepted another privilege upon his arrival in Hot Springs, Arkansas, a spring training site McGraw had used before moving on to Augusta, Georgia. "Travis Jackson, shortstop," one newspaper story noted, "will be offered the position of captain of the New York Giants when he arrives here tomorrow to enter preliminary training, John McGraw, manager, announced. McGraw, who arrived from Havana to take charge of the training of the Giants, refused to discuss the trade of Hornsby, who Jackson may succeed."[42]

"Jackson deserves the honor," commented McGraw, after Jackson's quick acceptance. "He is a heady, fighting ballplayer, and his steadiness under fire and his experience entitles him to the job. I know he'll make good."[43]

McGraw and the Giants came up a couple of strides short of the St. Louis Cardinals in the 1928 pennant race. The New York club battled down to the wire with St. Louis but dropped three out of four games to the third-place Chicago Cubs as the season was expiring to ruin their pennant hopes. Jackson hit 14 home runs for the second year in a row and drove 77 runs across the plate. The shortstop's defensive WAR calculated to a league-topping 3.5. He ranked fourth in WAR among NL position players at 5.4.

In 1929, the Cubs, who were contenders in 1928, handily won the National League pennant (led by MVP Rogers Hornsby). The Northsiders paced 10½ games ahead of Pittsburgh and 13½ in front of the Giants. Jackson not only improved his batting average to .294, but struck a career-high 21 home runs. His 94 RBI were only four fewer than his previous best.

On June 15, the Giants were involved in a wild and woolly game at Forbes Field, scoring in two extra frames to pull out a 14-inning, 20–15 win. Jackson was the hitting star of the 28-hit Giants attack, belting two home runs, a double and a triple, and knocking home seven runs. He also scored four runs. The Pirates, with 24 hits of their own, did not go down without a fight. In front of a substantial Saturday crowd of 22,000, Pittsburgh knotted the game at 11–11 with a three-run, ninth-inning rally. The battling home team extended the contest again, scoring once in the 11th, and then kicked up a fuss once more in the bottom of the 14th with three runs—after the Giants had dented the plate *eight* times in the top half of the inning. Some of the attendees exhibited bad behavior in the final inning, tossing empty pop bottles onto the field after Edd Roush was called safe at third on a close play. The triple by Roush started the Giants off on their big inning and led to the ejection of Pirates manager Donie Bush for arguing the Roush verdict. In the bottom of the 14th, with two outs and all appearing lost for the Bucs, fans in right field jumped out of the stands and delayed further the foregone outcome. The time of game was four hours and 17 minutes.

A little more than a month later, on July 12, Jackson hit the first of his two career walk-off home runs. The Giants shortstop whacked the first pitch he saw from Chicago Cubs pitcher Pat Malone into the lower left field stands at the Polo Grounds to provide the Giants with a 4–3 win, in ten innings.

Again in 1929, Jackson's glove work quantified as best in the circuit with a defensive WAR rating of 3.2. For the third year in a row, he led senior circuit shortstops in assists, with 552.

Jackson spent the winter working for a local drug store company in Memphis. He maintained the titular title of vice president and was also the manager of one of its retail outlets. As the next season approached, Jackson reported late for work to his primary job due to a contract squabble. He came to terms, which were not released, on March 5. Other notable 1930 Giants holdouts were Bill Terry, third baseman Freddie Lindstrom, pitcher Larry Benton, catcher Bob O'Farrell and outfielder Edd Roush. "Those fellows who stay away from training camp and neglect the early work are a detriment to the club," said McGraw in camp. "They slow up the whole team. They won't do it again next year if I have anything to say about it. At least if they do they will pay for it."[44]

McGraw would indeed make both Benton and Roush "pay" for their protracted demands for higher salaries. He traded Benton to Cincinnati in May and accepted Roush's sitting out of the entire season. The fact that Roush was getting up there in years (he was turning 37) and Benton was coming off a 12–17 season made the decisions easier to digest for both the manager and Giants fans. It is extremely doubtful that McGraw would have taken either course of action with prime stars Terry or Jackson.

Recurring knee problems and a bout with the mumps limited Jackson to 116 games in 1930. The exceptionally hitter-friendly year produced Jackson's highest single-season batting average—.339. He complemented the number with 13 home runs and 82 RBI in 431 at-bats. He posted an exceptional .915 OPS, thanks to a career-best .529 slugging average.

On April 21, the Giants' captain enjoyed his seventh multi-home run game, connecting against two Philadelphia Phillies pitchers at the Polo Grounds. Jackson's four RBIs helped pace the Giants' 8–6 triumph. As normally the sixth- or seventh-place hitter in the Giants lineup, Jackson still managed to knock in his share of runs. In five of his 15 seasons, he accrued 80 or more RBI. Considering the mashing of Lindstrom, Ott and Terry, who all hit ahead of him in the order, and the reduced number of games he played, 82 was an excellent total in 1930.

The Giants placed third, five games behind the champion Cardinals. McGraw's charges, under Dave Bancroft, played well down the stretch, winning ten of their final 12 games, but could make up no ground as the Cardinals duplicated the record in their last dozen contests.

A recuperated Jackson seemed to be especially looking forward to returning to the diamond for the 1931 campaign. "We have a great team this year with every position well covered and everybody in a winning mood," he stated on the eve of the season. "Don't count the Giants out when you are picking pennant winners."[45] But as it played out, the 87-win Giants were minimized in stature by the high-flying Cardinals, who, with 101 victories, soared 13 games above New York in the final standings.

The returned-to-health player was once more a shining performer with the glove. Jackson tabulated the highest defensive WAR ranking (2.8) in the league for the third time in four years. Playing the most games at shortstop (145), he totaled the most assists (496) at his position for a fourth time. "Jackson can get that ball away from him as fast as any infielder in the business," Rogers Hornsby had said in spring training in a discussion of infielders, "and he certainly can hand it to you to throw to first base for a double play."[46] For the second time in three years, the Giants infielder led the circuit in fielding percentage (.970).

Jackson collected the only five-hit game of his career on July 12. His five singles were part of a 13-hit attack that boosted a 9–4 Giants win over the Philadelphia Phillies in front of the home fans. The hits produced no RBI, as Mel Ott, batting ahead of Jackson in the order, cranked two homes, driving in five runs. In a side note to the 1931 season, the Giants and Yankees joined forces to help the increasing number of unemployed citizens in New York City, a reflection of the job-scarce times across the country. The Giants visited Yankee Stadium on September 9 and played its occupants in an exhibition game. The Yankees won, 7–3. A four-run eighth inning, featuring a Babe Ruth home run (the only one of the game), proved to be the difference. Jackson had three hits, including a triple. It was the first meeting between the two teams since the 1923 World Series. Jackson, Ruth and Yankees hurler Herb Pennock were the only players remaining on their respective teams from that October square-off.

Witnessing the proceedings were 60,372 fans, providing net proceeds of $59,642.50 for the intended "down on their luck" populace. The green batter's eye in center field was removed to better accommodate the invading throng. The contingent of news reporters covering the game also had to pay their own way.

The National League had slightly altered its ball composition in 1931 to try and balance somewhat the diamond scales that had tipped in the hitters' favor like never before in 1930. The American League had not changed their balls this season. For the first five innings, an American League ball was used. Three runs were scored by the two clubs (one by the Giants). The supposedly duller National League ball with raised stitches (making it easier for pitchers to grip) was brought into play afterwards, resulting in seven runs scored, five by the Yankees. Ruth's NL ball-smashed home run "cleared the screen in deep right center."[47] (The Cubs played the White Sox in a similar charity game in Chicago the same day, drawing nearly 35,000 spectators at Comiskey Park.)

The following season, the eventful 1932 campaign began for the Giants with a 13–5 home defeat by the Philadelphia Phillies. Jackson committed one of five team errors in the game and went 1-for-4 with a run scored.

On June 25, Jackson injured his knee sliding into second base on a double. His foot came off the base, and he was tagged out. It is unclear whether he overslid the bag or the pain from the injured foot caused him to come off it. On August 13, club physician William J. Walsh announced that Jackson, who had been sidelined since the injury and had not been responding to treatment, would be out for the rest of the season. The shortstop ended up with a batting average of .256. During his disabled time, Jackson served as third base coach. Utility infielders Eddie "Doc" Marshall and Gil English filled in at shortstop.

In late October, Jackson underwent surgery on both knees. He had damaged cartilage removed from one and bone chips from the other. The surgeries took place in Memphis, and Bill Terry announced that they were a huge success. "He'll be back at shortstop when the season opens,"[48] declared the months-on-the-job Giants manager.

Expected again to be Jackson's keystone mate when the season opened in 1933 was Hugh Melville Critz. A graduate of Mississippi Agricultural & Mechanical College, Critz was born September 17, 1900, in Starkville, Mississippi, and grew up west of his birth town in Greenwood. He was the oldest of three children, including younger brother Wiley Gillespie Critz and sister Julia Moon Critz. His parents were Hugh Sr., and Julia Gillespie. Referred to as Hughie, he had been in the major leagues since 1924.

Critz was an all-around athlete in college. His father Hugh helped his son prioritize his athletic path. "I told Hughie that if he intended to be a baseball player to leave football and basketball alone," said the elder Critz, who in 1930 would be appointed president of his son's alma mater. "I told him track was all right."[49]

It was under Hugh Critz's presidential tenure that Mississippi A&M changed its name to Mississippi State University. Hugh Sr., was a long-time professor at Mississippi A&M and a cotton dealer. His son became an apprentice salesman under him. After he reached the big leagues, Hughie told how he had gravitated away from business to concentrate on his major league-culminating trail.

Dealing in cotton may be pretty soft, but the money wasn't flowing in satisfactorily, so I hooked up with a semi-pro nine. Following the encouragement I received on this team, I joined the Greenwood club through the influence of some friends. After receiving somewhat of a reputation, I was swapped to Memphis from where I went to Minneapolis in 1923. I played there the following year and in 1924 I reached the big leagues with the Reds. I was always an infielder. Although I took trials at third and short, I stuck to second mostly.[50]

When second baseman Sam Bohne was injured in May 1924, Cincinnati had insufficient reserve strength to fill the void. The Ohio team reached out to the Minneapolis Millers to obtain the 23-year-old Critz to shore up their infield on May 29. In the negotiations with Cincinnati, the Minneapolis club received pitcher Bill Harris, $15,000 and two players to be named. The infielder gained two hits in his first big league game on May 31—against Grover Cleveland Alexander, no less. He also recorded six assists and one putout, and started his first double play (4-6-3).

Playing in 102 games, Critz hit .322 in his rookie season, including 14 triples. Critz never hit for so high an average again, but by 1926 he had established himself as the top-fielding second baseman in the National League. He led all second sackers in games played in 1925 and 1926, with 144 and 155, respectively. He claimed the most assists at his position in 1926 with 588, and topped the circuit with a .981 fielding percentage.

In 1927, Critz held out for a bigger paycheck. As holdouts were concerned it was quite long, actually spilling into the beginning of the season. The fourth-year player was seeking a $12,000 salary from the Reds. Owner Garry Herrmann unbudgingly countered with $10,000. The season began with Critz unsigned, and the Reds lost their first three games, all at home. Critz, who sported a .286 lifetime average after three seasons—greatly assisted by his rookie success—had become a fan favorite with Reds followers, as the

Second sacker Hughie Critz was a solid pickup by John McGraw in 1930. His play stabilized the right side of the Giants' infield for several years.

following news item from Cincinnati attested: "Cincinnati fans have draped themselves in sandwich boards and paraded Redland Field, flaunting the demand: 'We Want Critz!' Politicians have been sent to Herrmann and demonstrations staged in the streets."[51]

Herrmann relented and paid Critz his desired amount. The two came to terms on April 17. Critz started his first game on April 22. He had the misfortune of starting off slowly, hitting below .200 in his first 15 games. The second baseman was benched in late May due to a lack of hitting. But he rebounded over the second half of the season and hit .278 in 113 games. What was described as a "lame shoulder" also cut into Critz's playing time.

According to a *United Press International* dispatch the first week of January 1928, the Giants offered Rogers Hornsby to the Reds for pitcher Adolfo Luque and Hughie Critz. The deal was rejected by Herrmann and the Reds. The same report also told of an alleged Hornsby offering to the Chicago Cubs in exchange for Kiki Cuyler. The Cubs turned it down. "The Rajah" was subsequently traded to the Boston Braves by the Giants.

In a complete about-face from the previous year, Critz returned his signed 1928 contract before the middle of January. The 1927 salary stalemate had hurt both parties—Critz on the early performance end and Herrmann on the public relations side. Obviously wanting to avoid a repeat occurrence, both parties were evidently willing to be more flexible. No salary figures were released.

Critz again proved himself the most reliable National League second baseman, playing in 153 games. Critz and keystone cohort Hod Ford had developed into a dynamic defensive tandem. Shortstop Ford had formed the Reds' up-the-middle-duo with Critz since he was acquired from Minneapolis with two months remaining in the 1926 season. The spectacular leather flashed by the pair earned them the nickname of "Heavenly Twins" in Cincinnati.

Critz smacked the baseball at a fine .296 clip in 1928, with 190 hits. The former Magnolia State collegian compiled two extended hitting streaks over the course of the campaign—one of 20, and the other, 24 games.

There were no compensation contentions for Critz in 1929, either. In spring training, the 28-year-old was named captain of the Reds, something that must have been satisfying.

The Reds produced their highest scoring output of the season on June 5. The team scored in seven of eight innings and tallied a 21–4 triumph over the Philadelphia Phillies at Redland Field. Critz accounted for nine of the runs, scoring three times and driving home a career-best six runs on a triple and three singles.

1. The Infield Led by "Memphis Bill"

Less than a month afterward, Critz suffered a spiking on a hard slide by the Cubs' Riggs Stephenson. The spiking was so severe the second baseman was hospitalized, and it was thought for a while that an operation might be needed. Reds manager Jack Hendricks voiced an opinion that the spiking had been intentional on the part of Stephenson. The incident took place July 2 at Wrigley Field. The team captain did not return to action until August 17.

Critz played in 106 games and put up the best fielding percentage (.974) at his position for a second time. His batting average was not on par with his fielding, as he hit .247.

In late January 1930, there were reports that New York's John McGraw was intent on making a trade to upgrade his infield's weakest defensive link—second base. Critz was mentioned as a primary target, as well as the Phillies' Fresco Thompson. Andy Cohen and Andy Reese had been sharing the Giants' second base duties since 1928, the first season after the Hornsby trade.

Critz' 49-point batting average drop in 1929 had made him expendable. A slow start with the bat to the 1930 campaign lowered his home market stock even more. He was hitting .231 when the Giants came calling in earnest. The Reds traded Critz to New York for former 25-game winner Larry Benton on May 21. In that 1930 calendar year, Critz would turn 30 and Benton would celebrate his 33rd birthday. The trade turned out to be one of McGraw's best, as Benton was a well-below-.500 pitcher with Cincinnati in five campaigns, while Critz solved the Giants' second base worries for several more years. (McGraw's spite worked in his favor in the deal. Benton had signed late and had gotten off to a slow start with a 1–3 record and high ERA. The right-hander had been one of "those fellows who stayed away from training camp and neglected the early work" that McGraw had said in the pre-season were detrimental to the ballclub.)

Critz had to be excited over joining the Giants, viewed as annual flag challengers. During his six years with the Cincinnati Reds, the club was a contender only in 1926, when the second-place squad finished two games behind the St. Louis Cardinals.

Critz stood 5'8" and weighed 150 pounds. "He's just one of the little fellers in baseball," one New York writer said, "but he casts a shadow afield almost as big as the grandstand. Where the ball is Hughie Critz is practically sure to be nearby."[52] Critz was the sparkplug type of player who would attract the attention of one John McGraw. He had a mental approach to his profession that was also favored by the Giants' strategic disciplinarian. "You've got to be clever and always act intelligently in this game," noted Critz. "Years ago when I started in the Cotton State League, I hit upon the idea."[53]

Critz's standing as an elite fielder had not diminished, a sentiment that was held by most around the league: "Surely Hughie is that certain second-sacker John McGraw has been 'watch-towering' for ever since Frankie Frisch and Rogers Hornsby were shorn of their Giant uniforms. And so outstanding is Critz's infield chores that even the accompaniment of Terry, Jackson and Lindstrom will not dim this infield gem, who swerves to the right and darts to the left with machine-like efficiency."[54]

Another baseball insider who rated the addition of Critz as a positive for the Giants was Hank Casserly. The newspaperman disclosed that, as a result of the trade, some of his colleagues were prepared to elevate the Giants' new infield foursome over the famous Dead Ball Era one based in Philadelphia:

> The New York Giants are not winning too many ball games at the present time, but the acquisition of Hughie Critz from the Reds should bolster the McGraw infield and give the old veteran manager a great quartet. Some of the experts have labeled the great quartet the $200,000 infield, and with Bill Terry, Travis Jackson and Freddie Lindstrom working with Critz, the Giants must be rated a far greater pennant threat in the older major league than at the start of the season.[55]

Critz collected four hits in his first three games for his new team, but in the third game, May 25, he booted a grounder with runners on second and third in the tenth inning to allow the winning run to cross the plate at Ebbets Field. The Robins won, 4–3, behind Adolfo Luque's four-hitter. Critz, however, settled in from there, and for the third time in six years he bested all second baseman in games started with 152. The 30-year-old infielder posted a .974 fielding percentage, tops in the league, as were his assists (510) and putouts (398).

Critz hit .265 for the Giants (.260 overall) on the season. He must have felt as if the season-long hitting parade of 1930 had passed him by, especially since everyone else on the Giants infield hit .339 or higher. A September stretch run by the Giants to overtake the league's top teams, St. Louis and Chicago, fell considerably short.

The entire Giants infield was late coming into the fold in 1931 because of shared contract issues. Critz finally arrived at the Giants' camp in San Antonio on March 1. When the season commenced, the second baseman had several good days with the lumber. A four-hit day against the Phillies on April 24 and a 5-for-5 hit-fest versus the Boston Braves on May 1 helped boost Critz's average well over .300 early in the season. In the former game, the teams played to a 12-inning, 7–7 tie, ended by darkness at the Polo Grounds. Against the Braves, Critz hit a solo home run and sprayed four singles, as Bill Walker pitched a 5–0 win at home.

In June, Critz was sidelined with what was described as a sore arm, then a bad shoulder. He had injured his shoulder on a play at second base, presumably sliding as he tried to avoid contact with an infielder making a double play pivot. The Giants lost their starting second baseman for weeks at a time during the summer, as he tried to grit through playing on a semi-regular basis. On August 31, Critz announced that he was leaving the club in an attempt to rehabilitate his sore arm back home. He played his last game August 25. The Giants were in second place, eight games behind the eventual National League champion St. Louis Cardinals.

The Giants had contingency plans for 1932 to move Freddie Lindstrom back to the infield if Critz's arm failed to improve. This was something McGraw did not want to do. McGraw had plugged in Bill Hunnefield at second base in 1931, obtaining him off waivers from the Boston Braves. Hunnefield had apparently not made an impression with McGraw during his fill-in time at second base, for he was optioned to Jersey City prior to the start of spring camp. Critz returned his 1932 signed contract prior to the Giants opening camp in February, with plans on further working his arm into shape.

Happily for the eight-year veteran, his throwing appendage responded to all early trials and he returned to the Giants' starting lineup. In fact, he led the league in at-bats with 659, playing in 151 games. He recorded 182 hits, the second-highest total of his career.

Critz started off hot with the bat. He collected his second career five-hit game on April 19, one of the safeties a double. He drove in one of the Giants' runs in their extra-inning, 8–7 home loss to the Boston Braves. Bill Terry knocked home all the others on the strength of two home runs and a triple. The second baseman was leading the league in hitting at .382 after games of May 8. But Critz's return to the field and his good hitting did not have the expected effect on New York. From the outset, the team could not find its traction and was a second division club for the entire season. Though his final batting average settled at .276, Critz was still comfortably in the top ten in hitting in the league on June 2, the consequential day John McGraw stepped down as manager.

2

The Outfield Headed by "Master Melvin"

It is not often a player arrives at a big league training camp with his father. Then again, not often does a player who is a week shy of his 17th birthday receive such an opportunity as Melvin Ott did in February 1926. The proud parent, Charles Ott, a cottonseed oil factory worker and former semi-pro baseball player, accompanied his son from their hometown of Gretna, Louisiana, to the New York Giants' spring training facility in Sarasota, Florida.

The opportunity had been given to the young Ott by one John McGraw himself. The Giants manager had received Ott the previous September when the 16-year-old showed up at the Polo Grounds with a letter of recommendation from a well-to-do McGraw acquaintance named Harry Williams. Fearing his true age would compromise his chance, Ott told McGraw that he was 17, and was given various tryouts. Ott impressed the Giants' authoritarian enough that he told the boy he would send a contract to him over the winter with orders to report to spring training in Florida.

> I was large for my age. When I was only 11 years old I played ball nearly every day in the year. I also played basketball and football. I became very fast and strong. Then when I was only 12 years old, I use to go around a good deal with my father and uncle. They took me to ball games in New Orleans and almost everywhere they went. Being with older men so much must have made me old for my years. I remember I spent more of my time with them than with boys of my own age.[1]

McGraw not only recognized Ott's raw talent immediately, he quickly foresaw a hindrance the player would have to confront on the defensive side. Ott had been a catcher in the majority of his brief, non-organized baseball playing, and he had presented himself as one to McGraw. During training in Sarasota, McGraw hinted at his plans for Ott, while singing his praise. "A youngster by the name of Ott is the best looking recruit in the camp," McGraw told one writer. "I am afraid he is too light for a catcher. The outfield may be

2. The Outfield Headed by "Master Melvin"

his right place. But of one thing I am positive, he can hit."[2] McGraw's assessments were correct on all counts, especially about the hitting.

Melvin Thomas Ott was born March 2, 1909, the second of three children to Charles and his wife Caroline. Mel had an older sister, Marguerite, and a younger brother, Charles, was to follow. At a young age, Mel developed the sharp hand eye coordination that would help him excel at baseball. Mel was an avid marbles player as a boy in Gretna, a suburb of New Orleans. Although not physically imposing by any means, he eventually grew to 5'9" and 170 pounds.

The biggest obstacle Ott encountered on the way to eventual stardom came from an unexpected place.

> The hardest job I ever had in baseball, harder even than making good for McGraw, was in getting my mother's permission to leave home and go away to New York. It was all right with my dad. He was an old time [semi-pro] ball player and proud of my chance to go with the Giants. But with my mother it was different. Dad and I had a tough time getting her to consent to that New York trip. And then, besides, she did not want me to play baseball for a living.[3]

Ott's mother would soon have a change of heart. Ott himself had not taken the decision to abandon high school lightly. His comments on the matter indicated that education was something to be valued. "I had thought to go through [to] college," he stated, "but I believe that winning a berth on a big league ball club is about as helpful to a boy in the development of his character, his wits and resources as any course in college."[4]

The Hall of Famer-to-be began his career on April 27, 1926, after McGraw took him north with the big club at the tender age of 17. He struck out as a pinch-hitter at the Baker Bowl in a game the Giants rallied late to win, 9–8. His role on the team, until the latter part of August, was strictly that of an emergency hitter—except for one game in which he pinch-ran. He was hitting .375 (9-for-24) in that capacity when he received his first major league start on August 21. At Sportsman's Park, Ott took an 0-for-4 collar as the Giants were defeated, 3–1, by St. Louis. "My first fielding chance," Ott later recalled, "struck my right wrist and bounced over my shoulder for a two-base error."[5] Ott played ten games in the field, all in left field. In 60 at-bats, the precocious player hit .383.

In 1927, the Giants turned over their starting outfield. Star center fielder Ed Roush was obtained from Cincinnati in exchange for High Pockets Kelly. Roush bumped Ty Tyson from the position he had held most of 1926. Right fielder Ross Youngs was stricken with Bright's Disease and played his last game in August of 1926. Left fielder Irish Meusel was not brought back. (In 1926, both Youngs and Meusel had mentored the young Ott as a big-league

Mel Ott demonstrates the distinctive batting stance that helped him accumulate unprecedented power numbers for many years in the National League.

outfielder in training. Youngs took the time to instruct Ott on how best to play the caroms off the right field wall at the Polo Grounds.) George Harper and Heinie Mueller were obtained in trades to roam right and left fields, respectively. Ott and Ty Tyson were the backup flychasers.

2. The Outfield Headed by "Master Melvin"   41

Ott hit the first of his 511 home runs on July 18. It was an inside-the-park hit that eluded Cubs center fielder Hack Wilson's shoestring catch attempt. Ott circled the bases as the ball rolled deep into the Polo Grounds' center field pastures. Ott played in 82 games and hit .282 in 163 at-bats. He struck out an outstandingly low nine times against the much older opposing pitchers. The player received his first taste of a pennant chase as the Giants came on strong in August and September to give the champion Pittsburgh Pirates a strong run for their money.

In spring training 1928, the idea of using Ott as a second baseman, in case Rogers Hornsby's replacement, Andy Cohen, did not make the grade, was toyed with by McGraw. Ott worked out at the bag, but in the end the tinkering was ended. Ott, who was described as "thick-legged," was not suited for the position. He was a "boy with the legs of a piano and the smile of a cherub,"[6] as *Brooklyn Eagle* writer Harold C. Burr described him. (Ott did play five games at second base early in the season when Andy Cohen came down with a bad case of the flu.)

McGraw had been bringing his young prodigy along slowly. Smartly, he made sure to slot Ott, a left-handed hitter, as exclusively as possible against right-handed pitchers in his rookie year, slowly exposing him to southpaws after that. In 1929, he finally unfettered Ott to try and make a mark against all types of National League hurlers. The Giants revamped their outfield again in 1928. Ott was placed in right field for all but a few of his games, alongside promising center fielder Jimmy Welsh, who was obtained in the Hornsby dismissal to Boston. Lefty O'Doul, whom the Giants purchased from the Pacific Coast League, was stationed in left. Edd Roush was injured much of the season and was lost to the Giants following surgery to repair an abdominal muscle tear in August; he played in only 46 games. George Harper was traded to St. Louis for catcher Bob O'Farrell. Heinie Mueller was sent to Toledo in the American Association.

Ott was the most productive of the new outfield troupe. Playing in 124 games, he hit 18 home runs and pushed 77 runs across the plate. The home runs were the most on the club. It was the first of 18 straight seasons Ott would lead the team in four-base wallops, a major league record not likely to be challenged under the game's long-established free-market practices. Ott improved his average to .322. Despite his good efforts, and those of others, for the second year in a row the Giants came up a pair of games short in the quest for a pennant.

On March 8, 1929, Ott clocked the first home run of spring training for the Giants in an intrasquad game against left-hander Floyd Johnson, a prelude to the breakout season that was in store for the youthful player. On April 3, the Giants battered the Cleveland Indians, 10–1, in an exhibition game played at New Orleans. Half of the crowd was said to have come from nearby Gretna to see their favorite son play.

Ott was not only the natural favorite of the residents of the Mardi Gras City and vicinity, but already had nary a rival as the best-liked teammate on the Giants. The reserved and polite Southern comportment he displayed from the first day he joined the Giants, along with the bashfulness of his youth, completely endeared him to all. "His voice when he talks to you is low and deep, but his enunciation is clear," explained one writer. "He has ... a charm that is most natural and unassuming."[7]

It was not only teammates and sportswriters that Ott won over. John McGraw, that crusty Giants autocrat, actually developed a soft spot for Ott, who now, entering his fourth big league season, was *still* not old enough to vote. Ott's respectful, wide-eyed youth—and obvious talent—proved too irresistible even for the curmudgeon of Coogan's Bluff. During his first training camp, McGraw had shepherded Ott around, to the elbow-nudging surprise of everyone. McGraw made no effort to hide the special interest he had in the high school-age boy. "It was almost as though McGraw were playing baseball again in the person of the youngster,"[8] said one New York writer of the initial relationship. The personal attention given to Ott by McGraw elevated Ott to being McGraw's apparent ward, from which came the benevolent nickname of "Master Melvin." From their first meeting, through all the remaining days of his life, Ott would refer to his first big league manager as "Mr. McGraw."

McGraw assigned Freddie Lindstrom to room with Ott on the road when the youngster broke in, in a type of guardian role, even though Lindstrom was only three years older than Ott. Trouble was, Lindstrom sometimes needed "guarding" himself. McGraw became displeased with Lindstrom and read him the riot act on more than one occasion for allegedly being a bad influence on Ott. The arrangement had been most agreeable to Ott. He would reveal that Lindstrom was his baseball hero, stemming from Lindstrom's youthful participation in the 1924 World Series. When Carl Hubbell joined the team later, Ott began rooming with him.

It did not matter where and with whom Ott was setting down his suitcases in 1929, when he established himself as the most prolific hitter on the Giants and baseball's newest star. Ott produced a special game on May 16, in the second game of a doubleheader at Braves Field. The story lead in one newspaper bitingly reminded everyone that the Giants were off to a slow start, before spotlighting Ott.

2. The Outfield Headed by "Master Melvin"

> The Giants became tired of losing games one at a time. They did twice as good yesterday. They lost two to the Boston Braves, 4–3 and 5–4. The McGrawmen, minus McGraw, who remained in New York, for sinus trouble treatments, seemed well on their way to win the second game when things began to pop, pop good and hard from the Braves' bats. Mel Ott, the kid outfielder of the Giants, did heavy execution with the stick.... In five trips to the plate in the second game, Ott banged out four hits, a single, double, triple and a homer.[9]

Two days later, in the same locale, Ott homered in the last inning of both games of another doubleheader. In the first game, with the Giants trailing by two runs and one out, Ott's ninth home run of the campaign tied the contest, 4–4. But the Braves scratched across a run in the bottom of the stanza to pull out the 5–4 win. In the nightcap, Ott hit a solo home run in the top of the tenth inning to break a deadlock; the Giants held on for a 6–5 win.

Ott's most recent slugging escapades elicited noteworthy praise in the press. "Ott is just 20 years old now," wrote Tommy Holmes, "and he leads the sluggers of both major leagues with ten home runs. He is a pleasant, round-faced, modest kid whom the Giants say may never change, no matter how many home runs he may hit. The boys on the club call him 'Baby Face' and 'Sunshine' [because] he is always smiling and always cheerful."[10]

At the Baker Bowl a month later, June 19, Ott drove in six runs with two home runs and two doubles, leading the Giants to a 15–14, extra-inning slugfest win. It was the first of eight times Ott would knock home at least half a dozen runs in a game in his career. Ott's second double sent home the game-winning run in the 11th inning. It was the first game of a doubleheader. The Giants continued their free-swinging ways in the second engagement, winning 12–6. Ott had two more doubles and a single. The outfielder hit a blistering .537 in ten games at the Baker Bowl in 1929, including five home runs and *21* RBI.

At the end of the season, on October 5, the Philadelphia club refused to pitch to Ott in the second game of a Baker Bowl doubleheader—the Giants' next-to-last game of the year—in order to conserve the slim home run lead their own Chuck Klein had over Ott, 43 to 42. "The Phillies administered the bases on ball treatment to Melvin Ott," explained one wire report. "He was passed once in the opener and five times in the second game. Ott has one more game in which to tie or better Klein's mark—at Boston tomorrow—but because of the size of the Braves' field, his chance is slim."[11]

Klein had broken the tie with Ott in the first game, socking his 43rd homer against Carl Hubbell. Ott went 1-for-3 with a walk and scored a run in the Giants' 5–4 defeat. In the nightcap, Ott singled in his first at-bat—and then was walked intentionally his next five trips to the plate. Ott biographer Fred Stein provided further commentary: "The last walk came with the bases loaded, forcing in a run, and Mel was so disgusted, with the Giants having a lopsided lead, he deliberately stepped off first base and allowed himself to be tagged out."[12]

To be clear, there was nothing strategic behind the walks. The Giants broke the game open early, with nine of their 12 runs coming in the first four innings. The Phillies were held to three runs in nine innings. Burt Shotton was the Phillies manager orchestrating the poor display of sportsmanship. Chuck Klein went 0-for-5 in what was his and the Phillies' last game of the season.

Ott batted leadoff in the Giants' final game, October 6, at Boston. But Ott did not homer. He posted a 2-for-4 day at the dish, with one walk, and finished one circuit clout behind Klein. The only other discontent Ott could have drawn from the season was the Giants' inability to contend for the pennant after the middle of July.

Over the course of the season, the baby-faced basher hit .328 in 150 games. He drove in a mountainous 151 runs, second in the league. His slugging totals were career highs, as were his 138 runs scored. The young swatter quickly earned the respect of National League pitchers by drawing a circuit-leading 113 walks. Showing all-around ability, Ott led all right fielders in assists with 25. He initiated a league-best 12 double plays with outfield throws. His offensive WAR was 6.8, third-best in the National League. Including his defensive merits, Ott tied with Lefty O'Doul for the second-highest WAR composite at 7.4, behind only the great Rogers Hornsby's 10.4.

After a brief, non-contentious holdout, Ott signed his contract for the 1930 season, announced on February 11, 1930, by James Tierney. The Giants' club and press secretary had been the first team official the overwhelmed Ott had met when he first arrived in New York from Louisiana in the late summer of 1925. The teenage Southern yokel had inadvertently showed up at the Giants' mid-town Manhattan offices. It was Tierney who directed Ott to the Polo Grounds, looking like one big city writer would later describe as "a rosy-cheeked young kid, sloshing around ill at ease in his first pair of long trousers."[13] Ott then had to wait a few days until the Giants returned from a road trip before he met with and was tried out by McGraw.

There was no public sparring over the contract disagreement in 1930. The respectful young boy had developed a mild-mannered, if not bland, persona as a young man—one which too often frustrated the New York media. Not many players could have hit 42 home runs more quietly in the pre-eminent media center of the country than did Ott in 1929. Ott's dissatisfaction over the salary matter can be detected only in the late return of the contract.

In the spring of 1930, McGraw once again tinkered with making Ott a second baseman, a decision borne from the manager's unhappiness with Andy Cohen, and others, at the bag. Ott practiced and played games around the keystone. But by the end of camp, as the Giants began their usual spring exhibition tour through the South, McGraw's own adulation of Ott appeared to have indirectly put the notion to rest, judging from this report from New Orleans:

> If the New York Giants stay here much longer, they'll lose the services of Mel Ott, the one time wonder boy who clouts them far and often. This is Ott's native city and apparently he could be elected mayor without making a speech. Everywhere the Giants go, Ott is pointed out, the hero of the hour. And the city has taken to John McGraw, as well, ever since he declared Ott to be "a phenomenal outfielder and the greatest natural hitter in the business."[14]

Ott's popularity was not limited to his biological home environs. He was gaining an ever-increasing following at the Polo Grounds. A section of the bleachers above the right field wall had been dubbed "Ottville," where fans of the power hitter could congregate and cheer on a united front.

In 1928, Ott's first year as a regular, he hit in every place in the batting order from second to seventh. In 1929, Ott hit mostly cleanup over the first three months of the season, then was moved down one notch in late July when McGraw seemingly decided on Terry as his fourth-place hitter. In 1930, Ott hit fifth in the majority of his games, with Terry batting ahead of him, a placement he would mostly stay in for the remainder of McGraw's tenure.

On June 7, 1930, Ott connected for two three-run home runs against St. Louis Cardinals pitcher Bill Hallahan, both bopped into the "Ottville" bleachers. It was a rainy Saturday afternoon in New York. Harold C. Burr provided a clever newspaper lead for the game, entwining Ott's performance with the day's big sporting event, which took place in another of New York's boroughs. "There was more mud at the Polo Grounds yesterday than at Belmont Park, but young Melvin Ott proved himself as good a mudder as Gallant Fox," wrote the *Brooklyn Daily Eagle* staffer, referencing only the second horseracing Triple Crown winner to date. "Master Melvin drove in six runs and prevented another by an outfield throw [to the plate] in the course of a gray and soggy afternoon."[15] The first home run was part of a four-run first inning and the other capped a five-run seventh frame in the 9–7 victory, the Giants' seventh in a row.

Despite these two three-run blasts, there was not as much *home run* cheering from "Ottville" in 1930 as in the previous season. Another grand exception came on August 31. In a game reflecting the sometimes football-like scores that pervaded baseball that season, Ott belted three home runs in succession and drove in six runs against the visiting Boston Braves. The road team, pelting out 18 hits, was victorious, 14–10. Despite the two dozen runs scored, the game—the second of a Sunday doubleheader attended by 40,000 fans—was played in two hours and 15 minutes. The long balls—hit in consecutive at bats in the fourth, fifth and seventh innings—were nos. 20, 21 and 22 on the campaign for the outfielder.

Ott hit only three more the rest of the way. Considering his total from 1929, the 25 home runs seemed considerably below the slugging curve of the league that season. Not deficient in any way were Ott's spectacular league-leading .458 on-base percentage, 119 RBI and 122 runs scored. The Giants were eliminated from the pennant race on September 21, after splitting a doubleheader with Cincinnati.

Ott was one of the first regulars into training camp in 1931. He arrived with a different family member than in the past—his wife, Mildred. Right after the 1930 season ended, Mel discreetly framed plans for becoming master of his own house. It was not until six weeks afterward, however, through published publicity photos, that the majority of the country became aware of the life-altering decision. "Married so quietly September 30 that few people heard anything about it," read the caption of one of the published photos, "Melvin Ott and his bride, the former Mildred Wattigny of New Orleans, recently returned to the home of Ott's parents in Gretna, Louisiana, after a honeymoon trip to the west. Ott is the 'baby' outfielder of the New York Giants."[16] The player had announced his engagement earlier in the season and wed only two days after the Giants' campaign ended.

Ott started the new season on a good note and in a new position. His ninth-inning, two-run home run at the Baker Bowl provided the Giants with a pair of insurance tallies in the team's 9–5 Opening Day win over Philadelphia on April 14. Ott was stationed in center field for the entire game. He had played the middle pasture in years past, so it was not a new experience for him. Ott stayed in center until an injury to Freddie Lindstrom, the Giants' new right fielder, upset the realignment plans. Lindstrom broke his ankle sliding into a base on July 9. Ott then returned to his old right field spot, and fourth outfielder Chick Fullis was put in center through the remainder of the campaign. Freddy Leach, picked up prior to the 1929 season, continued in left.

In the second game of a doubleheader at the Polo Grounds on July 12, Ott slammed two home runs, plating five runs. The Giants defeated the Philadelphia Phillies, 9–4. With his two "sweeps" of the bases, Ott prevented Travis Jackson, hitting behind him and banging five hits, from accruing any RBI. Hurling the route, Freddie Fitzsimmons wrapped up a double-victory celebration on the day for his team, after the Giants were big winners in the opener, 13–6.

Ott missed a week of games at the beginning of August with a shoulder injury. He was second, behind the Phillies' Chuck Klein, in circuit clouts with 17 at the time. Ott was also forced to miss the final five games of the season due to a beaning. On September 18, at Sportsman's Park, he was struck on the back of the head by a pitch from Cardinals hurler Burleigh Grimes. The blunt force of the pitch rendered Ott unconscious, and he was rushed by ambulance to St. John's Hospital. He was diagnosed with a concussion.

The beaning was unintentional, as the following reaction from the blow's deliverer—witnessed by one of the sportswriters on hand—confirmed: "Grimes rushed in from the pitcher's box, almost in tears. While Ott was being carried to the clubhouse, Grimes sat in the dugout, and it was only on the insistence of Cardinals manager Gabby Street that he continued in the game."[17] Grimes visited Ott in the hospital after the game and was pleased to find him responsive. While at the medical center, the popular player received telephone calls, telegraph wires and baskets of fruits and flowers from well-wishing fans from all over, including St. Louis.

Ott played in 138 games and hit .292, with 29 home runs and 115 run driven home. His home run total was two behind league-leader Klein. The outfielder scored 104 runs and bested all NL batters with 80 bases on balls.

Ott's first child, Margaret Carolyn, was born December 1, 1931. Six weeks later, the new father made the newspapers in an atypical way. "Melvin Ott, outfielder and heavy hitter of the New York Giants," detailed one daily, "revealed here today he has duplicated teammate Bill Terry's action in balking at a stiff salary slash for the 1932 season. He said he was returning his contract to the Giants unsigned and hoped to secure 'an adjustment.' Ott declared that the proposed salary cut was not 40 percent as in the case of Bill Terry, but it was 'much bigger than I expected.'"[18]

Either the Giants quickly made the desired "adjustment" or Ott reconsidered the initial terms, because only three days later it was pointedly announced by the Giants that Ott had signed on the dotted line. It was completely out of character for Ott to complain publicly about his employers. The convenient crutch raised by the economic despair that engulfed the country was something on which the Giants could heavily lean, but a potential public relations fallout involving their most popular player was not something they wished to risk, either. The team must have promised Ott something more than specified under the original terms for him to come around so rapidly. Unless, of course, he had a dramatic change of heart. The 1932 Giants were intent on making amends for a disappointing previous season, in which they finished 13 games behind the St. Louis Cardinals. The Giants, under two different managers (or three, if interim manager Dave Bancroft is counted), failed futilely in the attempt.

Ott was moved to right field, and the physically recovered Freddie Lindstrom was placed once again in center. The Giants tried several outfielders in left: Ethan Allen, Len Koenecke and Chick Fullis. Four years after the fact, the Giants were still trying to live down McGraw's disastrous trade of left fielder Lefty O'Doul to the Philadelphia Phillies, following the 1928 season, for outfielder Freddy Leach. While a fine player, Leach retired after the 1932 season. The flashy O'Doul became a star hitter and a two-time batting champion.

On June 1, Bill Terry and Ott homered back-to-back in the last game officially under John McGraw's long rule, a 4–2 defeat to the Philadelphia Phillies at the Polo Grounds. On June 4, in the first game under Terry's command, Ott homered in a 10–4 win over the same Phillies. Three days afterward, Ott crashed two home runs, including the game-winner in the bottom of the ninth inning, giving the Giants a 4–3 victory over the Cincinnati Reds. It was the first of four walk-off home runs hit by Ott in his career, and not surprisingly, it was deposited into "Ottville." Terry, on deck, was the first to greet Ott at the plate. The happy skipper offered a handshake, a slap on the back and a hug to the game's hero. The circuit wallops in the exciting June 7 game were Ott's eighth and ninth on the season, on his way to leading the National League with 38 (tied with Chuck Klein).

Ott had developed an ideal home run swing for his home ballpark. The bathtub-shaped playing field of the Polo Grounds had uniquely short distances down each line. It was 279 feet to the farthest point of the chalk line in left field and only 257 feet along the same straight trail in right. From these starting points, the high walls—constraining the bleachers and plastered with advertising—fell back at right angles, reaching distances of well over 400 feet, until they curved toward each other in an attempt to meet in the middle. Disrupting the intersecting trajectory of the high walls were the centerfield bleachers, with low-lying parapets and dual green "batter's eye" screens. Separating the screens in dead center was the rectangular recess that led to the road and home clubhouses, and executive offices, via two staircases. The five-foot-high, Captain Edward L. Grant Memorial, erected in 1921, was situated in the middle of the recess and in the field of play. The upper-deck bleachers in the outfield corners jutted out over the field, making high fly balls sometimes tricky propositions for fielders. The vast majority of Ott's home runs at the Polo Grounds were driven to right field. He devised an uppercut swing well suited for base-clearing results in the hitter-friendly park. "Like a sharpshooter he picked out a spot in the lower right field grandstand just east of the white foul pole and hit it twice,"[19] noted one sportswriter, following an Ott two-home-run day. The "Louisiana larruper," as some in the New York press referred to him, fashioned perhaps the most recognizable batting swing of the era. Ott strode into the pitcher's offering with his front foot well off the ground, which allowed him to shift his weight maximally behind his swing, adding distance to his drives. The mechanical lift and drop of his foot was the primary reason this "Little Giant" was able to hit so many home runs.

The home run crown in 1932 was the first of six for the 23-year-old Ott, who was genially referred to in one local paper as "the child clouter." The seven-year veteran also led the league with an even 100 walks and an on-base percentage of .424. Ott raised his average to .318 and played in all 154 games. He finished tied for fourth in RBI with 123. Ott outperformed every other senior circuit player with a Wins Above Replacement rating of 7.9. Interestingly, the three top WAR players were all Giants, with pitcher Carl Hubbell, at 7.3, nosing out his manager's 7.2 mark. In a year's time, these same three core players would lead the Giants' turnaround from a seventh-place team into unexpected champions.

Another core player of McGraw's Giants was Freddie Lindstrom. The infielder-turned-outfielder homered, along with Ott and Travis Jackson, in Bill Terry's first game as manager, June 4, 1932. Though still a relative boy at 26 years of age, as a veteran and star player, Lindstrom viewed himself as the frontrunner to any managerial vacancy on the Giants. When Terry was placed at the head of the club, Lindstrom set in motion overtures to be traded. It was a decision he would later regret. As amicably as possible, Terry accommodated the nine-year veteran's request after the season. In a

Kiddo Davis was unspectacular but steady on both sides of the ball in the Giants' outfield during the team's championship season.

three-team, five-player deal involving Pittsburgh and Philadelphia, Lindstrom, who hit .271 for the Giants in 144 games in 1932, wound up with the Pirates. The Giants received pitcher Glenn Spencer and outfielder George "Kiddo" Davis.

Upon graduation from New York University in 1926, George Davis was signed to his first professional baseball contract by New York Yankees scout Paul Krichell, who had signed Lou Gehrig a few years earlier. The youngest of eight children, four of whom were boys, Davis spent six years in the minor leagues before reaching the majors as a 30-year-old rookie in 1932 with the Philadelphia Phillies.

The son of a Welsh father named George and a Scottish mother named Bessie Rutter James, George Willis Davis was born February 12, 1902, in the immigrant family's home of Bridgeport, Connecticut. George was a "late child," his mother having given birth to him a few months prior to her 41st birthday.

Davis played one game in 1926 for the Yankees as a late-inning substitute in right field for Babe Ruth. "Garland Buckeye was pitching for Cleveland that day," Davis recalled, "and it was regarded as a disgrace by the Yanks that he beat 'em, so I guess that's why they stuck me in."[20] The Yankees were routed by the Indians, 15–3, at Dunn Field.

Davis did not bat in his debut game (June 5), and did not play another game in the major leagues until his 1932 rookie season with the Phillies. With Davis unable to crack the Yankees' stellar outfield, the New York team lost contractual control of the player in the minor leagues. "When I joined the [Yankees] club, Bob Meusel, Babe Ruth, Earle Combs, Ben Paschal and Cedric Durst were their outfielders," remembered Davis. "Paschal could really hit. Durst could go and get 'em for miles, and the other three guys were pretty good, too."[21]

Davis spent four years with the St. Paul Saints in the American Association, after two seasons split between several New York lower-level affiliates. His contract was purchased by Philadelphia after he concluded his 1931 campaign with the Saints, hitting 26 home runs, with 214 hits, and batted .343.

The right-handed-hitting Davis produced an excellent rookie campaign for the Phillies as their starting center fielder. He hit .309 in 137 games with 39 doubles and scored 100 runs while managing only five home runs. On the defensive side, his 12 errors were the most at his position. Brooklyn manager Casey Stengel had this assessment of the rookie, who stood 5'11" tall and weighed 180 pounds: "He doesn't look like a runner, but he's fast on the bases and in centerfield. He doesn't look like an outfielder who can throw well, but you can't take liberties with his arm."[22] Davis recorded 15 assists that season.

The NYU graduate was traded to the Giants in December of 1932 as part of the Freddie Lindstrom deal. "Davis is one of the most deceptive players in the National League," one New York writer noted shortly before the acquisition. "He doesn't look like a ballplayer or athlete of any kind. Davis is tall and spare. He hasn't much body on a long pair of legs. His shoulders are thin and his arms are short. He bats with a herky-jerky left-handed style and looks awkward running with his slim shoulders hunched around his ears."[23]

Davis was the unspectacular but steady center fielder of the Giants in 1933. He cut his error total to three, which gave him the top fielding average (.988) among his peers. While he did not shine with the bat, he did not hinder the overall composition of the championship team. He played in between Mel Ott, in right, and left fielder Jo-Jo Moore.

The first transaction Bill Terry made as manager of the Giants was to option Len Koenecke to Jersey City and recall 23-year-old outfielder Jo-Jo Moore. He did this on June 20, eight days after cutting infielder Doc Marshall to get down to the new 23-man team player limit. Koenecke had been McGraw's expensive minor league purchase but did not develop as anticipated. He could not win a starting outfield job and was hitting a "soft" .255 when he was demoted.

Moore had played a meager seven games with the Giants over the past two seasons. McGraw was said to have thought him too much of a "lightweight," at 5'11" and under 150 pounds when he first came up, unable to withstand the grind of a long season. Terry, on the other hand, must have seen potential in Moore. He wasted no time in putting Moore in left field and kept him there for the rest of the 1932 season. The rookie hit .305 in 86 games. Terry also placed Moore in the leadoff spot in the order after barely two weeks with the club. Terry moved Critz into the two-hole. McGraw had been batting Critz leadoff since his acquisition from Cincinnati.

Moore was a Texas League pickup of McGraw at the conclusion of the 1930 season after playing with the San Antonio Indians. Their manager, George Burns, an ex-Giant, recommended Moore to his former commander. Before joining San Antonio, the outfielder was briefly property of the Waco Cubs, and before that, the West Texas League's Coleman Rangers. In 1931, Moore showed quite well with two Giants affiliates. He batted .347 for the Newark Bears in 79 games and .359 for the Eastern League's Bridgeport Bears in 30 games. He was then moved over to Jersey City in 1932.

Moore's early minor league playing locales were the by-product of his birth state. Joseph Gregg Moore was born on Christmas Day, 1908, in Gause, Texas. He was the only child of Charles and Maude Rowena Moore. Gause was a very small cattle town about 45 miles southwest of Marlin, a regular spring training haunt of the Giants in the 1910s. The young Moore's dream of becoming a big-league ballplayer extended also to playing for the New York Giants, his favorite team growing up. His family moved to Crystal City in southwest Texas and Joe attended high school there. After graduation, he attended Texas A & M. But he left school not long afterward to sign on with Waco. Because of his slender appearance and fleetness afoot, he was nicknamed the "Gause Ghost." The nickname never really stuck because Moore filled out his frame. By the time he reported to training camp in 1933, he had gained 25 pounds from his welterweight beginnings. The home cooking of one Miss Jewell Ely may have played a hand in the weight gain. Moore had married his Gause sweetheart in January of 1931.

3

The Pitching Staff Sustained by "The Meal Ticket"

John McGraw's Giants limped into the month of September 1928 with a season-high eight straight losses and ten losses out of 11 games. As a result, the team had dropped from a two-percentage-point lead in the National League on August 20 to 6½ games off the pace on the last day of the month. McGraw's club then shifted into high gear and made a strong pennant push, winning 25 out of its last 33 games.

Leading the charge from the mound was Carl Hubbell, a 25-year-old rookie pitcher who had joined the Giants in late July. Hubbell won seven games in September, all but one as a starter. The Giants' valiant effort to raise another pennant over the Polo Grounds came up short against the circuit champion St. Louis Cardinals, but Hubbell's 7–1 record in the month hinted at the great promise he was to fulfill as an illustrious pitcher.

Five of his September victories were complete games. A relief win, on September 22, was delivered with five scoreless innings against the front-running Cardinals (although two inherited runners scored following his entrance). The Giants emerged 8–5 winners in front of 40,000 Polo Grounds fans and moved to within a game of first place. Hubbell's performance drew the praises of at least one wire reporter. "Less than two months ago the Giants bought this lean and lanky southpaw, Hubbell, from the Beaumont club for a reputed $40,000," stated *Associated Press* editor Alan Gould. "He looked like $140,000 star out there today and if the Giants should come through to win an eleventh pennant for John McGraw he can claim a full share of the world's series spoils without the slightest argument."[1] (The sale of the pitcher, which was originally said to be for $25,000 and one or two players to be named later, was announced by the minor league club on July 14. Hubbell debuted for the Giants 12 days later.)

Hubbell won his seventh game of the month, and tenth of the season, on the final day of the campaign, September 30. He defeated the Cardinals again, 4–2, on a six-hitter. The Giants had been eliminated from the race the previous day.

Beaumont had purchased Hubbell's rights in April from the Detroit Tigers. Detroit had obtained Hubbell's services from the Oklahoma City Indians at the end of the 1925 Western League season. Hubbell spent several spring trainings with the Tigers before being farmed back to the minors. The team never gave the young left-hander a major league tryout. Out of player options by the time 1928 rolled around, the Tigers sold Hubbell to Beaumont rather than risk losing him to the minor league draft.

Hubbell later commented that his time spent with the Tigers was far from instructional. "Nobody helped me in anything, anything at all," said the pitcher. "They didn't have pitching coaches."[2] Hubbell also singled out Detroit's two managers during his years there as being less than altruistic. "[Coach] George McBride did all the talking to me," he said. "I don't think [manager George] Moriarty knows yet that I was with the club, and Ty Cobb, who managed the Tigers the first time I reported to them, was even less interested in me, if possible."[3]

The first team to show professional interest in Hubbell was the Class D Cushing squad of the Oklahoma State League in the summer of 1923. He used this team as his stepping-stone to Class A Oklahoma City. The young pitcher had first made a name for himself hurling for his Meeker High baseball team. (Meeker Senior High School is today located on East Carl Hubbell Blvd.) Meeker, Oklahoma, was Carl Hubbell's hometown by way of his family's farm settlement, which lay a couple of miles outside of town.

Carl Owen Hubbell, born June 22, 1903, was one of seven children, six of whom were boys. Around 1907, George and Margaret Hubbell of Red Oak, Missouri, settled in Meeker. (Official registries list Carthage, Missouri, as Hubbell's birth town. George Hubbell disputed this, stating Red Oak, a town 20 miles northeast of Carthage, was his son's place of birth.) Patriarch George became a cotton grower, with all of his children pitching in around the family farm. For one of them, the years of outdoor labor provided an advantageous sports benefit. "I had a well developed arm when I started playing ball," said Carl. "I was either chopping cotton or getting in the wood all the days of my life until the year before I graduated from high school."[4]

Hubbell was spotted by part-time Giants scout Dick Kinsella after a particularly fine outing with Beaumont. According to stories passed down over the years, Kinsella's sighting of Hubbell was by happenstance. As an Illinois delegate to the Democratic National Convention in nearby Houston, Kinsella likely saw Hubbell and the visiting Exporters shut out the Houston Buffaloes, 7–0, on five hits on June 12, 1928. Hubbell's next start delivered another white-

3. The Pitching Staff Sustained by "The Meal Ticket" 55

wash, this time in Waco over the Cubs. Hubbell improved his record to 8–8 on the season, pitching for the last-place Exporters. He had 15 complete games, with a decision in each of his 16 starts. On July 11, Hubbell won his ninth straight victory, defeating Houston again, 5–2. His record stood at 12–8. Three days later, Kinsella, who devoted his baseball services to the New York Giants, had raved enough about Hubbell to convince John McGraw to purchase him.

Hubbell's first game with New York, less than two weeks after his sale by Beaumont, was a forgettable one. He was knocked out of the box in the second inning by the Pittsburgh Pirates at the Polo Grounds. His pitching line was 1⅔ innings, seven hits, five runs, three earned. The final score was 7–5, with Hubbell the losing pitcher. On the plus side of the ledger was Burleigh Grimes, whom the Giants had traded the prior season. The veteran right-hander was on his way to a career-high 25 wins for the Steel City team. Following the inauspicious start, Hubbell was relegated to bullpen appearances for the next week and a half.

On August 5, Hubbell was summoned in relief of ineffective starter Jim Faulkner, with one out in the third inning of an important game against the St. Louis Cardinals. With four runs charged to Faulkner, Hubbell kept the Cardinals off the board for 11⅔ innings, as the homestanding Giants came back to tie the game 4–4 and send it into extra frames. In the top of the 15th, in his 13th inning of work, Hubbell surrendered four hits and two runs, which gave the Cardinals a hard-fought 6–4 victory. Six days later, Hubbell tossed his first "official" shutout, blanking the Philadelphia Phillies at the Polo Grounds, 4–0. The left-hander scattered six hits, with one walk and five strikeouts. He followed that with a 3–2 complete-game win on August 18 over the Cardinals and Pete Alexander at Sportsman's Park. It was one of four wins Hubbell notched against the National League champion Cardinals on the campaign.

Hubbell's rookie season concluded with a 10–6 record and a sharp 2.83 ERA in 124 innings. He completed eight of his 14 starts.

The Giants received Hubbell's signed second-year contract on January 29, 1929, announced by James Tierney, indicating the pitcher was eager to try and build on his fine rookie season. The frontline pitching staff Hubbell was expected to augment was led by 20-game winners Larry Benton and Freddie Fitzsimmons, and included the 11–4 Joe Genewich.

In spring camp in San Antonio, John McGraw engineered an intra-squad game on March 5 that was a departure from the norm. McGraw instituted a one-inning game between a team of regular players and a squad of second-stringers and rookies. Each team batted until it made 27 outs. The "A" team hit first. Second-year hurler Bill Walker and Hubbell, pitching for the "scrubs," split the duties as evenly as possible from the mound. Allowing only five hits between them, their "inferior" team defeated the Giants' "regulars," 3–0. Larry Benton and Curly Ogden opposed Walker and Hubbell. Since each team stayed on the field until it registered 27 outs, it would seem to have been an unnecessarily taxing endeavor for only two pitchers, especially at this early point in training.

In Hubbell's first year, his first name was sometimes misspelled with a "K" instead of a "C." He was also repeatedly referred to as a curveball pitcher, a misidentification on the part of the press of his screwball's wicked roll. As the 1929 season began, his trademark pitch had not come to full light yet in all sectors, but predictions that he would shine from the mound were readily obtainable. "Carl Hubbell, young New York Giant southpaw, is expected to win a lot of games for John McGraw this year," one such report read. "That is the burden he is put under for his sensational work last season. A sharp curve ball and a good 'hard' one are the tools he uses to put his act over in the National League."[5]

Carl Hubbell sporting the National League's uniform for the inaugural All-Star Game in 1933. Hubbell pitched two innings in the game and was a gigantic force on the mound for New York in 1933.

Hubbell's "act" was particularly stupendous on May 8. In his fourth start of the season and only the 18th of his major league career, the left-hander no-hit the Pittsburgh Pirates, 11–0, at the Polo Grounds. Eight thousand fans were treated to the first no-hitter by a Giants pitcher since Jesse Barnes authored one on May 7, 1922, and the first by a National League southpaw since Rube Marquard of the Giants in 1915. Hubbell had to overcome back-to-back errors in the ninth inning by his mates to close out the grand feat. Opening the last frame, left fielder Chick Fullis dropped a catchable ball, and Travis Jackson bobbled a grounder and was unable to record an out. With runners on first and second, Hubbell, one could say, was presently faced with "picking his poison" from the upcoming Pirates hitters. He bore down and struck out Lloyd Waner, the pitcher's fourth strikeout of the game. He then induced Paul Waner to hit into a 1–6–3 double play.

Three days later, prior to the scheduled home game against the Chicago Cubs, Giants management presented Hubbell with an inscribed wristwatch commemorating the no-hit achievement. John McGraw was not present for the no-hitter or the gift-giving ceremony. A sinus attack had put him out of commission.

Hubbell, 3–0, followed the brilliant outing with several clunkers. He was the losing pitcher in the game on May 16 in which Mel Ott hit for the cycle against Boston. The pitcher allowed two runs on three hits in the bottom of the tenth inning and was defeated by the Braves, 5–4. He turned things around and won on May 23 against the same Braves, 11–4. The easy victory marked McGraw's return to the team after a 16-game absence.

The sophomore hurler pressed on to exhibit the best pitching on the club through the first months of the season. Hubbell went 5–1 in June, and had a 9–3 record with a 4.09 ERA at the close of the month. "The rise of Hubbell is amazing," wrote one columnist. "Lacking color usually attributed to left handers, he does not appear aggressive nor is he cock-sure. But he has poise, pitching poise. Hubbell says little but pitches a 'lot.' His taciturn manner may have had a great deal to do with the Tigers failing to see his worth."[6]

It was soon afterward that the Giants began losing their grip as pennant contenders. The team fell from 3½ games out of first place on June 30 to 10½ games out a month later. Even as the Giants slipped further behind the accelerating Chicago Cubs in the standings, Hubbell emerged as the top man on the Giants' pitching staff, ahead of Benton and Fitzsimmons. Finishing with an 18–11 record, Hubbell won the most games on the team, while his 3.69 ERA placed him in the top ten in the league. Hubbell tossed 19 complete games in 35 starts. His no-hitter was his only shutout.

Emerging as the team's fourth starter was another left-hander, Bill Walker, a former Denver Bears pitcher for whom McGraw had paid $30,000 in 1927, but who had been sidelined a good part of the prior season due to an illness. Walker, a 14-game winner, was the 12–3 winning pitcher in the Giants' next-to-last game of the season versus the Philadelphia Phillies. It was the second game of the doubleheader in which Phillies pitchers intentionally walked Mel Ott five times. Philadelphia was trying to protect its own Chuck Klein and his 43 home run total from being tied or surpassed by Ott. Conversely, Walker repeatedly challenged Klein and retired him all five times he came to the plate.

Klein had hit his 43rd home run against Hubbell earlier in the first game, a 5–4 Phillies victory and Hubbell's 11th defeat. Lefty O'Doul collected four hits against Hubbell, each one of them cracking off the bat as stinging reminders to John McGraw of the player he traded away. The Giants manager had sent O'Doul—and an undisclosed amount of cash—to Philadelphia in the off-season for outfielder Freddy Leach. O'Doul outhit Leach by 108 points on the way to winning the National League batting title with a sensational .398 average and a staggering 254 hits. Hits number 253 and 254 were claimed against Walker in the nightcap.

In January 1930, the 26-year-old Hubbell tied the knot. The occasion apparently was not widely broadcast at the time, judging from the first national notices of the event, released more than two weeks after the fact. "Carl Hubbell, New York Giants' pitcher who hails from Meeker, Oklahoma," began one such notice, "slipped a 'fast one' over on his friends, it was learned today. Hubbell and Miss Lucille Herrington of Shawnee were married at McAlester, January 26. The baseball hurler and his bride formerly attended high school together. They are at home in Shawnee [OK]."[7]

Hubbell was a late arrival to spring camp. Coincidentally, he arrived in San Antonio on February 25, the same day John McGraw showed up following his winter vacation in Cuba. Hubbell said he had taken a few extra weeks to recuperate from an operation on his broken nose.

The first intrasquad game was held March 4, with Hubbell and rookie Roy Parmelee splitting six innings of work and leading the Giants' "grays" team over the "whites," 7–1. The bigger news from camp was the protracted holdouts of Bill Terry, Edd Roush, Freddie Lindstrom, Larry Benton, catcher Bob O'Farrell, and Freddy Leach.

On April 6, nine days before the Giants opened the season, Hubbell went the distance in an exhibition game against the Memphis Chicks in Memphis. He won, 7–3. His first regular season start came two weeks later, April 20. He defeated 43-year-old Pete Alexander and the Philadelphia Phillies, 2–1. It was one of the final starts of Alexander's monumental career. A capacity crowd of 45,000 came out to the Polo Grounds to see the first Sunday baseball of the season. Thirty thousand fans clicked through the turnstiles the same day at Ebbets Field, additional proof that disposable income had not begun to dry up yet in the wake of the six-month-old stock market crash.

Both Walker and the right-handed Fitzsimmons started ahead of Hubbell to open the season. While it was understandable for McGraw to want to have a lefty-righty-lefty starting rotation order, it is unclear which left-handed starter had the better spring. Hubbell was the Giants' winningest pitcher in 1929 and, on that basis alone, he deserved the Opening Day nod. Could McGraw have been trying to send an underlying message to Hubbell

3. The Pitching Staff Sustained by "The Meal Ticket" 59

over his late arrival at camp? Walker, on the other hand, had led the National League with an ERA of 3.09 in 1929, although pitching 90 fewer innings than Hubbell.

The two southpaws ran much more neck and neck in 1930, matching each other's win totals with 17. Hubbell tossed three shutouts to Walker's two. Hubbell logged 17 complete games in 32 starts; Walker posted 13 in 34 opening assignments. Walker had the edge in innings pitched, 245⅓ to 241⅔. Both pitchers were called on to relieve on five occasions. Hubbell's 3.87 ERA was the second-best in the National League, while Walker's 3.93 placed him third.

Of the two games Hubbell saved that season, the first was a true fireman's rescue. On July 7, two days after picking up his seventh win, Hubbell was summoned from the bullpen to secure the final out of a high-scoring Baker Bowl clash between the Giants and Phillies. Freddie Lindstrom's two-run single in the top of the ninth inning had given the visitors a 13–12 lead. The Phillies threatened in their final turn, putting two men on base against the Giants' third reliever in the game, James "Tiny" Chaplin. Hubbell came in and struck out Chuck Klein. The Phillies slugger had homered previously and was tied with Hack Wilson for the league lead in home runs with 24.

On July 24, the third-year pitcher received credit for a rain-shortened shutout (1–0) at what one hometown writer sarcastically referred to as the "Water Polo Grounds," due to the amount of precipitation that fell during the 6⅓-inning game. The same writer wondered why the visiting Pirates club did not employ stalling tactics in the fifth inning to try to delay the game from becoming official. Hubbell retired the first two batters of the frame, then walked the next hitter. The fourth batter lined deep to right field. "It was all quick and commonplace," wrote Harold C. Burr, while providing a glimpse into the normal pace of this era's games. "The [Pittsburgh] boys did not even step out of the batter's box to spit on their calloused hands."[8] The game was eventually called with one out in the top of the seventh. The Pirates had loaded the bases prior to the decisive deluge.

Hubbell entered September with 12 wins. He closed the season with four straight victories, the last one coming in relief on the season's final day, September 28. Acting manager Dave Bancroft used all of his top starters in an attempt to stay in third place, one game ahead of their urban rivals, the Brooklyn Robins. Against the visiting Philadelphia Phillies, Walker started but was ineffective. Fitzsimmons was called upon to record the final out of the fifth with the Giants trailing, 5–0. The reliever was removed for a pinch-hitter, and Clarence Mitchell pitched the next two innings for the Giants, keeping the Phillies off the board. The Giants closed the gap to 5–4 before the Phillies scratched across an insurance run against Joe Heving in the eighth frame.

Hubbell, who had thrown a 5–3, complete game win against the Phillies the *prior* day, came on to pitch a scoreless ninth. The Giants rallied for two runs in the lower half of the stanza to tie the game. In the tenth, Freddy Leach singled in the game-winner, 7–6, for the home team. Hubbell retired all six men he faced to earn his 17th win against 12 losses.

Having won 45 games in less than two and a half seasons probably propped Hubbell into making a stand for more money on his 1931 contract. The pitcher was marked absent during the early roll calls of spring camp in late February. "Although official verification or denial is lacking," explained one wire service communique, "it seems that at least two battery men are holdouts—Carl Hubbell, southpaw pitching ace and Frank Hogan, gargantuan catcher. They failed to report with other battery men at San Antonio on Monday. Manager John McGraw declared some time ago that tardy players would be fined one day's pay for every day they were late in reporting. At this rate, Hogan, Hubbell, et al are losing money almost as fast as the stock market bears."[9]

The latter remark referenced the stock market's partial rebound and the false sense of recovery being emitted by the previously beleaguered commodity brokers of Wall Street. "The markets rallied several times in 1930 and 1931 in anticipation of recovery," wrote Eric H. Allen in *1931: The Year of the Great Worldwide Financial Crash*, "but each rally was followed by further decline when a true recovery failed to materialize. It was only after the currency collapses in the fall of 1931 that the depression achieved historic status."[10]

Hubbell, as it turned out, was more like a straggler than holdout. He was front and center again, participating in the Giants' first intrasquad game on March 6.

Nineteen-game winner Freddie Fitzsimmons was McGraw's choice to open the 1931 campaign on April 14 in Philadelphia. The right-hander picked up a 9–5 win over the Phillies. McGraw's choice for starter the next day was somewhat of a head-scratcher. The testy skipper selected 20-year-old Hal Schumacher, a former college athlete from northern New York. The young pitcher did not fare well, and McGraw had to use four relievers to finish the game his young, unproven hurler had started, Hubbell among them.

Walker, Clarence Mitchell and Fitzsimmons, again, received starts before Hubbell was chosen to open his first game. It came in the Giants' seventh game, the second contest of a doubleheader on April 20. Hubbell lost a tough 1–0 decision to the Boston Braves, permitting the run with two outs in the bottom of the ninth inning. This effort aside, and a two-hit shutout win over the Braves on May 26, Hubbell's pitching in the opening weeks of the campaign did not help gain his manager's favor.

"The long-legged left-hander, with the prominent Adam's Apple,"[11] as sportswriter Tommy Holmes described Hubbell when he first joined the Giants, began displaying better pitching around mid–June. From June 18 to July 9, Hubbell tossed five straight complete games, winning three of them. He spun a second two-hit shutout on June 24 over the Cubs at the Polo Grounds. The third victory, July 9, was a 9–3 road decision over the Philadelphia Phillies. Halfway through the game, Freddie Lindstrom broke his ankle sliding into third base.

On July 23, in his 17th start, Hubbell defeated the Cincinnati Reds, 4–2, in ten innings. Hubbell's record improved to 6–7, and his ERA dropped below 3.00, a threshold he would not re-cross for the remainder of the season.

Hubbell won eight of his remaining 13 decisions, including his third and fourth whitewashes of the year. His 14 victories trailed both Fitzsimmons (18) and Walker (16) on the staff. Walker, who had been living up to his purchase price, led the National League in shutouts with six and in ERA at 2.26. Hubbell's 2.65 ERA was second in the league to his left-handed teammate. He completed 21 out of 30 starts and surpassed 240 innings pitched for the third year in a row.

The former Oklahoma farm hand never set out to invent a new pitch. In fact, as a minor league hurler Carl Hubbell was simply trying to perfect an old one, when he forged an increased twist of the wrist that led to the birth of his signature pitch. "Carl says the screwball showed up in his delivery when he tried to develop a sinker," affirmed one early profile on the pitcher. "However, each time the ball took that out and away dip that batters find so difficult to see, let alone gauge."[12]

The wrist twisting was of an aberrant nature—clockwise—in the opposite direction of a curveball's wrist-spinning propulsion. "Most pitchers aren't loose-jointed enough to throw it," Hubbell said. "They can't get the wrist turned over."[13] Hubbell gripped his screwball similar to his fastball, except that his two longest fingers were spaced farther apart over the seams.

Hubbell, it would seem, was anxious to continue unleashing his deviant pitch on National League hitters, as he promptly signed and returned his 1932 contract to the Giants. On January 16, team secretary James Tierney made sure to alert the media that Hubbell and Mel Ott's signed contracts had been received on the same day. Tierney delighted in advising that Hubbell's contract had been received from Meeker, Oklahoma, and Ott's from Gretna, Louisiana. Ott's acquiescence was particularly well received by management as the superstar-in-the-making had only days earlier verbally expressed discontent with the initial Giants offer.

"Due to his fine year," leaked one report of the pitcher's signing, "it was generally assumed Hubbell received a raise."[14] With the way player salaries were being sheared, the report's assumption may have been too optimistic. The best-case scenario for Hubbell was probably that he was not offered a pay cut from the prior year, something more feasible for the team's higher-ups to absorb because Hubbell was not making that much to begin with. No salary amount for either player was revealed by their employer.

In February, on his way to join the rest of his team in Los Angeles, the Giants' new spring conditioning locale, Hubbell spent a few minutes with local newspapermen during a stopover between connecting trains at Rock Island Depot in Amarillo, Texas. He said he supported Bill Terry's trenchant holdout position, and that his greatest thrill was his no-hitter. "He's a left-hander, but doesn't act like one," opined one scribe. "He looks all the world like a youngster on his way to see things for the first time. He has an eager and impetuous manner. Laughs easily and wholesomely."[15] The pitcher also confessed that Brooklyn gave him the most trouble, collectively, while Chuck Klein, individually, was his toughest opponent.

In Los Angeles on February 28, Hubbell participated in a benefit game to raise funds for that summer's United States Olympic Team. Two well-known comedians of the day, Buster Keaton and Joe E. Brown, were named honorary captains of two clubs composed of Hollywood film actors and diamond luminaries, such as the Waner brothers, Rogers Hornsby, Tris Speaker, Sam "Wahoo" Crawford, Pie Traynor and Gabby Hartnett. The game was played at Wrigley Field, with 7,500 spectators in attendance. The Cubs' Charlie Root pitched for silent screen star Keaton's team, while the retired Pete Alexander and Hubbell hurled for the convivial Brown's 10–4 winners.

The next day, February 29, John McGraw unveiled his high-priced outfielder, Len Koenecke, for the first time. "If that boy isn't a ballplayer then I never saw one,"[16] McGraw had said following the player's much ballyhooed purchase the previous winter.

"I ought to make good," said Koenecke, who had arrived the prior evening and was brimming with confidence. "I hit .353 in the American Association and had plenty of triples. None of these cheap home runs for me."[17]

Koenecke was in McGraw's starting lineup on Opening Day at the Polo Grounds, April 12. His 0-for-4 debut was as bad as the Giants' all-around performance on the day. McGraw's team was whipped, 13–5, by the Philadelphia Phillies. ERA champ Walker surrendered seven runs in one-plus inning of work. In the Giants' second game, also at home, Hubbell started and was knocked around for seven runs, six earned, in 7⅓ innings by the same Philadelphia club. He was the losing pitcher as the Giants fell, 7–6. McGraw's clan lost their next game to begin the season 0–3.

After absorbing a second loss, as a reliever, Hubbell earned his first victory on April 24, on the road over the Brooklyn Dodgers, 7–2. He went the distance, backed by 16 Giants hits.

Two weeks later, on May 8, Hubbell tossed a six-hitter over the St. Louis Cardinals at Sportsman's Park in the first game of a doubleheader. The 4–1 victory was the last win registered by John McGraw. The managerial icon swallowed a 6–5 defeat in the second game, then traveled with the team to Chicago, where all but one game of an intended three-game series was rained out. The Giants lost the sole encounter, 9–2, with McGraw absent. From Chicago, the team trekked to Cincinnati, where McGraw was felled by what was originally reported as "indigestion." He gained the strength to visit Redland Field only long enough to give Bill Klem a piece of his mind for making the Giants play through rainy conditions the prior day in a Giants loss. McGraw left Cincinnati ahead of his team to return to New York.

In the Giants' first game back from their road trip, on May 26, Hubbell took on the Dodgers again and established a career high for strikeouts. The pitcher fanned 15 Brooklynites, but was stuck with a 3–2 defeat, in 12 innings. Hubbell struck out at least one batter in each inning, and would not have reached his strikeout level had the Dodgers not been caught batting out of order. A sixth-inning, run-scoring single by Al López was nullified when López, the eighth-place batter, stepped to the plate ahead of High Pockets Kelly, who was listed on the lineup card as batting ahead of him. The Brooklyn blunder, however, had not been detected earlier by an inattentive Dave Bancroft, or his coaches, when Kelly, the seventh-place hitter, batted out of turn for a second time and homered against Hubbell in the fifth inning. With more keen observation from the Giants' bench authority—which did not realize the visitors' batting flub until the *third* time around the order—Hubbell might have won the game, 2–1, in nine innings, albeit without his personal strikeout mark. (Kelly's blast would have been annulled.) Batting in the proper spot, López later crossed the plate with the winning run in the top of the 12th, scoring on one of the nine hits permitted by Hubbell. Lefty O'Doul provided his club with its first run, a solo homer off Hubbell in the fourth. (O'Doul whiffed three times in the extra-inning contest, the *only* time in his 11-year career he struck out that many times in one game.) Watty Clark was the impressive complete game winner for the visiting team.

Four days hence, in the first game of a Decoration Day doubleheader, Hubbell downed the Braves, 6–2, at Braves Field. He allowed one earned run on eight hits. The next time the southpaw took the mound, the Giants' bench authority had radically changed.

The first game Hubbell won for his new manager, Bill Terry, came in his second try, on June 10. He defeated the Cincinnati Reds, 4–3, at the Polo Grounds, his sixth win against three losses.

Hubbell won 18 games and lost 11 for the seventh-place Giants. Though he did not throw a shutout, his 2.50 ERA for the season was the second-best mark in the league to Chicago Cub Lon Warneke's 2.37. The Giants' leading pitcher tossed 22 complete games in 32 starts. His 7.3 WAR ranking was bested only by teammate Mel Ott's 7.9.

Remaining relatively constant, in the years since Carl Hubbell joined the Giants, was the team's starting pitching staff. Since 1929, the year Hubbell became a regular, two other hurlers, Bill Walker and Freddie Fitzsimmons, steadfastly alternated with Hubbell from the hill, leading up to the Giants' championship success in 1933. Walker, plagued by arm trouble, was traded by Terry, along with three others, after the club's dismal 1932 campaign. Walker had completed a poor 8–12 season, coughing up the most gopher balls in the league with 23. His ERA had swelled to 4.14 in 177 innings. The Giants received catcher Gus Mancuso and pitcher Ray Starr from the St. Louis Cardinals in the exchange.

Fitzsimmons, the third pitcher in the Giants' triumvirate of starters, suffered through arguably his worst pitching season in 1932. In 31 starts and 4 relief appearances, he was tagged for the most earned runs in the league with 117. He posted an 11–11 record with a 4.43 ERA in 237⅔ innings. This season notwithstanding, Fitzsimmons had been a standout pitcher since joining the Giants' rotation in 1926.

Frederick Landis Fitzsimmons was born July 26, 1901, on his family farm in the Prairie Township sector of Tipton County, in rural central Indiana. The Fitzsimmons ancestral lineage dated back to pre-colonial times. Freddie's great-great-great grandfather Thomas, on his father's side, served in the Continental Army during the Revolutionary War and was among the troops present for British General Charles Cornwallis' surrender at Yorktown. When Fitzsimmons was a young child, his family—consisting at the time of father Richard, mother Margaret Ellen and older sister Mary Louise—pulled up roots and eventually settled in Mishawaka, Indiana, part of metropolitan South Bend.

By his own accounts, Fitzsimmons' vocational aspirations were formed from an early age. "Like most other ball players my ambition as a boy was to be one, and I pointed myself on such a career," Fitzsimmons said. "In those days, I was ambitious to play the infield and my idol was Hans Wagner, although I must confess I had a spot in my heart for Grover Cleveland Alexander."[18]

The Fitzsimmons family eventually grew by three more boys. By age 17, the oldest male, Freddie, was employed by the Dodge Manufacturing Company, an industrial machine parts maker in Mishawaka. It was through this affiliation that Freddie received his first taste of organized baseball playing. (His high school did not have a baseball team in the years that he attended.) A subsidiary company of Dodge sponsored a team in one of the so-called factory leagues that were spread across the area. Freddie latched on with the subsidiary team in 1917 and continued playing what was considered semi-pro ball for two more years. Still a teenager, Fitzsimmons eventually moved out of Mishawaka to Kenosha, Wisconsin, for an opportunity to play with the local industrial team there.

In 1920, the Indiana native signed his first professional contract. He joined the Muskegon Muskies, a Class D Central League squad. The young pitcher signed for a $125 a month salary. He eagerly did so at the Muskies' home ballpark—apparently before a scheduled game. "I was so crazy to sign the contract," Fitzsimmons later recalled, "that I paid fifty cents admission at the gate to report to ... [the] manager ... before he changed his mind."[19]

The Muskies' manager was Doc White, a former 13-year pitcher in the big leagues and the winning pitcher for the Chicago White Sox in the clinching game of the 1906 World Series. Fitzsimmons' biographer, Peter J. DeKever, wrote that Fitzsimmons maintained later on that White was most responsible for rounding him into a major league-quality pitcher. White stressed to him the need to throw different types of pitches and that having less reliance on his fastball, in the long run, would help extend his career.

One of the different pitches Fitzsimmons threw was a knuckleball. Unlike many knuckleball pitchers who develop the pitch out of necessity—trying to prolong a career or overcome other pitching shortcomings—Fitzsimmons fashioned his knuckler from an early age. A boyhood friend of his put him on the path to the "dipsy-do" pitch, which cemented Fitzsimmons' chosen diamond position. "When I was 15 years old," he recounted as an established major league pitcher, "I was playing catch on the street one night with a youngster who said he could throw a knuckleball. He held the ball with his forefinger doubled against his palm and he could make it do funny things. He taught me what he knew about it. I practiced and having used it with considerable success against sandlot teams, I decided to become a pitcher."[20]

Fitzsimmons also commanded a fine curveball in his pitching repertoire, which helped him win 33 games for Muskegon in two and a half seasons. In September of 1922, Fitzsimmons' contract was purchased from Muskegon by the Indianapolis Indians. He won three and lost four over the final few weeks of the season for his new team. In 1923, upset over being refused a cut of his

Freddie Fitzsimmons captures for posterity his stylishly dressed wife Helen prior to the first game of the 1933 World Series.

contract's purchase price, he tried to get back at Muskegon by not reporting to Indianapolis. In the off-season, Fitzsimmons worked side by side with his younger brother Gordon as a member of the Mishawaka Fire Department. He was prepared to make this a year-long endeavor. Fitzsimmons' father, who was also a civil servant—on Mishawaka's police department—eventually convinced his eldest son to reconsider and not squander his baseball talents over a fit of pique.

Fitzsimmons eventually relented and reported to Indianapolis. The time away from the club cost him, however, as he lost a starting slot in the Indians' rotation. He managed nine wins, along with four defeats, in 173 innings; his ERA was 4.53. After the season, Fitzsimmons was induced to travel to Cuba to pitch in the winter league. His time on the island was apparently short, as records show him appearing in only four games with the Marianao club, losing his only decision.

In a full season with Indianapolis in 1924, Fitzsimmons posted a 14–17 record with an ERA of 4.55 in 279 innings. He found his groove the following year, when he won 14 of 20 decisions, with an improved 3.77 ERA, in less than a full season. Earlier, in spring training, the Indians had matched up against the New York Giants in an exhibition game. Fitzsimmons pitched five relief innings, allowing four hits and one run, in the game won by the Indians, 4–3.

Several months later, with the Giants battling Pittsburgh for the National League's top spot, John McGraw took a quick jaunt from Cincinnati, where his club was playing the Reds, to Indianapolis and bought Fitzsimmons. The personal detour was proof that Fitzsimmons had impressed McGraw and that the manager had not forgotten about him. (Fitzsimmons had pitched a one-hitter earlier in the season for Indianapolis, which McGraw presumably had heard about.) The August 8 monetary exchange between McGraw and Indianapolis included sending Giants outfielder Frank Walker to the Indians. Fitzsimmons immediately reported to his new team. The first major league game the young pitcher witnessed came as a member of the New York Giants at Redland Field.

In six minor league seasons, Fitzsimmons had won 73 games and had thrown nearly 1,300 innings. He was 24 years old, yet a pitcher more seasoned than most when he debuted for the Giants on August 12. "This man can throw the knuckler about as well as anyone," McGraw had proclaimed. "He knows how to pitch. I will stake my reputation on it."[21] In a performance that almost mirrored the one McGraw had seen in the spring exhibition game, Fitzsimmons relieved Giants starter Virgil Barnes in the fifth inning and hurled shutout ball for four innings against the Pittsburgh Pirates at Forbes Field. The home team held on to win, 5–3. The Giants' reliever obtained his first big league hit, a single, in his first at-bat.

Four days later, in the second game of a doubleheader at the Polo Grounds, Fitzsimmons received his inaugural start as a major leaguer. He dispersed ten hits but only two runs in defeating the Boston Braves, 6–2. The pitcher also was responsible for half of his team's scoring output, delivering three RBI with two well-timed hits. Fitzsimmons relieved on one other occasion and started eight games over the remainder of the season, as the second-place Giants failed to muster a challenge against the league-topping Pirates. Fitzsimmons pocketed his first shutout win, 3–0, on September 26, a neat four-hitter against the Pirates at the place of his major league introduction. A week later, in the Giants' final game, he lost by the same score to the Phillies at the Baker Bowl. His final rookie numbers were 6–3 with an ERA of 2.65, six complete games and one shutout in 74⅔ innings.

Early in the winter, the Cincinnati Reds, in an attempt to fill a void at first base and trim some age from their pitching staff at the same time, tendered an offer to the Giants for High Pockets Kelly and the rookie right-hander, Fitzsimmons. The deal would send two-time, former batting leader Edd Roush and veteran pitcher Adolfo Luque to New York. "I like Roush, he's a great player, but he has had bad legs for two or three years," John McGraw said in declining the proposal. "Luque is 35 and has seen his best days, while Fitzsimmons is just breaking in."[22]

Fitzsimmons was also acquainting himself with a new life removed from the ranks of bachelorhood. A *Sporting News* profile alluded to the happy fact as follows: "The Giants hurler is a black Irishman, much too good-looking to be a pitcher, for he has a shock of black hair, parted in the middle, dark eyes, a nice voice and is five feet 11 inches in height and weighs 185 pounds. But—don't get excited, he's not on the eligible list."[23]

Fitzsimmons had been married in January 1925. The previous spring, the young man had met Helen Borger, a young woman who happened to live across the street from a place Fitzsimmons and some minor league teammates had rented for the season. Though they had yet to meet, from a distance he was secretly the player who most appealed to Helen, she would later reveal. The social divide was finally bridged through old-fashioned hospitality. Helen sent over a plate of fudge brownies to the ballplayers that she had baked. Fred returned the plate in person to the baker and introduced himself. Less than a year later, he married the Indianapolis girl—who admittedly knew nothing about baseball. (Helen eventually grew to love the sport. Throughout her husband's career, especially down the road with Brooklyn, it was often written that she was one of the most well-thought-of spouses on the team.) The young couple moved to Arizona.

In 1926, Helen's husband soon began getting more acquainted with baseball at the major league level. The pride of Mishawaka had to earn his way into McGraw's starting rotation. He finally did, a month into the season, after five relief appearances. Fitzsimmons' first win as a starter that season came in his third start on May 26. He defeated the Brooklyn Robins, 5–3, at the Polo Grounds. All the visitors' runs were charged to Fitzsimmons; Jimmy Ring recorded the final five outs.

A few weeks later, June 17, Fitzsimmons hurled a tenacious 13 innings to emerge victorious over the Pittsburgh Pirates. Giants third baseman Freddie Lindstrom gained the headlines with a walk-off, three-run home run to give the Giants a 6–5 triumph. All five runs allowed by Fitzsimmons were unearned. In the process, Fitzsimmons stopped the 22-game hitting streak of the Pirates' Kiki Cuyler. The extra-inning win was Fitzsimmons' fifth against four losses.

McGraw, for several seasons now, had been expanding the starting pitching chores on his team to include more and more men. In 1926, Fitzsimmons received 28 starts. With a 14–10 record, he won the most games on the staff, and his 2.88 ERA was bettered by only Virgil Barnes' 2.87 mark, for lowest on the team. The sophomore hurler's 219 innings were third-most on the squad.

Fitzsimmons' record was not a reflection of the Giants' team performance. McGraw's club lost more games than they won for the first time since 1915. The no doubt angry manager shook up the team—and all of baseball—when he traded the previously AWOL Frankie Frisch for Rogers Hornsby as the calendar year was expiring. McGraw also obtained Burleigh Grimes from Brooklyn as part of a three-team trade involving the Philadelphia Phillies. Grimes was a perennial holdout every spring with Brooklyn and commanded an elevated salary. But after his team finished three games under .500 in 1926, McGraw and his boss Stoneham became more receptive to increasing salary budgets. In Grimes they obtained one of baseball's best and most reliable hurlers over the past several years. Grimes had lost more games than he had won the past two seasons, which must have made him more expendable.

Fitzsimmons slotted behind Grimes and Opening Day starter Virgil Barnes as the Giants' number three moundsman in 1927. Three days after saving Barnes' and the Giants' inaugural day victory over the Philadelphia Phillies on April 12, Fitzsimmons started the club's third game and defeated the same team, 6–3, at the Baker Bowl. The right-hander yielded 11 hits and five walks, but only one earned run, in the taxing nine-inning endeavor, in which the Giants committed three errors and turned two double plays.

Fitzsimmons was sharper in his next start on April 20. It was the Giants' home opener, and he tossed a seven-hitter. "With Mayor Walker and 40,000 other fans in the stands," rendered one newsprint account, "the New York Giants opened their home season under ideal weather conditions with a 5 to 1 victory over the Phillies. The game developed into a pitchers' duel between Fred Fitzsimmons and Hub Pruett, the latter weakening at the finish."[24]

In June, McGraw pulled off a fine trade, landing pitcher Larry Benton from the Braves, along with two other players, for second-tier pitchers Hugh McQuillan and Kent Greenfield and highly regarded infielder Edward "Doc" Farrell. (As a Giants prospect, Benton had been traded away by McGraw in 1922, as part of a package deal to Boston for McQuillan.) Benton won 13 games for New York in 1927 (17 combined between the two clubs).

Fitzsimmons matched up against his boyhood idol on June 18, in what must have been a memorable occurrence for him—at least at the start. At Sportsman's Park, Fitzsimmons shared the mound with Pete Alexander. But in one of his poorest performances, Fitzsimmons was chased in the third inning after surrendering a three-run homer to the Cardinals' Jim Bottomley. Alexander pitched the distance in gaining a 6–4 win. Giving up five runs, Fitzsimmons was charged with the loss; his record leveled to 5–5. (Fitzsimmons had previously crossed swords with Alexander in relief on May 8, 1926, when the legendary pitcher was with the Cubs. Fitzsimmons provided 3⅔ innings of middle relief in the game also won by Alexander by the score of 6–4. The Giants pitcher was not involved in the decision.)

On July 9, Fitzsimmons spun his first shutout since his rookie season. With no margin for error in the game, he defeated Jumbo Elliot and Brooklyn, 1–0, at the Polo Grounds. Bill Terry doubled in Edd Roush with the only run of the game, as 45,000 fans watched the Saturday afternoon pitchers' duel, lasting one hour and 25 minutes. The Giants right-hander improved his record to 8–6 with the five-hit, no-walk gem.

Fitzsimmons had an even better second half of the season, including a particularly strong September—although John McGraw did not see it. Rogers Hornsby managed the Giants over the final four weeks of the campaign. The 26-year-old pitcher won five games in the month, four as a starter and all complete games. His 31 starts were second on the staff to Grimes' 34, as was his win total (17–10 to Grimes' 19–8 mark). He was outdistanced in innings by Grimes, 259⅔ to 244⅔, and trimmed in ERA, 3.54 to 3.72, by the famed spitballer. Fitzsimmons came out of the bullpen on 11 occasions, finishing seven games.

Fitzsimmons' 17th win of the season occurred on September 27, a 6–2 decision over the Phillies at Baker Bowl. It kept the Giants 3½ games behind first-place Pittsburgh. But three days later, the Giants were eliminated from the chase and eventually finished two games short of the league's big prize.

The following season, 1928, the husky Hoosier won 20 games and lost nine, in arguably his best major league season and his sole 20-win campaign. Joining Fitzsimmons in the charmed circle was Larry Benton. The reacquired Giants pitcher produced a career year from the mound, winning 25 games while losing nine, with a fine 2.73 ERA in 310⅓ innings.

Fitzsimmons accepted 31 starts and nine emergency calls from the bullpen. The 40 appearances generated 261⅓ innings and a 3.68 earned run average. He won two of his first three starts before suffering his first loss on May 14. The setback occurred at Wrigley Field, where he could always count on a good support group of friends and family from his Indiana home territory. He allowed six runs, though only two were earned, and was defeated by Charlie Root, 8–2. After the game, John McGraw was hit by a passing car outside the park while attempting to flag down a taxi.

Of the 16 complete games Fitzsimmons tossed in 1928, three were extra-inning efforts. On June 14, he was defeated by the Pirates, 4–3, in 11 innings. Absorbing his third loss against six wins, the right-hander allowed ten hits, including a Sparky Adams triple in the final inning, preceding a Paul Waner sacrifice fly.

Five weeks afterward, on July 21, Fitzsimmons engaged in a valiant pitching display lasting 14⅔ innings against the Chicago Cubs at Wrigley Field. In the grueling effort, the longest of his big league career, Fitzsimmons was defeated by a game-winning hit by Cubs first baseman Charlie Grimm, the 13th safety permitted by the gutsy Giants pitcher. The final score was 2–1. Art Nehf threw the first 13 frames for Chicago. It was the first game of a doubleheader, played in three hours and five minutes. The nightcap lasted ten innings, also won the Cubs, 5–4. Both extra-inning games took just over five hours to play.

On the first of September, Fitzsimmons twirled his only shutout of the season. The Giants had lost eight games in a row, their longest losing skid of the year. Brooklyn writer Tommy Holmes presented a tart lead in the next day's *Eagle* that may have stamped Fitzsimmons with his uncharitable nickname. It read: "The task of halting the slump of the Giants was one for strong hands, honest hearts and broad backs. The stupendous nature of the task was not below the undivided concentration of the Harlem Beef Company, Inc., to wit: Fat Fred Fitzsimmons and Francis 'Hefty' Hogan."[25] Holmes was referring to the Giants' batterymen who combined to deliver a 1–0 win over the Brooklyn Robins. Hogan, the catcher, was listed as 6'1" and 240 pounds. Fitzsimmons, from the reference, had added to his 185-pound program weight. Freddie Lindstrom helped end the Giants' losing ways with an RBI single in the third inning, accounting for the only run of the contest. The win was the pitcher's 16th, with eight losses.

Fitzsimmons' 20th win came on September 18 at the Polo Grounds, a ten-inning affair in which the right-hander was crowned the victor when Bill Terry hit a "long, looping drive that just cleared the concrete wall out in deep right field"[26] for a home run. The victory kept the Giants on the heels of the front-running St. Louis Cardinals. But the Missouri team would not be caught; in the end, McGraw's aggregation came up a pair of games short in the standings.

Despite Benton's great year and the impressive coming-of-age season for Fitzsimmons, McGraw had weakened his pitching staff by trading Burleigh Grimes to Pittsburgh, for curveballer Vic Aldridge, two months before the season. McGraw's reasoning had been that Grimes did not win enough games early in the season. Grimes, who had not signed his Giants contract at the time of the one-for-one February 11 swap, was, as previously mentioned, a big winner for the Pirates in 1928. Aldridge registered a 4–7 record for the Giants, who had only two other pitchers with double figures in wins: Joe Genewich (11–4) and rookie Carl Hubbell (10–6).

In the winter of 1927, Fitzsimmons and his wife had left Arizona and moved to Arcadia, California, making it their new winter home and joining Helen's brother, John, in the thriving poultry business that surrounded the area. The former farm boy quickly began operating his own chicken and dairy ranch. In the lean years that would follow, the investment that provided the staple foods of milk and eggs would prove a financially solid one.

Accompanied by his wife, Fitzsimmons journeyed by rail from his California ranch and was among Giants pitchers who participated in the first workout of spring camp, February 15, 1929, under the auspices of coaches Ray Schalk and Bert Niehoff. The men ran the show in San Antonio until John McGraw arrived from Havana. Carl Hubbell, Joe Genewich, and Larry Benton were also in the punctual group.

This outward diligence in training seemingly did not help Fitzsimmons' physique when it came to the measuring eyes of some sportswriters—even when he was at the top of his game. That summer, Fitzsimmons put together a string of outstanding performances against one particular team. "[All] Fat Fred Fitzsimmons of the Giants has to do to beat the Reds is walk to the mound," probed one report. "This year he compiled one of the most remarkable 'jinx' records which has come to light in modern times. In four consecutive appearances against the men from Ohio, Fitzsimmons scored four shutouts and pitched 36 consecutive scoreless innings."[27]

Three of the whitewashes were at Redland Field, where Fitzsimmons won four out of five decisions that season. Two came in the same series, on June 8 and 11. The shutouts against the Reds supplied his quota for the year and surpassed by one his career total to date. The shutouts also served to temper Fitzsimmons' final ERA of 4.10, due partly to the increased hitting pervading the major leagues. The rest of the Giants' pitchers combined for five shutouts.

Larry Benton recorded three shutouts, and although his ERA was only slightly higher than Fitzsimmons at 4.14, his 12–17 record fizzled in comparison to his 25-win campaign of a year earlier. Fitzsimmons' 15 wins (with 11 losses) were second on the club to Carl Hubbell's 18. As in prior seasons, Fitzsimmons was called from the bullpen often, on seven occasions. He made 30 starts and completed 14. Lefty Bill Walker enjoyed a breakout year, winning 14 games and losing seven as a part-time starter. His 3.09 ERA was the lowest in the league. The same league in which the Chicago Cubs were head and shoulders above the rest of the field.

3. The Pitching Staff Sustained by "The Meal Ticket"   73

Fitzsimmons signed and returned his contract for 1930 to the Giants' offices before the end of January, and was again one of the pitchers and catchers engaging in early spring workouts at San Antonio, under the watchful eye of coach Dave Bancroft. The Giants were anticipating the arrival of highly touted pitching prospect Roy Parmelee, who was hoped, for his sake, would arrive before John McGraw.

Bancroft took a Giants squad, with the arrived McGraw's blessing, to Houston, for an exhibition game against the Chicago White Sox on March 8. Despite being in camp for only three weeks, and with the opening of the season still five weeks off, Bancroft let Fitzsimmons pitch the entire game. The burly right-hander was defeated, 5–3, in the game played at Buffalo Stadium.

A month later, Fitzsimmons was mistreated by the White Sox again in a game played in Fitzsimmons' backyard of Ft. Wayne, Indiana. The final was 8–1, although it is unclear how long Fitzsimmons pitched. (No other Giants pitchers were mentioned in the *Brooklyn Eagle*'s recap.) The Giants committed four errors and made only one hit. Though the Giants seemed to play the game as if distracted, only Fitzsimmons had a legitimate excuse for his mind to be elsewhere. His wife was expecting their first child any day. Two days after the 8–1 drubbing, Fitzsimmons became a father with the birth of his daughter Helen Louise on April 11.

Eight days afterward, Fitzsimmons picked up his initial win of the new campaign in the Giants' second game. Fitzsimmons relieved starter Hub Pruett to open the ninth inning, with the Giants trailing the Philadelphia Phillies, 2–1. Pruett had given up only one hit—a two-run home run to Chuck Klein—when he was removed for a pinch-hitter. Fitzsimmons pitched a scoreless ninth, and then benefitted from the Giants' two-run rally to take home the easy victory.

The Giants started the 1930 season with seven straight victories, Fitzsimmons winning the seventh in his usual role as starter. In keeping the Giants undefeated on April 27, the staunch right-hander displayed his all-around pitching savvy. In front of a packed house at Ebbets Field, he defeated the Brooklyn Robins, 10–4. "The real hero of the game," wrote the *New York World*'s William Hennigan, "was Fred Fitzsimmons, now a California chicken fancier. The pudgy knuckleballer started and finished the battle in a blaze of glory. Fitz was doing something nearly every time you looked up and in the fifth inning he 'brought down the house' by grabbing [Wally] Gilbert's terrific line drive with his bare hand and doubling [Johnny] Frederick off first base."[28]

The Indiana hurler earned the reputation of being a top fielding pitcher, and he had the numbers to back it up. In 1930, Fitzsimmons led all NL pitchers in putouts for the third time in five years. In 1926 and 1928, he had defended his position without making a single error.

Fitzsimmons won only once in May, as hitters throughout baseball exhibited an ability to strike the ball with more positive results than ever before. The lone victory came at home on May 21. Fitzsimmons started and won, 11–4, against the Philadelphia Phillies. The same day, McGraw traded former 25-game winner and more recent holdout Larry Benton to Cincinnati for Hughie Critz.

In June and July, Fitzsimmons picked up his pace, checking off eight wins, two of them with relief stints of four innings each. In back-to-back complete game victories at the Polo Grounds on July 26 and 30, Fitzsimmons connected for his first big league home runs. His first four-base wallop was one of three the Giants hit in his 10–4 triumph over the Pittsburgh Pirates. It was powered into the left field stands in the eighth inning with no one on base and the game in hand. The second home run, a two-run shot, provided late-game insurance runs in Fitzsimmons' 5–2 defeat of the Boston Braves.

The New Yorkers entered August five games off the National League pace, in third place, behind front-running Brooklyn and three games in back of the Chicago Cubs.

That summer, night baseball began gaining popularity throughout several regions of the country. More than 40 cities were cited as having parks that had hosted games after sundown. A two-game series under the lights in Sacramento, California, between the Sacramento Senators and Oakland Oaks, had drawn 62,000 people. Wrigley Field in Los Angeles had been equipped with floodlight-type lamps. (Ironically, almost 60 years passed before its more famous namesake in Chicago would be.) All-time attendance records for Wrigley Field and Houston's Buffalo Stadium had recently been set with night games held at those venues. The Jersey City Skeeters, the Giants' quasi-affiliate, had played evening games not very far from the Giants' home stadium. The following report on the current mini-rage identified the practical aspects that would drive the sport into the nighttime arena in the near future:

> Club owners in the cities where the night game has been adopted are almost unanimous in declaring that the quality of the game has not deteriorated, while the attendance has sharply increased. They point out that many people attend the night games who cannot get away from their occupations in the daytime, and that it is more comfortable in the cool of the evening than during the heat of the day.[29]

McGraw was not at all a fan of baseball under artificial light, and Stoneham was adamantly against it. Mel Ott, when asked to comment on the novel minor league trend, prophetically put it best. "If the crowds justify it," he said, "we might as well get used to it."[30]

With the first major league night game still five years away, Fitzsimmons would not have to worry about toeing the rubber beneath anything but natural sunbeams for the time being. In his first August start, Fitzsimmons did most of the shining, tossing his only shutout of the season to blank the Brooklyn Robins, 4–0, on six hits. The August 4 victory was the 12th in 15 games for third-place New York and reduced its deficit in the standings to four games. After the Ebbets Field encounter, beat writer Tommy Holmes suggested that the Robins' defeat was due as much to a team batting slump as the opposition's pitching. He ungraciously wrote: "Instead of a fat perspiring fellow like Fred Fitzsimmons toiling and spinning on the mound like a composite of Walter Johnson and Christy Mathewson ... one catches the image of Babe Herman, Glenn Wright, Del Bissonette, Jake Flowers and others in the throes of a batting slump."[31]

The reference to Fitzsimmons "spinning" described a unique delivery that the pitcher had developed. From the set position, with his hands together at the waist, he lifted his left leg and showed his back to the batter with a twirling motion. (Reds pitcher Johnny Cueto is a contemporary clone.) The motion allowed Fitzsimmons to "hide" the ball and throw it seemingly from out of his uniform. The pitcher landed with a small hop and feet spread apart, giving him fielding mobility to his left or right.

Fitzsimmons had an eight-game winning streak halted on August 20 by the St. Louis Cardinals. From that point, with a 13–6 record, the Giants ace won six and lost only once, with one victory coming in relief. Fitzsimmons completed his final six starts of the season, winning five. His 19th win was at the expense of Brooklyn, a team he usually had good success against. Fitzsimmons defeated the Robins at Ebbets Field, 8–2, on September 23. The Giants had already been eliminated from contention by a St. Louis Cardinals team that had moved past three teams, the Giants included, in a surge to the top of the National League standings.

Fitzsimmons threw 17 complete games in 29 starts. His ERA of 4.25 reflected the assertive hitting displayed in the league throughout the year. His 19 victories led the staff, although 17-game winners Bill Walker and Carl Hubbell had moderately better ERAs. Fitzsimmons' 12 relief appearance were more than Walker and Hubbell combined.

In 1931, a purportedly less lively baseball helped level the pitching plane in the National League. Also seeking an adjustment of sorts in 1931, in the way of salary compensation, was Freddie Fitzsimmons. It was not until March 4, following a long distance phone call with John McGraw, that he left his California residence to prepare for a new campaign.

Now in the fold, Fitzsimmons was expected to head the same Giants starting staff from a year ago, consisting of himself, Walker, Hubbell and spitballer Clarence Mitchell. Tuning up for his first Opening Day start, Fitzsimmons hurled ten innings against the Chicago White Sox on April 9 in an exhibition tilt held in Charlotte, North Carolina. It was three days after he had pitched a complete game versus the same Chicago team in Jackson, Mississippi.

On Opening Day, April 14, Fitzsimmons pitched six innings against the Philadelphia Phillies at the Baker Bowl, permitting four runs. Hughie Critz's three-run home run in the top of the seventh inning not only got his starter off the hook but put Fitzsimmons in position to win the game. The Giants scored five runs in the inning and won, 9–5.

Five days later, the Giants scored the same number of runs and Fitzsimmons held down the Braves for the entire game to take a 9–2 decision. After a no-decision, Fitzsimmons won three straight games, the last two by shutouts. He defeated Boston, 2–1 (the run was unearned), on the Giants' home turf, and then blanked Brooklyn and Chicago in succession. In the encounter versus the Braves, he scored the game's first run after doubling and drove in the game-winning run with a single. In an 8–0, road whitewash over Brooklyn, only three Robins tagged him for hits. In the second shutout, on Sunday, May 10, at the Polo Grounds, Fitzsimmons threw a four-hitter in front of sell-out crowd of 55,000. He walked none and struck out four Cubs' hitters. The 5–0 victory was garlanded by a second-inning, grand slam home run by the winning pitcher himself.

The St. Louis Cardinals put an end to Fitzsimmons' superior pitching in his next trip to the mound. In the first stanza of their meeting with the hot hurler, May 17, the club ended Fitzsimmons' 23 scoreless-inning streak and a string of 34 innings without allowing an earned run. The Cardinals sent the Giants' top pitcher to his first defeat, 6–1, with five runs charged to Fitzsimmons. The defeat was particularly disappointing for the capacity-exceeding throng of 56,000 at the Polo Grounds.

The early season magic quickly left Fitzsimmons, as he lost four more games in succession, one of them, 2–0, to the Boston Braves in a game shortened to six innings by Sunday curfew. In the other losses, he was not effective.

Showing a penchant for streakiness, Fitzsimmons then won five straight decisions in six starts, beginning June 12. (In the no-decision, he was knocked from the box in the second inning, but the Giants rallied to spare Fitzsimmons a potential loss.) His best-pitched game in that stretch was a 10–0 win over the Pittsburgh Pirates on June 20 in which he also hit his second home run of the season. Newly converted outfielder Freddie Lindstrom kept his pitcher's shutout intact, hauling in two difficult catches in right field.

Fitzsimmons flung his fourth and final whitewash on July 25; it was a

5–0, four-hit suppression of the Cincinnati Reds in the first game of a doubleheader at Redland Field. The fourth-place Giants, with a win in the second game, made up a half-game in the standings to St. Louis, but still found themselves 8½ games behind the eventual champions. Following back-to-back wins over Brooklyn on August 4 and 9, Fitzsimmons hiked his record to 14–7. On August 24, Fitzsimmons became a 15-game winner when Bill Terry hit an inside-the-park home run that ended up in the visitors' bullpen against the left field Polo Grounds wall. A failed, falling-down attempt to catch the ball by Chicago Cubs left fielder Danny Taylor allowed Terry to steam home with the winning run for a 2–1 Giants victory.

On September 5, meeting Brooklyn again, Fitzsimmons tried for his 17th triumph. He obtained it, but not without also receiving some hard knocks—to his person. The starter was cruising along with a 4–1 lead and three hits surrendered, in the top of the seventh inning. With two outs, opposing pitcher Fred Heimach hit a ground smash back to the box, hitting Fitzsimmons in the groin. Fitzsimmons found the ball and threw Heimach out at first; then he keeled over in pain and lost consciousness temporarily. Biographer DeKever wrote that "the team doctor and other Giants gathered around him, ready to take him off the field on a stretcher."[32] But he insisted on staying in the game and was helped back to the dugout. As luck would have it, the aggrieved hurler was due to bat first in the home inning. The first pitch from Heimach hit Fitzsimmons in the face. He went down in a heap. "I didn't even see the ball," the battered player later recounted. "When I come to, they're waving smelling salts under my nose."[33] Fitzsimmons then retired from the action, and his team went on to win 5–1.

Four days later, the tough Irishman was back on the hill, doing his part for New York City's disenfranchised residents, in the charity game between the New York Yankees and Giants at Yankee Stadium. Pitching the bruised Fitzsimmons indicated McGraw's desire to win the exhibition. The Giants' gritty pitcher hurled the first six innings, permitting three runs, to a strictly first-string Jacob Ruppert team. For the first five frames, Fitzsimmons used American League baseballs, unchanged in composition from last season—unlike NL balls, which were purposely designed to be less lively in 1931. During those five innings, the Yankees scored two runs. When the "duller" National League balls came into play, the Bronx Bombers plated five runs, including a long home run by Babe Ruth, who was hitting with a bandaged right thumb. The Yankees won, 7–3, as Lefty Gómez pitched the entire game for his squad, scattering ten hits and spacing single runs in three stanzas. He allowed one run with his own American League balls and two with the National League's.

Back at it in four days' time, on September 13, Fitzsimmons won his 18th game, beating the Reds in Cincinnati. The 9–4 victory gave the Giants, a team all but mathematically eliminated from pennant contention, a split in a doubleheader. When Fitzsimmons' next start came around, a no-decision against the St. Louis Cardinals on September 18, the team was playing for pride.

With a handful of games left on the schedule, three young pitchers were offered starting assignments: Jim Mooney, Roy Parmelee and Hal Schumacher. Only Schumacher won, and that was due to considerable offensive support. Fitzsimmons took the mound in the Giants' final game on September 27. He responded with the worst showing of his career. The Dodgers knocked Fitzsimmons all around Ebbets Field mercilessly with 12 hits and nine runs in two and two-thirds innings. The final was 12–3.

The ugly defeat could not blight Fitzsimmons' all-around good year. The final day's bombing pushed his ERA over 3.00 to 3.05. But his 18 wins (against 11 losses) led the team's pitchers. He also topped everyone with 253⅔ innings, derived from 35 appearances, all but two as a starter. He threw 19 complete games, tied with teammate Bill Walker and two behind Carl Hubbell's 21. His four shutouts tied Hubbell for the second-most on the staff, behind league ERA champ Bill Walker's six. The new, raised-stitch design of the National League baseballs seemed to have stemmed the prior year's prolific offensive numbers. It should be noted that Fitzsimmons hit a career-high four home runs that season.

Freddie Fitzsimmons had now won 109 games for the Giants, in not quite six and one-half seasons—tops on the Giants during that time. His standing as a consistent winner somehow became lost, or diminished, in the Giants' eyes, when management sent him his contract for 1932. For the second year in a row, Fitzsimmons was displeased with the compensation offered, so much so that he wired his dissatisfaction from California on January 15, also advising the press as to the matter.

The following newspaper notice, a few days later, implied a desire on the Giants' part to come to terms in a timely manner with not only Fitzsimmons, but two other discontented stars: "It is felt the Giants will make a strong effort to come to terms with their three avowed holdouts, Bill Terry, Freddie Lindstrom and Fred Fitzsimmons before they start for spring camp at Los Angeles on February 14."[34] The year was fraught with broad salary cuts for all professional players, as the owners leveraged the nation's steep economic downturn to the fullest against their covenant-bound employees.

Lindstrom negotiated with the Giants in the press, as was the practice of the day, and came to terms rather quickly—on January 20. That left Fitzsimmons, Terry, second baseman Hughie Critz, and left fielder Freddy Leach as the remaining unsigned Giants regulars. Leach, the player McGraw obtained in the disastrous Lefty O'Doul trade, would sign and would be sold to Boston the following month, clearing the way for expensive recruit Len Koenecke.

Fitzsimmons was still not on the payroll when the Giants' pitchers and catchers reported to Los Angeles in mid–February. He was present, though, at the train depot to greet the advance group led by secretary James Tierney, when the players derailed. It took the later arrival of John McGraw to convince Fitz to sign his contract, and that was only following a closed-door meeting between the pitcher and manager on February 24. McGraw sent the terms of the contract back to New York for Stoneham's approval, which came through on the 27th.

Fitzsimmons wasted no time in getting into the swing of things. On February 25, he endured an extended workout in an intrasquad game, displaying that he had kept in shape on his chicken ranch during the off-season. "The prize for best condition in the New York Giants' training camp should go to Fred Fitzsimmons," judged one report. "The big pitcher played 12 innings at third base with the Giants yesterday, although it was his first day in camp. One of the best fielding pitchers in baseball, Fred turned in a neat job at the hot corner."[35]

After what had to be considered an all-around pleasant experience, the New York Giants left the City of Angels, carrying the disconsolate news that one of their own had lost a child. Second-year infielder Johnny Vergez's infant son had died from polio. For those who believe in such things, perhaps it was an omen for what was to turn into a disconsolate 1932 season for the New York Giants.

Fitzsimmons lost three of his first four decisions. The third defeat occurred in Cincinnati on May 16. The Giants and Fitzsimmons were forced to resume a game that had been halted by sudden rain showers, without the weather having cleared up. Umpiring crew chief Bill Klem insisted the Giants return to a still rainy field, to ensure there would be sufficient daylight to complete the game. Picking up with the bases loaded, the Reds broke the game open with six runs in the inning against Fitzsimmons to win, 6–2. McGraw, who was not in attendance due to a bout with "indigestion," filed a protest to league president John Heydler over Klem's actions. It was dismissed.

> The Giants' boss claims that every time the veteran arbiter works a game where the Giants are concerned he immediately assumes a churlish and domineering mood. [Yesterday], the regal gentleman in blue chased the Giants out of the dugout during a downpour and made Fitz work with a slippery ball, and held his watch on them, threatening to forfeit the game if they did not stop their whining and get on with the play.[36]

The skies cleared up after the Reds' big inning ended.

Two and a half weeks later, McGraw's illnesses forced him to step down as manager. On June 4, Fitzsimmons provided enough steady pitching for new field boss Bill Terry to pick up his initial win as manager. In the first game of a doubleheader, Fitzsimmons tossed 8⅓ innings before tiring and giving up three runs in the ninth inning. The game was well in hand and the Giants won, 10–4. The Giants won the second game as well to furnish Terry with a most auspicious first day at the office.

But wins were too few and far between the rest of the way for the Giants. Fitzsimmons managed 11 victories for himself, along with the same number of defeats. He allowed the most earned runs in the league with 117 and, correspondingly, his ERA bounced up to 4.43. He threw no shutouts. His 11 complete games (in 31 starts) were the fewest of any of his seven full seasons. The Giants finished in next-to-last place.

In a doubleheader on the last day of the season, Terry gave the start in the meaningless second game to Roy Parmelee, a young, hard thrower who had been trying to earn a place with the team for a few seasons. Parmelee was defeated, 6–3, although the four runs charged to his record were all unearned. Carl Hubbell won his 18th game in the opener.

Leroy Earl Parmelee was born in Lambertville, Michigan, on April 25, 1907. He attended Lambertville High School, where he was converted

The fourth man in the Giants' starting rotation, Roy Parmelee contributed 13 victories. He lost a tiring heartbreaker, 1–0, in 15 innings, to Cincinnati's Red Lucas on July 16, 1933.

from an infielder to a pitcher. Parmelee half-heartedly joked with a sportswriter early in his career that his baseball coach in high school told him that he knew right away the youngster was best suited for the mound. When the sportswriter asked how the coach knew, the pitcher answered, with a smile, that he hit the first batter he pitched to in high school on the head.

The story confirmed the lack of control, often associated with young pitchers, that also plagued Parmelee throughout in his career. A right-hander, Parmelee attended Eastern Michigan University and pitched in and around the local recreational baseball leagues of the area. At the age of 19, he was signed professionally by the minor league team he had grown up watching play. "I was playing twilight ball and pitched a couple of shutouts," Parmelee disclosed. "One was a no-hit affair. Bill Clarkson was scouting for Toledo then, he signed me. I was farmed out that year and the next."[37] In his youth, Parmelee would often cross the state border that Lambertville hugged with neighboring Ohio to watch the Toledo Mud Hens. In 1927, his first professional season, Parmelee was optioned by Toledo to two lower level clubs. He was still with the Mud Hens in June of that season when the New York Giants came to town to play an exhibition game. Casey Stengel, the Mud Hens' manager, chose Parmelee as one of the pitchers in the game. The 20-year-old hurler allowed three runs in three innings, all the runs coming in one frame.

In 1928, Parmelee was again farmed out, to the New England League's Salem Witches, where he posted a 10–18 record. Coming back to Toledo for the full 1929 season, Parmelee recorded a 12–14 won-lost ledger. Pitching 234 innings, his ERA was 4.77. Toward the end of the minor league season, his contract was purchased from Toledo by the New York Giants. One would think Stengel was whispering in McGraw's ear for the young pitcher to draw such a plum assignment.

Parmelee made his big league debut as a relief pitcher at the Polo Grounds on September 28, 1929. In two innings of work, he allowed three runs on five hits. He did not walk a batter. On October 6, in the last game on the schedule, the high-ranking prospect received a start. At Braves Field, the 22-year-old pitcher picked up his initial major league win. Parmelee was removed from the game after five innings, ahead 5–4. Ray Lucas preserved the lead for his youthful cohort, hurling four scoreless innings. The Giants added four more runs to win handily.

The following season, Parmelee earned a place with the Giants coming out of spring training. The 1930 season was probably the worst for a young pitcher to try and make his mark. Home run totals in the National League jumped from 754 to 892. Six teams batted over .300. The collective ERA of the eight teams was just under five, at 4.97.

One slightly extreme example of the mistreatment of pitchers came in Parmelee's first action of the year. On April 29, scoring at the Polo Grounds occurred on a scale rarely seen at the old Manhattan ballpark. "The innings were so long that the outfielders came back to the bench with a full set of whiskers and went unrecognized by their teammates," exaggerated one sportswriter. "Base hits rang out like the rattle of thunder. Runs trouped across the plate in droves."[38] The Giants were defeated by the Brooklyn Robins, 19–15. Parmelee, the fifth Giants pitcher in the game, threw the final seven innings in relief of four very ineffective predecessors. He gave up the last six Brooklyn runs, half of them earned. He was not involved in the decision.

Parmelee's start of the season was one to forget. He lasted one-third of an inning, allowing six runs on four hits and two walks. The 16–8 Giants loss, charged to Parmelee, took place at Forbes Field on May 7. When club rosters had to be trimmed to 25 by June 15, Parmelee was one of the players excised. The inexperienced pitcher spent part of June and July, and all of September, with the Newark Bears. For Newark, Parmelee went 5–4 with a 3.71 ERA in 80 innings, much better than his 0–1 record and 9.43 ERA in just 21 innings with the Giants.

The high hopes the Giants maintained for Parmelee's development were made clear in the spring of 1931, with a visceral assessment of the pitcher's raw aptitude by the Giants' headmaster himself. "It depends wholly on his control," said John McGraw. "He's got more natural stuff and talent than any young pitcher I've seen in many years. He's strong, too, and can work early and often. If he can learn to control his 'stuff,' and Chief Bender is working hard to correct his faults, he will represent just about all the pitching help I need."[39]

The former Athletics pitcher and 212-game winner Bender was a new coach hired by the Giants for that 1931 campaign. But not even Bender's shared pitching wisdom could prevent Parmelee from being demoted to begin the season at Columbus in the American Association.

A few years earlier, in the lower minors, Parmelee had been tagged with one of two nicknames he carried. Generic in nature, it surfaced in an American Association weekly recap in *The Sporting News* that read: "Not the least of the reasons for the improved showing of the Columbus entry has been the pitching performances of Bud Parmelee, the mastodonic moundsman acquired from the New York Giants."[40] The prehistoric reference to Parmelee's size was due to his tall, broad-shouldered physique.

After winning eight games with Columbus, Parmelee was recalled by the Giants early in August. Following several relief appearances, Parmelee received his first start of the season on September 2—and first decision. His deliveries proved too much for the Boston Braves. The big Michigander pitched a four-hitter, winning 3–1, in the back end of a Braves Field twin bill. Lauding the effort Joe Vila wrote,

> Parmelee, a 200-pounder, more than six feet tall, is a natural born pitcher, but has been retarded by wildness ever since the Giants purchased him from Toledo three years ago. He has been farmed out for the purpose of correcting his chief fault.... McGraw always insisted if Parmelee could get control of the ball, he would become one of the finest right-handers in the game. It was McGraw's supreme confidence in the big fellow that sent him to the box in Boston, with such gratifying results.[41]

The first game was won by Carl Hubbell, 9–2. Five days later, the same two pitchers combined to give the Giants another pair of victories, this time over the Philadelphia Phillies, in New York. Hubbell won the opener, 6–0, and Parmelee followed with a 2–1 triumph, walking six. He was reached for only four hits, and the run he allowed was unearned.

Parmelee was defeated, 3–2, by the Pittsburgh Pirates on September 11, pitching the eight-inning distance. Two days after the Giants clinched second place, a far distance behind champion St. Louis, Parmelee made his fifth and final start on September 20. His record dropped to 2–2 as he was beaten, 7–6, by Lon Warneke and the Chicago Cubs. Apart from his five starts, Parmelee appeared out of the bullpen eight times and compiled an ERA of 3.68 in 58⅔ innings.

In a sign that he wished to continue his development, Roy Parmelee's 1932 endorsed contract was received by the Giants' administrative offices on January 20. It almost certainly called for the minimum salary, which hovered around $6,000. During the third week of February, Parmelee and catcher Bob O'Farrell met a contingent of Giants players, traveling by rail, in Chicago, on their way to the West Coast.

After a strong showing in camp, McGraw included Parmelee on his staff that headed east. That decision may have been placed in doubt on March 29. Parmelee opened an exhibition game against the Seattle Indians and was bombed. The game was played at Santa Cruz. Every major business in the picturesque central California town took out advertising space in the *Santa Cruz Sentinel*, welcoming the Giants. The day was declared an unofficial holiday with most merchants in town closing shop early in anticipation of the afternoon ballgame. Mr. and Mrs. McGraw, along with secretaries James Tierney and Eddie Brannick and team trainer Edward Jones, were given a motorcycle police escort into town to their hotel. Accompanying them was Santa Cruz mayor Fred Swanton.

The big game was a disappointment, with the Seattle Indians crushing the Giants, 18–4, in front of a capacity crowd. The local press complained afterward that McGraw had repaid the town's hospitality by fielding a team of "scrubs."

(The only regular who played for the Giants was catcher Shanty Hogan. Jo-Jo Moore also played but he was shortly destined for the minors.) The Giants' A-team was in San Francisco, confronting the Seals. Parmelee was the starter in Santa Cruz, and he lasted 1⅓ innings, allowing seven runs on nine hits. *New York Herald-Tribune* writer Rud Rennie reported that "the Giants paid $25,000 for Parmelee [in 1929] and the Indians made him look like a lead dime."[42]

McGraw was not only embarrassed by his team's performance but also by Community Park's naïve public address announcer. McGraw's arrival at the park, sometime after the first pitch, was pointed out to all by the announcer over the loud speaker: *"There he is, ladies and gentlemen! The man we have all been waiting for! The famous Mugsy McGraw!"*[43] The Giants' manager turned beet red with anger at hearing his detested nickname so audibly dispatched. According to the ever-present Frank Graham, the seething McGraw yelled to acting manager Tom Clarke to yank Parmelee, directing a few unprintable words at both his coach and the exiting pitcher.

Once the season began, Parmelee was relegated to short-term bullpen work for the first two months. As part of the June 15 roster cut, he was one of two players optioned to the minors by manager Terry in order for the Giants to comply with that season's mandatory 23-player roster limit.

Parmelee had a spectacular three-month showing with the Columbus Red Birds of the American Association, posting a 14–1 record. The scintillating record earned him a recall to the Giants in September, as the team limped to the finish line. He made three appearances, all starts within an eight-day span. The right-hander lost all three. The decisions were Parmelee's only ones on the season, in which he pitched only 25⅓ innings with an ERA of 3.91. On September 25, the last day of the season, in the second game of a doubleheader, Parmelee was defeated 6–3, by the Philadelphia Phillies. At the Polo Grounds, he gave up four runs, none earned. He allowed only two hits in seven innings, with six walks and ten strikeouts.

It was a pitching line the Giants chose to view as indicating more promise than qualms.

Hal Schumacher was another young pitcher on the Giants. He found work more regularly, early in his career, than did Roy Parmelee.

Schumacher came from a large, German immigrant family that resided in upstate New York. The youngest of nine children, Harold Henry Schumacher was born on November 23, 1910, in Hinckley, a town about 125 miles from the Canadian border. He was the third child of Andrew and Margaret Schumacher to be born in the United States. Prior to Schumacher turning three, his family resettled in Dolgeville, a small town 23 miles northeast of Hinckley. The Schumachers' eldest son, Joseph, was killed in the battle of

3. The Pitching Staff Sustained by "The Meal Ticket"

Chateau Thierry in World War I. Joseph was a skilled baseball player and had legitimate hopes of playing professionally. When he was killed, father Andrew lost interest in the game until Hal reached the major leagues.

From a young age, Harold, or "Hal," was a bright student with a natural disposition for athletics. An early write-up on the future pitcher indicated that he applied himself rigorously to all of his endeavors, as a way of honoring his fallen brother, whom Hal had looked up to. Hal became a two-sport player in high school (basketball and baseball), and after graduation he earned some extra money playing for a semi-pro team based in a neighboring town. Commendably, his primary focus at this time was his education. After high school, he attended St. Lawrence University in Canton, one of many state enclaves of higher learning erected within the scenic landscapes of northern New York. At St. Lawrence, Schumacher continued his baseball playing and began making a name for himself with his pitching performances.

John McGraw's old 19th century manager at Olean, Al Kinney, was the first to spot Schumacher's potential. He let his now-famous former player know about the college right-hander. McGraw dispatched a scout, who signed Schumacher in 1931, in his junior year. For Schumacher, who was facing tuition problems, the signing could not have come at a better time. The young man turned pro with the intent of returning to school in the off-season to obtain his degree.

The 20-year-old Schumacher literally went from the college campus to training camp to the major leagues, in the course of a few months. He made the team as easily the youngest member of the pitching staff in the spring of 1931. (Schumacher was the third-youngest player in the NL that season.) The cantankerous John McGraw clearly took a liking to the green conscript, for he named Schumacher as the starting pitcher in the Giants' second game of the season—April 15, against the Philadelphia Phillies. McGraw's fellow upstate New Yorker did not make it out of the second inning. He was smacked around for an inning and one-third, allowing seven runs on seven hits. The Giants were defeated, 10–7, at the Baker Bowl, in a game in which McGraw used five pitchers and the Phillies two. Schumacher was the loser.

The young hurler pitched sparingly after that. Instead of sending him to the minors to aid his development, McGraw kept him in the bullpen for the first four months of the season. He gained entry into six games, all in relief, pitching a total of only seven innings. On June 22, against the Cubs, he had a performance similar to his Opening Day fiasco, which ballooned his ERA to 25.31. Finally, on August 6, the Giants demoted the 0–1 Schumacher to Rochester in the International League and optioned him shortly afterwards to the Eastern League's Bridgeport Bears.

With Bridgeport, Schumacher won four games and lost two, hurling 54 innings in eight appearances. Recalled by the Giants in late September, the pitcher who had started the Giants' second game on the schedule tied together his first big league season by starting the Giants' next-to-last game on September 21. Schumacher defeated the Chicago Cubs at Wrigley Field, 15–7, evening his meager record. A good crowd of 22,000 was on hand for the Monday afternoon game between the second- and third-place teams in the National League, with both squads long eliminated from title contention by the St. Louis Cardinals. The fine gathering saw anything but fine pitching. Schumacher went the distance, and six of the seven runs he surrendered were earned. He allowed ten hits, struck out seven and walked *nine*, in registering what must have been an off-the-charts pitch count. Five Cubs pitchers issued five free passes and were reached for *27* hits by Giants hitters. Despite the number of base runners and runs scored, the game was played in under two and a half hours.

In mid–February 1932, the suitcase-packed Schumacher met the Giants' Limited train at Utica, New York, on its way to the West Coast for spring training. The train had departed from New York City and would make a stop in Buffalo to pick up pitcher Joe Genewich, who had sat out all of last season, unable to come to salary terms. In Chicago, Freddie Lindstrom, Roy Parmelee and Bob O'Farrell boarded the Giants' special transport to the West Coast.

On February 18, the train reached Los Angeles. The Giants derailed under cloudy skies and the threat of rain. The following spring training report captured the arrival:

> The vanguard of the New York Giants moved into spring training quarters here today and immediately laid plans for a first workout at Wrigley Field this afternoon. James Tierney, secretary, brought 16 players, mostly pitchers and catchers, along with coach Tom Clarke. They were greeted here by coach Dave Bancroft and Fred Fitzsimmons and Herman Bell. Tierney said manager John McGraw, en route from Havana, would arrive in a day or two and take complete charge of training. "We had a fine trip," Tierney said, "and are all set for a good season. I hope we get some good weather."[44]

The weather was good, and the stay for the Giants was, with few exceptions, pleasant. Genewich did not make the club and never pitched again in the major leagues. McGraw, except for the episode with the PA announcer in Santa Cruz, which had gotten him extremely hot under the collar, regarded his time out west so favorably that he booked the team a return engagement in 1933.

In one of the final games of spring camp, Schumacher hurled a 5–0, five-hit shutout over the San Francisco Missions at Seals Stadium on April 1. If that did not seal a spot on the staff, an outing a week later certainly did. On

Hal Schumacher produced a sterling campaign for Bill Terry's champions, although toward the end of the season he was physically worn and gaunt-looking.

April 8, in an exhibition contest at Navin Field, he defeated Detroit, 2–1. The complete game was the Giants' fifth victory in seven meetings with the Tigers, including spring sessions in California.

The Giants began the 1932 campaign by dropping their first three games. In the fourth game, Schumacher took the Polo Grounds mound for the first time as a starter and was splendid. The former college pitcher had to share some of the spotlight with one of his infielders, as this game overview explained: "Johnny Vergez and Hal Schumacher enabled the Giants to gain their first victory of the season Sunday, a 6 to 0 win over the Boston Braves. Vergez, slender Portuguese [sic] third baseman, blasted a homer into the left field Polo Grounds stands with the bases loaded. Schumacher, pitching his first complete game in the majors, shut out Boston on two hits."[45]

Schumacher was out of kilter in his next start, five days hence, April 22. At the Baker Bowl, he faced only eight Philadelphia Phillies batters. He was touched for three hits, two walks and three runs, all unearned. The Giants had scored seven runs in the top of the first inning. But McGraw did not like what he saw from Schumacher or did not want to take any chances. He pulled the young pitcher after two-thirds of an inning and brought in new bullpen member Hi Bell, who secured the last out of the inning. Bell pitched four more innings, allowed three runs, and was given credit for the 13–8 victory.

Perhaps McGraw's decision was spurred by an out-of-sorts delivery he detected from his starter. "Schumacher is a fast ball pitcher," read one analysis, "and throws a sinker. A downer, he calls it. His delivery is kept low, and, of course, provides plenty of work for the infielders."[46]

Young Hal could not find his good form again during the season. He threw but one more complete game, late in the year. When Terry took control of the club, he removed the rookie from the starting rotation. In September, Terry allowed Schumacher to make three starts, all in doubleheaders. The best of the lot, by far, was on September 13. At the Polo Grounds, Schumacher topped the league's best pitcher in the Cubs' Lon Warneke. It took 11 innings and the score was 3–2. Vergez tripled in Gil English with the winning run.

Schumacher's final record was 5–6, with a respectable 3.55 ERA, in 101⅓ innings. He pitched 27 games, 13 as a starter.

4

The Bullpen Stabilized by "The Pride of Havana"

Adolfo Luque's long journey to become a valuable member of the New York Giants began outside the United States and was interposed with many head-to-head, hard-nosed battles against the Giants themselves, prior to Luque donning the team's orange and black for the first time in 1932. Born August 4, 1890, in Havana, Cuba, Luque initially encountered the New York Giants—and John McGraw—in the late fall of 1911. Pitching for Club Habana, Luque hurled three games against the barnstorming Giants, winning once and dropping two decisions. In the victory, Luque showed some of the combative fire that characterized him through much of his extended major league career. He was ejected from the game in the seventh inning by North American umpire Cy Rigler. He was ahead, 3–2, which was the game's final score.

At the time, Luque had not yet turned pro. As an enlisted soldier, he had been pitching as a member of a regimental army baseball team. A former Cuban League player, later a promoter, Agustín "Tinti" Molina, secured Luque's early release from military service through an acquaintance named Carlos Macía, who had been a well-known 19th-century player in Cuba and was a high-ranking civilian administrator attached to the *ejército* team. Luque signed his first professional contract with Club Fe, one of Cuba's earliest teams. He pitched two seasons with the team. His records show that he did not win a game in six decisions.

In 1913, before his second winter league season, the inexperienced ballplayer had been recruited to play abroad with a squad in the New York–New Jersey League called the Long Branch Cubans. The club was owned and managed by a local Cuban businessman named Antonio Hernández Henriquez and composed of mostly Cuban nationals. The Cubans ran away with the Class D league, winning the pennant by 19 games with a record of 65–29. Winning the most games on the team was Luque (22–5), including back-to-back victories as a starting pitcher on July 5 and 6 against the Newburgh

Dutchman. A right-hander, Luque had begun the season as a third baseman. He ended up playing every position on the diamond, including two games behind the plate. His 27 decisions came in 28 mound appearances.

In August, Luque, along with outfield teammates Angel Aragón and Luis Padrón, was purchased by the Boston Braves. The deal was disputed publicly by Frank J. Farrell, president of the American League New York franchise formerly known as the Highlanders. Farrell contended that he had reached an agreement with Hernández Henriquez to buy the players prior to the Braves. "I have two witnesses to prove that the manager of the Long Branch team accepted [my] offers," stated Farrell. "I promised to pay $750 each for Luque and Aragon, and $500 for Padron. In case any made good, the purchase price was to be raised to $1,000. I was promised immediate delivery of the players. The next thing I heard they were sold to Boston."[1]

Farrell's verbal agreement apparently did not hold up against the counter-offer from the Braves which was likely more lucrative. As was customary, Luque closed out the season with league champion Long Branch and reported to Boston for spring training in 1914. He made the Opening Day roster. (Aragón, it appears, was returned to Long Branch, for later in the summer Farrell obtained him from the minor league team, and the outfielder debuted for the Yankees as the franchise's first Hispanic player on August 20, 1914. Padrón, an older player, never reached the major leagues.)

In a summer exhibition game with Long Branch in 1913, Luque had defeated the Pittsburgh Pirates. Less than a year later, on May 20, 1914, the 23-year-old pitcher made an unballyhooed big league entrance as the major leagues' first Latin American pitcher, facing the same Pittsburgh Pirates—this time at Forbes Field. Luque was not accorded much support on either side of the ball. He had to pitch around five Boston errors (four by shortstop Rabbit Maranville) and received only one run of offensive support. He was beaten, 4–1; he allowed five hits and three earned runs, pitching the first of his 206 career complete games.

Luque pitched one other game for Boston, ten days afterward, hurling two-thirds of an inning of scoreless relief. The following month, he was optioned to the Jersey City Skeeters of the International League. As a result, Luque became but a footnote to one of baseball's most historic teams. Boston, in dead last at the time of Luque's second game, would stage an amazing turnaround to win the National League pennant and World Series and be eternally dubbed "The Miracle Braves." Luque won only two games for the Skeeters and lost ten in 14 appearances. He played 57 games in the field, which may not have helped his pitching preparation.

Luque tried again to latch on with the defending world champion Boston

4. The Bullpen Stabilized by "The Pride of Havana" 91

Braves in 1915. Once again on the Opening day roster, he was given a start six days into the new season, April 20. Facing the Brooklyn Robins, he was pulled from the Fenway Park mound by Braves manager George Stallings after four innings with the score tied, 2–2. He had allowed five hits and walked three, with one earned run. The Braves were victors, 4–3, in ten innings. The next day, Stallings brought Luque in to pitch an inning of inconsequential relief. The major league player limit of 21 for each club was to be reached as of May 1. Luque and another pitcher, Gene Cocreham, were casualties of the requirement. Both hurlers were sent to the International League's Toronto Maple Leafs. The demoted Cuban pitcher won 15 and lost 9 for Toronto, throwing over 200 innings while continuing to play in the field when not on the mound.

In April 1916, the Braves released or lost their player control over Luque and he signed with the Louisville Colonels of the American Association. It

Something unthinkable for the modern ballplayer, but as part of their workout regimen, veteran Adolfo Luque, left, and young conscript Francis Healy cut the grass at Wrigley Field (Los Angeles). It was spring training 1932, John McGraw's last in charge of the Giants.

took another two and a half years before the hurler gained the notice of another major league ball club. One of those years, 1917, may have been misspent. Louisville manager Bill Clymer tried to convert Luque into an everyday player. The experiment failed and left Luque as an underachieving hitter and part-time pitcher, with a 2–4 record in less than 80 innings of mound work for the season.

In 1918, honing his pitching to an elevated level, Luque once again was not limited to any one position as a Louisville Colonel. The American Association shut down its operations in midsummer, in advance of U.S. government restrictions that were intended to bolster the country's war effort at home through a consolidation of resources. The United States had entered World War I in the spring of 1917. In May of that year, Luque and Cuban teammate Emilio Palmero had both been among a dozen "non-exempt" Louisville players who had been obliged to register for conscription. "Under the law," specified one newsprint announcement, "the [draft] cards issued today to the Cubans were sent to registration precincts in Havana where they reside."[2] Neither player was called to serve.

As the league closed its ballparks, and Luque was preparing to return to Havana, the Cincinnati Reds signed the 11–2 pitcher for immediate employment with their big league team. Luque's return to the big league mound came against his old team. At Braves Field on July 24, he tossed an inning of scoreless relief for Cincinnati. Two days later, Luque was pummeled in a complete game effort in the same place and by the same Boston Braves team; the final score was 11–5. It was the first game of a doubleheader, and Luque was called on to pitch an inning of relief in the second game, as the Reds played their second doubleheader in two days, with another twin bill scheduled for the next day.

After two more relief appearances, Luque was given a second start by Reds manager Christy Mathewson on August 8—in Mathewson's former stomping grounds. On an oppressively hot New York summer day, Luque defeated the New York Giants, 5–2. He had two hits in the game, and the only earned run he allowed came in the last inning, when he was nearly overcome by heat exhaustion. The umpires for the game were Charlie Moran (behind the plate) and Cy Rigler (first base). One was apparently sympathetic to Luque's physical plight near the end, as indicated by this partial game recount: "[In the ninth], after passing [Larry] Doyle, Luque went over in the shade of the grandstand and lay down for a minute while [Reds pitcher] Pete Schneider was oiling up his wing in the bullpen. Luque, however, would not give up and he returned to the mound to finish it. The heat was terrific, and it is a wonder that there were not more prostrations."[3]

Despite this exhaustive effort, the new Reds hurler was given only two days of rest before he was assigned another start. In the second game of a doubleheader on August 11, Luque was beaten by the St. Louis Cardinals, 5–3, at Redland Field. Four days later, in the same park, the 28-year-old pitcher edged the New York Giants, 6–5, the winning run scoring on a wild pitch in the lower half of the ninth inning. Luque leveled his record at 2–2.

The Reds' recent pitching addition started five more games on the season, which was cut short by adherences to World War I home front measures on September 2. Luque appeared in 12 games, made nine starts—three on two days' rest and one with a single day's rest—and completed all nine. His record was 6–3 for the third-place Reds.

The game the pitcher hurled with one day off between starts happened to be on the shortened campaign's final day. After downing the Chicago Cubs, 8–4, at Weeghman Park on August 31, Luque was assigned to pitch one of the games of a season-closing doubleheader on September 2. The resilient moundsman saved his best for last. He defeated the St. Louis Cardinals, 1–0, and in doing so delivered the first shutout by a Latin American pitcher in the major leagues. At Redland Field, Luque permitted six hits, one walk and struck out three. The hard-luck hurler for the Cardinals was compatriot pitcher Oscar Tuero, a not-yet-20-year-old native of Havana. Two of the hits surrendered by Luque were to Cardinals catcher Mike González (though playing left field in this game). A fourth Cuban, Manuel Cueto, started at catcher for Cincinnati before he changed positions with left fielder and regular backstop Ivey Wingo. It is unclear what prompted the change.

González, Cueto and Luque departed Cincinnati together the next day to return to their Havana homes.

All four of the Cubans, including Tuero, were back in the big leagues in 1919, but Luque boasted the best all-around success of the quartet. Much of that stemmed from a World Series triumph attained by his Reds team. Spurred by AL President Ban Johnson, American League and then National League owners agreed to a shorter schedule of 140 games for 1919, mostly as a salary cost-saving measure. The Cincinnati Reds, managed by Pat Moran, blazed a trail to the top of the National League. In spite of a final record of 87–53, John McGraw's team finished nine games behind the NL champions, who won 96 games and lost only 44.

Although not a regular member of the starting staff, Luque won his first five decisions, three coming as a starter. His best early effort was a 1–0 victory over the Brooklyn Robins on May 16. He allowed five hits and walked four. Soon Moran began calling on Luque less and less to throw the game's first pitch for his team. One time Moran gave Luque the starter's nod was on July

31, and he and Reds fans were the happier for it. Luque hurled the second of his two shutouts on the season, 2–0, yielding four hits to the Boston Braves at Redland Field. His performance was described in Boston's *Daily Globe* as "a baseball poem in nine well-pitched stanzas."[4]

After that, the Reds, who were battling the Giants for the top spot in the circuit, began pulling away and eventually coasted to the pennant. The Reds had two 19-game winners in Dutch Ruether and Hod Eller, and a 21-game victor in Slim Sallee. Ray Fisher won 14 games and Jimmy Ring added ten wins, along with Luque, who was 10–3 in 30 appearances, nine as a starter. The club's ERA of 2.23 was second in the league, behind Chicago's 2.21, as was its total runs scored of 578, to the Giants' 605 tallies. The Reds used only the six aforementioned pitchers in the World Series and conquered the AL champion Chicago White Sox, five games to three, in what became baseball's most infamous Fall Classic.

Luque appeared in two games, both in relief in Reds losses. In Game Three, on October 3, with an inning of work from the mound at Comiskey Park, Luque became the first Latin American player to appear in the World Series. In his next outing, in Game Seven, he hurled four scoreless innings. He pitched a total of five innings and allowed one hit and no runs, facing a total of 16 batters.

Garry Herrmann's world champions trained in Miami in 1920, sparing Luque much additional travel time following his boat ride over from Havana that spring. The Cuban was the fourth Reds pitcher to agree to terms, after Sallee, Fisher and Ring. He was one of the last pitchers to present himself at camp, arriving on the morning of March 9. He participated in a workout the same afternoon. Unknown to Luque, he and all other big league players were about to become frontline participants at the dawn of a new and exciting era of commercial communications and public consumption in the United States that helped raise and energize baseball to unrivaled levels of popularity.

The major leagues agreed to return to a 154-game schedule, and baseball fortuitously timed new rule changes that coincided with the first shouts of the Roaring Twenties. The spitball was abolished in 1920, as was the application of foreign substances to the ball. In an effort to regulate the new rule, umpires were encouraged to introduce new baseballs into games regularly (a departure from the past). The newer, cleaner balls helped the arbiters to monitor any defacement, or "scuffing," of baseballs by pitchers, which was also prohibited. (Some skilled hurlers could manipulatively command an erratic flight of the sphere, using the smallest surface nick, to gain an unfair advantage over the hitters.) The balls themselves, although made by different manufacturers, Spalding for the NL and Reach for the AL, were produced under the same exact specifications. The only outward difference was the blue and red stitching used for AL balls, opposed to red threading for the Senior Circuit. According to home run historian David Vincent, the integration of a better quality yarn produced a tighter winding around the core, which was responsible for a farther-traveling projectile when struck squarely. The more hitter-friendly ball and rules increased offense exponentially and ushered in what was to be known as the Live Ball Era.

In the first year of a decade full of rampant wealth creation from booming economic activity and consumer spending, 29-year-old Adolfo Luque embarked on a ten-year-long incumbency as a top Cincinnati Reds pitcher, replete with a nose-to-the-grindstone work ethic that may have appeared contrarian to the self-indulgent times surrounding him. The Reds left Miami on March 28 and played an exhibition game against the New York Yankees the next day in Jacksonville. The second of two Reds pitchers used in the game, Luque was tagged with the 8–7 loss when he surrendered back-to-back doubles to new Yankees addition Babe Ruth and outfielder Duffy Lewis.

Luque was actually mentioned as a possible Opening Day starter, because of the excellent form he showed in camp (he had pitched in the Cuban Winter League). Instead, he was given the ball in the Reds' third game of the season versus the Chicago Cubs. On a cold day at Redland Field, with the grounds wet from an overnight rainstorm, the pitchers did not have their way. Allowing five runs (three earned), Luque received a no-decision, following a mid-inning removal in the seventh. The Reds rallied with six runs in the lower half of the inning to win, 11–6. (Luque seldom did not receive a decision, with an 88.5 percent decision rate as a starter in his career.)

On the pitching-rich Reds, clearly there was little room for mediocrity. It took Luque six more weeks to receive another starting assignment. He was not totally inactive during the period; he appeared in eight games out of the bullpen. His carryover work as a reliever from 1919 to the first weeks of this season drew the attention of Brooklyn sportswriter Thomas S. Rice. "Adolfo is first aid to Moran's staff, and as a first-aider he has impressed us as being in a class by himself. He is not a very large man, and does not have the stamina to continue his horrifying stuff for a full game with any great deal of success, because he pitches himself out in a short while."[5] The latter observation would be completely disproved by the five-foot, seven-inch, 160-pound pitcher.

On May 25, Luque was unexpectedly called into a game, to start the third inning, after starter Rube Bressler fractured his ankle sliding into second base. The Reds scored five runs in the inning (the first driven home by Bressler's single) and cruised to an 11–2 home victory over the Boston Braves. Luque tossed the final seven stanzas and was nicked for two runs. A too-sympathetic official scorer credited the victory to Bressler, citing the Reds' five-run lead at the time of his departure. The slighted Luque obtained his first victory of the season four days later, starting against and defeating the Pittsburgh Pirates, 3–2, at Redland Field. The Reds were managed by Heinie Groh, as Pat Moran was stricken with a bad cold.

On June 2, with Moran back on the bench, Luque missed attaining his second complete game in a row when he twisted an ankle fielding a slow hit roller in the ninth inning against the Chicago Cubs at Cubs Park. The final two outs of the 5–3 Reds victory were secured by Slim Sallee. Luque was not seriously hurt, but postponements due to rain caused his next start to be skipped over.

In a relief effort on June 8, two eighth-inning errors by the Reds, while Luque was on the hill, allowed the deciding run to score in the New York Giants' 5–4 victory. The loss was Luque's first of the season. After a win as a starter and another relief appearance, both against Brooklyn, Luque secured, for good, his place in the Reds' starting rotation. On June 22, at the Baker Bowl, the right-hander beat the Philadelphia Phillies, 3–1, in 11 innings. He allowed nine hits, struck out eight and walked none in running his record to 4–1. The first-place Reds moved two games ahead of the Chicago Cubs with the win.

On June 26, Luque was involved in a physical altercation with umpire Bill Klem that would have brought a smile to John McGraw's face. It occurred toward the end of a long day with the Reds on the verge of dropping a twin bill to the St. Louis Cardinals. After ruling against the home team on a close play at the plate in a previous inning—which caused the playing field to be strewn with pop bottles tossed by indignant Redland Field fans—Klem grew impatient with Luque on the mound and commanded the pitcher to speed things up, adding a racial epithet. According to Luque, the umpire repeated the racial insult, which incensed the pitcher.

News of the incident spread across the country in a multitude of newspapers. "In the eighth inning of the second game," read one account, "pitcher Luque of the Reds attacked umpire Klem and dealt him several hard blows about the head. The assault took place while Luque was in the box with no one on base and the pitcher claimed it was due to vicious language used by the official. Luque and catcher Allen both made affidavits that Klem used such language."[6]

Luque was ejected and also absorbed a 4–3 defeat in the game. League president Heydler fined Klem $100 for using abusive language toward Luque, and docked the Reds pitcher the same amount for his attack on Klem. Luque did not draw a suspension. Heydler did suspend Reds catcher Ivey Wingo for five days for using abusive language at Klem, following the earlier call Klem had made, which resulted in Wingo's ejection and the littering of the field by the fans.

Luque's next start came on July 1. He was outdueled, 1–0, by the Cubs' Pete Alexander. A bad-hop triple led to the only scoring. As it happened, Bill Klem was officiating behind the plate. The following interesting tidbit was printed in the *Cincinnati Enquirer:* "Adolfo Luque looked up inquiringly in the eighth inning to see if anything was going to happen, but Bill Klem was as quiet as a guest being surreptitiously invited into the cellar. It was the eighth inning on Saturday that pandemonium broke loose on the lot. Hearing nothing from the vicinity of the plate, Adolfo went calmly about his business and got the Cubs in order."[7]

A victory slipped through Luque's fingers on July 5, when the Pirates scored twice in the bottom of the 11th inning against the plucky starter to pull out a 6–5 win. The Reds slipped out of first place shortly thereafter. Luque suffered a second 1–0 defeat on July 10, this one to the Braves' Joe Oeschger—he of the all-time co-endurance mound record of 26 innings pitched with Brooklyn Robins hurler Leon Cadore earlier that season. The second-place Reds opened a four-game weekend series, at home, versus Brooklyn on July 16. Luque pitched the Sunday game, and delightfully well, for the second-largest crowd at Redland Field (26,000) since Opening Day. The gallant pitcher collected two hits and drove in a run, and collapsed from exhaustion on the Reds' bench after recording the last out of the game. The 4–1 Reds victory may have historically distinguished itself by having each base manned by blue-suited magistrates for the first time in the regular season. "Recognizing the importance of the contest and knowing that the field would be jammed with fans," it was reported, "President Heydler sent four umpires to officiate at the game, July 18, which made it resemble a miniature world's series."[8] Two umpires were still the norm during this period.

The game was the first of four starts and five straight appearances Luque (6–5) made against the two New York National League teams. He won two, both against Brooklyn. He defeated Leon Cadore, 3–2, on July 29, with both pitchers hurling the distance at Ebbets Field. In between, he suffered a pair of setbacks to the Giants, at Redland Field, one in relief.

On August 1, when Reds scheduled starter Dutch Ruether complained of a stomach ache, Moran called on Luque to face the Giants, on short rest and ahead of more rested starters Ray Fisher and Slim Sallee. Fresh in Moran's mind may have been the recent July 22 game Luque had lost to the Giants, 2–1 (his first start against the club since 1918). One of the runs scored against Luque had been unearned, and the other was scored when a potential inning-ending double play was not executed. Reds shortstop Larry Kopf was signaled for missing second base prior to his relay throw to first.

In spite of threatening skies, a big Sunday crowd of 35,000 came out to see the second-place Giants and third-sitting Reds at the Polo Grounds. Luque took a 2–0 lead into the bottom of the ninth. He retired the first two batters and got ahead 0–2 on Ross Youngs. A third of the crowd remained, as it had begun to rain in the previous inning, but not hard enough to halt play. Luque had allowed five hits and one walk to the Giants up to this near-final point. After two pitches were called balls, Youngs hit an offering back up the middle. Second baseman Morrie Rath fielded and threw to first. On a close play, Youngs was called safe by first base umpire Hank O'Day. Spectators in the lower bowl, thinking the final out had been recorded, stepped over the retaining barriers and onto the field to exit the stadium. The game was delayed while the fans returned to their places. Then Frankie Frisch singled, High Pockets Kelly doubled, knocking in a run, and Vern Spencer capped the unlikely rally with a two-run single. Spencer was carried to the Giants' clubhouse by many of those fans who had come on the field earlier thinking the game had concluded.

Luque rebounded from the disheartening defeat to throw his lone shutout of the campaign. He three-hit the Phillies at the Baker Bowl, 7–0, on August 5. It was one of four victories he registered that season against the last-place Philadelphians. Luque also victimized the pennant-winning Robins four times without a setback. His record on the year for the third-place finishing Reds was 13–9, with a crisp 2.51 ERA (sixth-best in the circuit), in 207⅔ innings. He tied with the Pirates' Wilbur Cooper for the second-best WHIP at 1.098.

To prepare for the following season, Luque left Havana on March 2, 1921, along with Mike González, who was property of the New York Giants. Both men traveled to Texas, where they parted ways to join their respective teams, Luque in Cisco and González in San Antonio. Luque arrived in Cisco on March 6.

The Reds' top mound winners, Jimmy Ring and Dutch Ruether, had been traded over the winter. The Cuban hurler was appointed the Opening Day starter by manager Pat Moran, a first for a Hispanic pitcher in the major leagues. Luque did not disappoint the biggest Opening Day crowd to that point in Cincinnati baseball history—30,444. Though handicapped by the absence of two prominent "holdout" players—Heinie Groh and Edd Roush—the Reds defeated the Pittsburgh Pirates, 5–3. Luque was peppered for 12 hits, but only two earned runs. He also tripled and scored a run. Five days later, April 18, Luque turned in the first shutout in the National League that season, blanking the visiting St. Louis Cardinals, 4–0, on six hits. The shutout was one of three tossed by the Reds pitcher in 1921, which tied with several other hurlers for the league high.

Luque led the Cincinnati staff in appearances with 41 in 1921. He started 36 games, second behind Eppa Rixey's 37. He topped everyone in the mound corps with 25 complete games. He tossed 304 innings and earned a decision in all but one of his starting assignments. The only no-decision he received was a game in which he pitched 11 innings against the New York Giants, on September 13. He was removed for a pinch-hitter and the Giants won the game, 4–3, in the following inning. Luque's record was 17–19. But his 5.0 Wins Above Replacement rating was exceeded by only two other pitchers in the league, Burleigh Grimes and Pete Alexander. The Reds finished in sixth place in 1921. They scraped their way all the way up to second in 1922. The pitching was spearheaded by 25-game winner Eppa Rixey and young Pete Donohue, who won 18 games. Luque stumbled to a 13–23 record.

Most 20-game losers throughout baseball history were not as bad as their record. Luque was no exception. In fact, he was the second-hardest pitcher in the circuit to solve, holding opponents to a .268 batting average. Another telling indication of the deceiving record was Luque's 3.31 ERA, sixth-lowest among starting pitchers in the league. Moundmate Johnny Couch, for example, posted a 16–9 record with an ERA more than half a run higher, at 3.89. Poor run support and a porous defense on many a day he pitched conspired against Luque. He was stifled by 27 unearned runs on his ledger.

The Queen City pitcher absorbed four 2–1 defeats, three coming against John McGraw's Giants. On June 11, at the Polo Grounds, Luque, who recorded the stingiest home runs per nine innings mark among pitchers with 200 or more innings (.056), was victimized by a rare long ball he surrendered.

> Yesterday, Casey Stengel carved a home run out of the offerings of Senor Adolfo Luque of Cuba and Cincinnati, and this hit gave the Giants the run that allowed them to beat the Reds by 2 to 1. Condolences are in order for Senor Luque, generally rated by the experts as the hard-luck pitcher of two hemispheres. The Cuban labors under the spell of the darkest jinx in both leagues, and nobody knows it better than the Giants.[9]

On December 20, 1922, it was erroneously leaked that John McGraw had proposed a trade with the Reds, offering pitcher Jesse Barnes for Adolfo Luque. Reds president Garry Herrmann said he turned the deal down. McGraw almost assuredly did not appreciate the appearance of being rebuked, especially while still basking under the bright lights of his second consecutive World Series victory. McGraw was quick to explain that the Reds had first asked waivers on Luque in September, and rather than pay the waiver price, he offered Barnes, but nothing more came of it. A few days earlier, it had been confirmed that the Brooklyn Robins had asked waivers on two-time 20-game winner Burleigh Grimes. The Reds, in turn, refused to place a claim on him. Brooklyn then offered Grimes to the Reds, asking for 22-year-old Pete Donohue in return. Cincinnati countered by proposing Adolfo Luque for the spitballer. The Robins declined. Both Grimes and Luque would stay with their respective clubs in 1923 and become big winners, but even Grimes' stellar 22-win campaign fell considerably short of the Cuban's sensational season.

Behind three other pitchers in the rotation in 1923, Luque was granted only three starts in April. He won two of them. On his way to a third victory on the second of May, the pitcher was sadly denied, at the last minute, by an errant throw from one of his infielders. Holding a 1–0 lead over the Chicago Cubs in the ninth inning, he allowed a hit and walk. He then induced a potential game-ending, double play grounder. Second baseman Sam Bohne badly overthrew the shortstop, and the ball rolled away into foul ground. Both runners were able to score before the ball was retrieved. The Reds could not answer in their last turn to bat and lost, 2–1.

After two no-decisions, Luque took on the Giants at the Polo Grounds. He flung the first of his league-high six shutouts on May 18. John McGraw's men absorbed their first whitewash of the campaign, 7–0. The winning pitcher allowed five hits and retired the last ten batters in a row. The right-hander's next win, a 2–1 decision over the St. Louis Cardinals on May 27, snapped a Reds six game losing streak. Two ninth-inning errors by the Reds cost Luque a shutout and snapped a 22-inning scoreless streak. Luque improved his record to 5–1 with a 3–2 decision over the Chicago Cubs on May 31. The locked-in pitcher soon began another scoreless innings streak lasting 29 frames. Included in the faultless pitching were shutouts over both the Giants and Robins. Against the latter team it was an 11-inning blanking. The goose-egg parade ended June 24 against the Chicago Cubs, when Pete Alexander defeated Luque, 2–0, in front of more than 20,000 fans at Cubs Park.

Luque entered July with a 10–2 record and won seven more games, losing but once. Two of the victories were gained on the same day. In the middle of the month, the Reds were saddled with three doubleheaders to play within a week's time. Luque expressed typical bravado by offering to pitch both ends of a twin bill versus the Boston Braves on July 17. At Braves Field, he went six innings in game one, allowing two runs. He benefitted from a four-run Reds rally in the top of the seventh and was credited with a 4–3 win. Luque was cheered by the Braves fans when he took the mound to begin the second game. He proceeded to hurl a 9–5, complete game victory over the home team.

It was clear that a very special season was developing for Adolfo Luque, who was not only the new ace of the Reds' staff, but also of the entire circuit. "For this smiling gent from the land of free-flowing liquor and waving palms is just about the best pitcher in the National League these days," declared one report. "This is especially gratifying to Luque after going through a season of defeats that would put the ordinary pitcher in a padded cell or Class D league."[10]

Luque's record stood at 17–3 on the eve of a big five-game series with the front-running New York Giants, beginning on August 4. Manager Moran decided to alter the order of his starting rotation to give Luque two starts against the defending world champions in their four-day layover at Redland Field. The manager pitched stalwart hurlers Pete Donohue and Eppa Rixey out of turn in order to provide Luque with his two opportunities, on August 4 and 7. The second-place Reds were three games behind the Giants, and the Reds' top pitcher had beaten McGraw's team three times, twice by shutout. As a result, New York papers had dubbed Luque the "Giant tamer." For his part, Luque was gung-ho over the idea. But Moran, on whom the ultimate responsibility rested, should not be free from criticism for lack of sound judgment in adopting the scheme. Although it was an age in which pitchers were programmed to go to the post on short rest, there was no justifiable need to juggle his starters, in this manner, with two months of the season remaining. The short-sighted plan completely backfired on Moran, with disastrous results for his team and for Luque.

On his 33rd birthday, the Giants pummeled the league's best hurler, and a reliever, for 20 hits and 14 runs. Luque was knocked from the box in the fifth inning, surrendering half of the runs. The energized Giants, behind Hugh McQuillan, decisioned Rixey, 2–0, the following day, and then swept a pair of games on August 6, defeating Donohue and the Reds' fourth starter, Larry Benton. In his rematch on August 7, Luque was slightly better but was involved in a bench-clearing brawl that led to his ejection in the eighth inning.

Giants players sat along an open-air bench extending from the dugout. From there Luque was heckled by the opposition, never more so than when the visitors tacked on two runs in the top of the eighth inning to take a 5–2 lead. With two outs and two men on base, one or more Giants verbally crossed the line with their goading, enough to prod Luque to leave the mound and saunter over in their direction. The offended pitcher sought out one particular heckler, Casey Stengel, and began reigning blows upon him. Reds players joined the fracas, and park police and some fans jumped on the field to take part in the free-for-all. After he had been pulled away back toward the Reds' dugout, Luque "returned with a fiery look and a fungo bat grasped in his hands."[11]

Order was finally restored and the disarmed pitcher was sent off the field.

> On reaching the clubhouse, Luque, who was still white with anger, said that Stengel had hurled a highly improper epithet at him just after he pitched the first ball to Youngs. The Cuban stated that he would never, under any circumstances, stand for what Stengel is alleged to have called him, so he took the matter into his own hands. He only regretted that he had been seized and dragged away before he had succeeded in in subduing the temperamental Casey.[12]

At first, Luque was suspended indefinitely, until the league president could review all reports of the riotous incident. President Heydler reinstated the pitcher effective August 15, after seven days of forced inactivity. His return to the diamond coincided with the Reds opening a return five-game series against the Giants in New York. Luque opened the series as part of the first game of a doubleheader attended by 25,000 venom-dripping fans. In his first on-field action following his executive reprieve, Luque made a statement not only from the mound but also at the plate, and, in so doing, accomplished what few athletes are ever able to do amid similar scathing settings—sway the hostile horde in their favor.

> Adolfo Luque, booed and hissed by the crowd at the start of the first game, forced the rooters to come around his way when he set back the Giants in round after round and won his own game with a drive into the upper deck in left field in the fourth round. The crowd was cheering the game little Cuban before the contest was over, and the Giants, who aroused his ire by the rough remarks in the last game of the recent series at Redland Field, left him severely alone.[13]

Luque's two-run home run provided the winning margin for his eventual 6-3 win. The second-deck souvenir was also the initial home run of Luque's career and first hit by a Latin American pitcher in the major leagues. Luque did not pitch again in the four-day series, as Moran apparently discarded his previous plan to throw his number one pitcher at the Giants as often as possible, even on short rest.

Nine days later, August 24, Luque became the first Hispanic 20-game winner in the big leagues when he blanked the Robins in Brooklyn, 4-0. On the first of September, the surging right-hander improved to 22-5 with a 4-3 win over Pete Alexander and the Cubs. Luque had an outside chance at winning 30 games, but a 6-2 loss to the third-place Pittsburgh Pirates on September 5 all but eliminated the lofty goal. The star pitcher won his 26th game on September 23, against Wilbert Robinson's Brooklyn team. The day before the 5-1 home victory, Luque had been used as a pinch-runner against the same club.

There were six games now left in the Reds' season. Moran's team trailed the first-place Giants by four games, with games scheduled at Redland Field against the league-leading club on September 24–25. The home team won the first game. The Reds' scheduled starter for the second contest, Eppa Rixey, came up with a lame arm during his pre-game warmup tosses. Rixey, one of three Reds pitchers to win 20 games on the season (Pete Donohue was the other), had pitched 11 innings in his previous start. Luque, with 305 innings pitched under his belt, volunteered to take Rixey's place—on one day's rest. Moran acceded. John "Mule" Watson outpitched Luque, 3–2, and all but assured McGraw's Giants of a third consecutive pennant. Luque went eight innings and gave up all of the runs. The brave effort was not lost on the hometown faithful. "The fans applauded Adolfo Luque all throughout the contest," said one reporter. "They recognized his courage in going into the box unprepared and with very little rest and they wanted him to know that they appreciated it."[14]

In his last start of the campaign, on September 29, Luque won his 27th game with ease. It was an 11–1 victory over the St. Louis Cardinals and concluded the greatest season by a foreign-born pitcher in major league history. Luque's final numbers were: 27–8, 322 innings, 1.93 ERA, six shutouts and 28 complete games in 37 starts. The wins, ERA and shutouts were major league highs. Luque lost *seven* other shutouts simply due to unearned runs staining his complete games. He allowed two home runs all season. From an analytics point of view, Luque's 10.8 WAR was well above runner-up Frankie Frisch's 7.1 rating in the National League, and second in the majors to Babe Ruth's incredible 14.0. The pitcher's 201 ERA+ and 2.94 Fielding Independent Pitching computations were the best in baseball. (With 100 considered average, ERA+ measures a pitcher's value, taking into account adjustments for runs-scoring environment and ballparks. Teammate Eppa Rixey finished a distant second in the National League with an ERA+ of 139. FIP attempts to gauge a pitcher's performance utilizing strikeouts, walks and home runs allowed—the "three true outcomes"—within a set formula that converts the results to an ERA-resembling number. Rixey was also second to Luque with a FIP of 3.10.)

Luque expectedly never matched his historic "career year" again. In 1924, he won only ten games while losing 15, despite finishing in the top ten in ERA (3.16) and fourth in FIP (3.30). But number of wins was the primary measuring stick for a pitcher in this era, and something that would have been unthinkable just a year earlier was proposed for Luque after the 1924 season—a trade. Their eyes specifically focused on Bill Terry, the Reds, over the winter, offered Luque in exchange for the Giants' gleaming, young first baseman. McGraw countered by asking for one of the younger pitchers, Rixey or Donohue, which killed any potential swap.

Fortune was clearly not on Luque's side in 1925 either. The 35-year-old bested all NL pitchers in ERA (2.63) and shutouts (4), but toiled to a 16–18 record. In the off-season, Luque, along with Reds catcher Bubbles Hargrave, was again the subject of trade rumors with the New York Giants, this time involving their terrific second baseman Frankie Frisch. A second proposed Cincinnati–New York deal surrounding Luque was also turned down by John McGraw. The Giants manager would confirm that he declined to trade High Pockets Kelly and youthful Freddie Fitzsimmons to the Reds for outfielder Edd Roush and the league's most effective pitcher.

On April 12, 1926, the eve of Opening Day, Adolfo Luque became a bridegroom. He crossed the Ohio River with Mrs. Mae Dennison, a presumed Cincinnati widow or divorcee, into Newport, Kentucky, where the couple were married after obtaining a marriage license. The occasion was purposely kept low-key by the new husband for personal reasons delineated in this printed news brief: "Adolfo sought to keep his marriage a secret because of the death of his sister in Havana last winter and the present illness of his mother there."[15]

The union would last 18 months, ending in divorce petitioned for by Luque's wife. The baseball professional had been previously married. His first wife, Eugenia Valdés de Luque, had sued the pitcher for divorce two short months after his triumphant return to Cuba following his glorious 1923 major league season. The couple had an eight-year-old daughter at the time named Olga.

In 1926, Luque, at 13–16, suffered through a third consecutive losing campaign. His 3.43 ERA, .39 below the league average, suggested he deserved better results than he received, as did the 34 unearned runs to which he was subjected. The Reds battled the St. Louis Cardinals for the pennant into the final week of the season, but came up two games short.

In March 1927, John McGraw offered the Reds $15,000 to buy Luque. The Reds would not release him for less than $25,000. "That's where the negotiations stand," said McGraw. "All other information regarding the status of Luque must be referred to the Cincinnati ball club."[16]

The parties could not come to an agreement and Luque stayed in Cincinnati for the 1927 season. He ended his three-year losing record slide by winning 13 games and dropping 12, in 27 starts. In a shining outing on July 21, Luque defeated the Brooklyn Robins, 2–1, at Ebbets Field. It took 13 innings, with the winning pitcher tripling in the first run of the game in the top of the tenth inning. Luque's final 1927 win also came against the Robins, and also in extra-inning fashion. At Redland Field, the right-hander defeated Wilbert Robinson's team, 2–1, in 12 innings. Four days later, September 26, the staunch pitcher lost to the St. Louis Cardinals, 3–1, in 13 innings.

In 1928, after Rube Bressler was claimed off waivers by the Brooklyn Robins prior to the season, Luque became the Reds' last remaining member from their 1919 championship team. The Reds' number two pitcher behind Eppa Rixey, Luque compiled an 11–10 record in 29 starts. Tonsillitis caused Luque to miss nearly three weeks in early June.

One of the starts was Luque's second Opening Day assignment on April 11. The veteran had pitched exceptionally well in training camp, and Reds manager Jack Hendricks bestowed his longest-tenured pitcher with the privilege. "Luque has won the opening day assignment on his merits as a pitcher who is ready to hurl championship ball," informed one Cincinnati newspaperman. "His control has been excellent, his curves have been of the July variety, and his pitching brain, one of the best in baseball, just as keen as ever. His spirits are higher than they have been in many a spring."[17]

For years, Luque had been increasingly relying on his curveball and had become known as a top curveball pitcher. Tommy Holmes wrote a story titled, "Vance Has Great Hook Ball, But the Craftiest Curveball Pitcher is Luque." In the piece, Holmes explained that Luque had variations to his curve. "Luque deliberately throws two kinds of curves," Holmes quoted an unnamed National League outfielder as saying. "He has a 'ten cent' curve and a 'million dollar' one. He has marvelous control of the cheap hook and throws it frequently. And when you think you have solved the mystery of his dinky curve, Luque lets you see the real bender."[18]

With dignitaries A. Victor Donahey, the Governor of Ohio, and Kenesaw Mountain Landis, Baseball Commissioner, on hand, Luque no doubt used an abundance of his off-speed pitches to keep Chicago Cubs batters off balance, on his way to pitching a 5–1 victory at Redland Field. In front of 30,000 enthusiastic fans, he allowed seven hits and defeated Charlie Root, who had beaned Luque in 1926.

His best—and most valiant—performance of the season came in his last start on September 23. At the Polo Grounds, Luque battled Giants pitcher Joe Genewich for 13 innings in a 1–1 tie. In the bottom of the 14th, Luque allowed consecutive singles to Freddie Lindstrom, Bill Terry and Travis Jackson, and was beaten, 2–1.

Over the winter, McGraw tried again to obtain the seemingly unobtainable pitcher. But in mid–January 1929, from Havana, McGraw regretfully put the notion to rest, at least for another year. "I have given up hope that Luque will be with us," McGraw said, implying that culpability lay with the other party. "As much as I would like to have him, the Cincinnati Reds have delayed negotiations so that we have been forced to abandon the prospect for the present."[19]

In 1929: Carl Hubbell tossed a no-hitter; Pete Alexander retired; Harry Frazee and Miller Huggins died; Babe Ruth reach the unprecedented 500 home run plateau; Helen Wills won the French, British and U.S. singles tennis championships for the second year in a row; the brilliant, intractable Rogers Hornsby took the Cubs to the World Series; and the incorrigibly tight-fisted Connie Mack returned his Philadelphia Athletics to World Series glory. It was also the year that "marked 14 consecutive quarters of economic contraction."[20] As far as Luque was concerned, it was a year to forget for purely professional reasons.

Playing for the worst Reds team in more than 20 years (66–88), and met with the striking increase of offense throughout baseball and perhaps the stark reality of the shortfalls of his own aging constitution, the colluding factors levied upon Adolfo Luque his worst major league season. The graying, 39-year-old pitcher won five games and lost 16. His ERA jumped from 3.57 in 1928 to 4.50 (though still below the league average of 4.71). He pitched one shutout. It came at the Polo Grounds when he defeated the New York Giants, 7–0, on May 13. The pitcher hit his fifth and final career home run in the game. John McGraw, out with his sinus disability, was spared a close-up view of the proceedings.

In February of 1930, the Reds, non-contenders for the last three seasons, traded their elder statesman to the Brooklyn Robins for pitcher Doug "Buzz" McWeeny, six years younger than his counterpart. The transaction could be described as a mutual parting of the ways between a grateful team and dedicated player. McWeeny would not win a game for Cincinnati in 1930, while Luque, in his age 39 season, would have a final, fine showing as a starting pitcher.

The 14-year veteran tied for the second-most starts (24) on the Brooklyn team, behind Dazzy Vance, whose season from the hill stood out magnificently among his peers, in the onslaught of the heavy hitting throughout the league. Vance was 17–15 with a 2.61 ERA and four shutouts. The league ERA was 4.97. Luque won 14 games and was defeated eight times, and posted a 4.30 ERA. His 16 complete games were second on the team to Vance's 20.

Manager Wilbert Robinson's reasons for obtaining Luque were to shore up his bullpen and to have Luque impart some of his pitching wisdom to Brooklyn's younger pitchers. He did not plan on using Luque in his rotation, except as a spot starter. But the greybeard hurler won a starter's role in spring training. It was not long afterward that Luque's mound strategies had Robinson gushing with approval. "What a pleasure it is to watch old Lookee throw that onion," exclaimed the manager. "With most of our young fellers nowadays, it's a case of getting the ball over the plate. Not with that old Lookee, though. He just wonders whether he will make the next one high and on the outside corner, or low and cutting the inside of the pan."[21] Though the colloquial spelling of the pitcher's name was purposely done, presumably to mimic Robinson's pronunciation, it might be a good time to clarify that "Luque" is pronounced LOO-KEH. "Keh" as in ke-ttle.

On April 13, two days before the start of the regular season, Luque started the Robins' final exhibition game. At Yankee Stadium, the crafty pro struck out five of the first six Yankees to face him, among them Earle Combs, Mark Koenig, Babe Ruth, and Lou Gehrig. However, he grew wild in later stanzas and the Yankees scored five runs in five innings against him, before coming out on the winning end of an 8–5 score.

Prior to the season, Luque was reassuring about his condition and enthusiastic about his new team's prospects. "I am fine," he said. "What are gray hairs or age when one is strong? I am stronger than I have felt in five years. I will win many games. And this team will win, it has spirit."[22]

That team spirit was on display no more so than on August 5, in its own home confines. Evidently tiring at the end, Luque, the game's starter, let a win slip right through his fingers. Pitching against the New York Giants, he had the game practically signed and sealed for his backers. He led, 6–1, with two outs, two men on base, and two strikes on the game's would-be final batter. Remarkably, the Giants rallied to tie the game, plating two runs on two hits, ahead of a Bill Terry three-run home run, surrendered by Luque. After the Giants scored twice in the top of the tenth inning to take an 8–6 lead, the Robins scored three runs in their last at-bat to send Ebbets Field into "riotous bedlam"[23] and the entire Brooklyn bench into "a state of mad jubilation."[24] Removed after the Terry homer, Luque did not figure in the decision.

Brooklyn was in first place at the time, and the team stayed in contention until the last two weeks of the season. Luque won his 12th game on August 31, coasting to a 14–3, home victory over the Philadelphia Phillies. The winning pitcher collected three hits, scored a run and drove in one. The following newspaper fragment revealed an interesting picture of Luque prior to stepping to the plate, leaving one to juxtapose with it a comical comparison with the cesta-size gloves used by major leaguers today: "Luque, Brooklyn pitcher, bats with his glove in his back pocket and removes it only when he gets on base."[25] On September 10, Luque brought the Robins to within a game and a half of first place with a 6–0 blanking of the Chicago Cubs at Ebbets Field. It was the pitcher's 14th win and the 26th and final shutout of his career.

Catching the game was rookie Al López, the team's regular backstop that season. Born in Tampa, Florida, to Spanish immigrés, López's Iberian roots were invariably linked with Luque as the major leagues' only Hispanic pitching and catching duo. "The Brooklyn Robins," read one cheeky report, "have discovered a battery that can get along without signals unless some undiscovered Moe Berg turns up in the National League. With ancient Adolfo Luque pitching and young Alfonso Lopez catching, the instructions can be passed in their native Spanish with no one the wiser. They also may be able to get in a few words about the umpire without being banished."[26] The reference to Moe Berg was to a contemporary major leaguer who was said to be fluent in multiple languages.

López was still catching Luque's slants in 1931, but with less regularity as a starting pitcher. In his second season with Brooklyn, the inconsistent Luque was eventually dropped from the regular rotation. He made 15 starts, completing five. He appeared in four other games and posted a 7–6 record, with an ERA of 4.56—more than a run above the leveled-off league average.

Luque earned $12,000 from the Robins in 1931, matching his salary high with the Reds in 1924. Coming off his seven-win season, the club was not going to pay anywhere near that figure again; it released the battle-worn pitcher on January 22, 1932. All teams in the league passed on the chance of claiming him for the waiver price, and Luque became a "free agent." Three weeks later, the 41-year-old pitcher agreed to terms with John McGraw, who met with him while on holiday in Havana.

Not unexpectedly, following his release from Brooklyn, several stories circulated with speculation that Luque's career had come to an end. "Luque was always a colorful figure," wrote one syndicated columnist. "He was a fighter to the last ditch. When you saw him walking out on the diamond, you knew he was going somewhere. His attitude was such that one expected him to step on the face of anyone who got in his way."[27]

The McGraw-favored type of player, Luque had to scramble to reach New York to join an advance guard of players leaving on February 14 for the Giants' California spring training encampment. The hurler joined up with several pitchers and batterymates Shanty Hogan and Francis Healy. The train was scheduled to swing past Utica to pick up Hal Schumacher and stop in Chicago, where Freddie Lindstrom and Roy Parmelee, among others, were expected to hop on for the remainder of the western journey.

When the group of players arrived in southern California, the team's two current elder statesmen, Luque and 41-year-old Clarence Mitchell, were singled out in a discourteous news report that said when the two "stepped off the train, the folks at the depot could not figure out whether they were members of the New York Giants, arriving for spring training, or a couple of Supreme Court judges on vacation."[28]

The Giants had three dedicated starters, Carl Hubbell, Freddie Fitzsimmons and Bill Walker, to handle the pitching load for 1932. Jim Mooney was the expected fourth frontliner, with the 21-year-old Hal Schumacher anticipated to receive further big league grooming as a starter and reliever. The bullpen chores were expected to be split between Luque, Mitchell and Herman Bell, who, like Luque, was a newcomer to the team. Mitchell, however, was axed in June after Terry took over, bringing an end to an 18-year career.

Concluding a positive training stay in Los Angeles, the Giants headed east with elevated hopes for a competitive season, in spite of receiving the sad news, on the day of their departure, that Johnny Vergez had lost his infant child to polio. But the Giants were anything but a competitive ball club through the first two months of the season. On the morning of June 1, only one-half game separated them and the last-place Philadelphia Phillies in the National League standings.

The same day, the Giants played the Phillies at the Polo Grounds. Bill Terry and Mel Ott hit back-to-back home runs in the second inning, the only scoring in the game for the home team. Starter Walker took a 2–1 lead into the eighth inning, when the Phillies scored three times. In the bottom half of the frame, acting manager Dave Bancroft sent in Sam Leslie to pinch-hit for Walker, to no avail. In the last strategic move made under the regime of John McGraw, Bancroft called for Adolfo Luque to pitch the ninth inning. Luque provided an anxious half-inning, allowing two hits and a walk, but no runs. As they had in the eighth, the Giants failed to score in their final turn and lost, 4–2.

In their next game, a few days later, Terry would be making all strategic moves on the field for the New York Giants.

Herman Bell was about as unknown a pitcher as one could be when he reported to the St. Louis Cardinals' Bradenton, Florida, spring training facility in 1924. Bell had not pitched professionally the previous year, except for a fortuitous barnstorming exhibition with the St. Louis Cardinals following the 1923 major league campaign. The Cardinals signed Bell at the end of their barnstorming tour.

Born in Mount Sherman, Kentucky, July 16, 1897, Bell was reared in Sibley, Iowa. He was one of five children and the oldest of two boys. His father Nathan and mother Mattie, both Kentucky-born and bred, relocated their family to northern Iowa in the first decade of the new century.

In 1922, after pitching with several semi-pro teams in Iowa and Minnesota, Bell reached the organized baseball level as a 24-year-old hurler with the Tri-State League's Sioux City Packers. George Segris, owner of the Sioux

City club and an old friend of Cardinals manager Branch Rickey, recommended Bell along with fellow Iowan Wattie Holm.

Bell's unlikely journey to the major leagues reached its fruition when the inexperienced hurler unpredictably made the St. Louis squad in the spring. He debuted on April 16, 1924, in the Cardinals' second game of the season. The former sandlot pitcher allowed four runs in two innings of relief work as the Cardinals were beaten by the Chicago Cubs, 13–4, at Sportsman's Park.

On May 30, with six relief games and 14⅔ innings under his major league belt, Bell made his first career start and nearly matched his innings output to date. At Forbes Field, he started the second game of doubleheader, hoping to prevent the Pirates, 4–0 winners in the first game, from sweeping the day's activities. Bell produced an extra-inning effort that fell just short of the goal. The right-hander hurled a mighty 14⅓ innings before the Bucs pushed across a run in the 15th to win, 3–2. Bell permitted 12 hits in the two hour and 35 minutes-long game. He walked three and struck out the same number in the extraordinary endeavor.

Five days later, Bell picked up his first big league win, backed heavily by his teammates, 12–5. Allowing 12 hits and four earned runs, he downed the Phillies at the Baker Bowl. The Cardinals, 19–24 after the win, continued losing the majority of their games and slid into the National League cellar by midsummer. On July 19, four days after pitching seven innings of long relief and three days after his 27th birthday, Bell again exhibited iron-man pitching from the mound. The six-foot, 185-pound right-handed hurled complete game, doubleheader wins over the Boston Braves. The Sportsman's Park victories were by the scores of 6–1 and 2–1. The second game, dual four-hitters by Bell and Braves opponent Johnny Cooney, was completed in 74 minutes. On the day, the rookie pitcher allowed only six hits, walked two and fanned five. Both runs were earned. According to the following analysis from a source close to the St. Louis sports scene, Bell's grand accomplishment came as a total surprise:

> The facts concerning Bell's great achievement are still coming out. It seems that Rickey was greatly impressed by the youngster's first shot at the Braves and when the pitcher started on his way to the showers, Branch propositioned him. Rickey asked the young man if he would like to go back and win for himself a nice vacation. "Sure" was the ready reply. "Well, then you're the pitcher—hop to it," said Rickey. Rickey later said the real reason in sending the pitcher back in was to give him a system full of confidence.[29]

In his twin wins, Herman Bell had delivered one of baseball's greatest pitching exercises. In the first game, he pitched perfect baseball for seven and one-third innings. The Braves' Ernie Padgett doubled with one out in the eighth and was singled home by the next hitter, Cotton Tierney. Bell's lone walk came with two down in the ninth. In the nightcap, the native Ken-

4. The Bullpen Stabilized by "The Pride of Havana"

Hi Bell (pictured) and Adolfo Luque made up a terrific bullpen tandem for the Giants in 1933.

tuckian retired the first 16 batters he faced. Of the 18 innings Bell threw on the day, *12* were perfect. In his final inning of work on the long day, Bell had to bear down the most. The Braves scored their only run of the contest, using a walk and two singles. With the go-ahead runs on base, Bell coaxed Stuffy McInnis into a game-ending force out.

Bell next pitched again eight days hence, as a reliever in a 6–4 Cardinals loss at the Polo Grounds. He was reached for three runs in 5⅔ innings, following the exit of starter and loser Eddie Dyer. Bell received three more starts on the season and lost all of them. Bell's exalting doubleheader wins were his last on the season; his final record was 3–8, with a 4.92 ERA in 28 appearances. He completed half of his ten starting assignments.

The iron man performances notwithstanding, Bell apparently did not impress the Cardinals, or perhaps the club thought he required more "confidence building." The team optioned their novice pitcher to Milwaukee of the American Association in January 1925. With the Brewers, Bell expanded substantially on his pitching workload, hurling 323 innings in 50 appearances. He compiled an 18–19 record and 3.90 ERA. Bell rejoined the Cardinals in 1926 and was glad of it. The club won the National League pennant in a tight battle with the Cincinnati Reds, and then the World Series in seven games over the New York Yankees. The sophomore pitcher was a steady force in the St. Louis pen, with a 3–2 mark and 1.48 ERA in non-starting roles. He led the club in games finished with 12 and tied in saves with two. Bell was also used as spot starters by manager Rogers Hornsby, who had taken over for Rickey a quarter of the way through the 1925 campaign, following Rickey's front office promotion to vice president.

The reliever appeared in Game Four of the Fall Classic in a dicey, no-out, bases-loaded situation. Bell allowed two inherited runners to score before retiring the side. In two innings of work, Bell surrendered a two-run home run to Babe Ruth. Hornsby called on five pitchers in the Sportsman's Park encounter, a 10–5 loss. In the subsequent three games of the Series, St. Louis used only three other pitchers, including Pete Alexander in back-to-back games, to attain their hard-fought triumph.

The following spring, Bell's exploits, along with another player of local interest, were followed by newspapers in his adopted state. "Northwest Iowa's two baseball men, Wattie Holm and Herman Bell," disclosed the Hawkeye State's *Lake Park News*, "are showing up fine in spring training games for the St. Louis Cardinals.... Herman's nickname to his teammates is 'Hi.' The big right-hander is being groomed for much work this season."[30]

The broader role the Cardinals appeared to be planning for their third-year pitcher never materialized, however. With the exception of one start, Bell was relegated to bullpen duty. He pitched 57⅓ innings and posted a win-loss record of 1–3, with a 3.92 ERA. In 1927, the Cardinals were nosed out for the flag by the Pittsburgh Pirates.

Shortly thereafter, the hometown Iowa papers must have been slightly disappointed with Bell and his wife Emma for establishing residence in Long

Beach, California. The former Emma Goebel was the niece of current Alton, Iowa, mayor Peter Goebel.

In January 1928, St. Louis released Bell to Houston in the Texas League. A month later, the club traded Bell to another Cardinals affiliate—Rochester in the International League—for two pitchers. Bell spent the season with Rochester and led the team to the International League pennant. Bell won 21 games and lost only eight for the Red Wings, and he clinched the pennant with two wins on the final day of the season. The wins came in the same near-iron man, doubleheader fashion he had produced as a Cardinals rookie. On September 23, Bell hurled complete-game victories over the Montreal Royals, 5–2 and 6–0. He allowed three hits in the opener and five safeties in the second game. The nightcap was a scheduled seven-inning game. Royals fans grew restless in the lower half of the seventh and began throwing seat cushions onto the field with one out. The umpires forfeited the game to Rochester with the score and statistics reverting to the end of the sixth inning. Rochester lost a run they had scored in the top of the seventh inning.

The Red Wings' title came by virtue of a single percentage point. Due to rainouts, the club played four fewer games than runner-up Buffalo; the Red Wings (90–74/.549) won and lost two fewer games each than the Bisons (92–76/.548).

Bell was back with the parent club early in 1929. He was the last Cardinal player to agree to contract terms, signing on February 28. Some inconsistent showings, leading to an 0–2 record and 6.92 ERA, landed him back in Rochester for the final three months of the season, where he won 11 games. He did not rejoin the Cardinals following the demotion.

In 1930, St. Louis recaptured the pennant, and Bell made a strong return and became the top man out of their bullpen. He appeared in 39 games, nine of which were starts, and went 4–3. He led the league in saves with eight, while posting a 3.90 ERA. The Missourians were defeated by the Philadelphia Athletics in the World Series. Bell hurled one faultless inning in Game Six.

Eric H. Allen wrote that it was in 1931 that "the Depression truly became "Great."[31] Allen pointed out that "trade barriers worldwide" and "various economic and political forces which had significantly distorted the economy, and an inherently unstable monetary system that amplified economic adjustments resulted in an enormous and devastating downward economic swing."[32] In September 1931, the stock market experienced its greatest monthly decline in history—30.7 percent—following an "international monetary crisis"[33] that sheared the value of currencies and collapsed the credit of nations, the result of Great Britain's abandonment of the gold standard. (The English pound was the world's reserve currency.)

Hi Bell's St. Louis team was part of one of the few business entities not yet engulfed by the dark financial clouds swirling ominously around all the leading economic forecasters during this period. The Cardinals had made money every year since 1926, according to David George Surdam's *Wins, Losses & Empty Seats*. Five years on was no exception. "The team paid a reported 10 percent dividend after its first pennant in 1926," revealed Surdam, "and declared a dividend of 20 percent after winning pennants in 1928 and 1931."[34]

As noted in the shareholder payout, the Cardinals were the class of the league on the field again in 1931 and gained their revenge over the repeat AL-champion Philadelphia Athletics in the Fall Classic. Bell was not part of the championship run. Instead, he pitched all season long for his familiar minor league club in Rochester. Out of player options on Bell, the Cardinals could do nothing when a rival NL team pulled him out from their organization in October of 1931.

The following spring, that rival team—based in New York—publicized, through all the normal channels, the successful signing of the pitcher and his anticipated arrival with the big club:

> Though the Giants' vanguard has made arrival at Los Angeles, the New York office of the club continues to give out items of passing interest. Yesterday [traveling secretary] Eddie Brannick announced that Herman Bell had sent in his 1932 contract. Bell lives in Glendale, California and will join the Giants from there. Bell was picked up in the draft from the Rochester Red Wings. He's 34 years old.... However he captured 16 games while losing 11 with Rochester and not any old pitcher can do that.[35]

Bell saw action in the Giants' home-opening shellacking at the hands of the Philadelphia Phillies on April 12. He did not help things by giving up three runs in three innings of work. Bell's pitching improved from that point, although his team continued playing nearly as disastrously as in its 13–5 inaugural day loss. As it came to pass, Bell, with an 8–4 record, was one of only two Giants pitchers to post a winning mark (Carl Hubbell, 18–11) on the season. Using 25 rescue efforts and ten starts, he pitched the fifth-most innings on the staff with 120, and his 3.67 ERA was one of the team's lowest.

The first of two games he saved on the year came on May 30, in the second game of a doubleheader at Braves Field. Coming in with the tying run at the plate in the bottom of the tenth inning, Bell retired the Braves to preserve a 4–2 win for starter Sam Gibson and boost the Giants to a sweep of the twin bill. Though he was not present, it was the Giants' last win ostensibly under the regime of John Joseph McGraw.

5

The Championship Season—First Half

After its debut on Broadway in late 1932, Cole Porter's *Night and Day* became one of the top songs in America in 1933. The title of the popular musical number from the hit play *The Gay Divorcee* could have been borrowed to compare the New York Giants of 1932 to 1933.

It could be argued that the Giants of 1932 were not as poor a team as their 72–82 record indicated. Their team ERA of 3.83 was slightly below the National League average of 3.88. The club plated the second-most runs (755) in the circuit and hit a middle-of-the-pack .276 as a team. The Giants calculated out as an 82–72 squad, using Bill James' "Pythagorean expectation," which projects a team's win-loss record based on the differential of runs scored to runs allowed. The sixth-place team was considerably hurt by the league's second-worst record in one-run games: 18–31.

But the unchallengeable fact was that the Giants were not a championship aggregation. To his credit, new manager Bill Terry wasted little time in trying to change that realization. Terry attempted to improve areas he deemed as needing upgrades. On June 23, 1932, three days after the Len Koenecke dismissal, Terry acquired fading star hurler Waite Hoyt and removed aged pitcher Clarence Mitchell from the active list, retaining him as a coach, presumably to work with the pitchers. Hoyt, who had been released by Brooklyn almost two weeks earlier, was signed as free agent and arrived at the Polo Grounds in time to be fitted with his first National League uniform.

All the Giants, on the day of Hoyt's acquisition, debuted numbers on the backs of their uniforms for the first time in franchise history, according to longtime New York Giants historian Fred Stein. "McGraw, ever the traditionalist," wrote Stein, "had refused to follow the lead of other major league clubs that had begun to have identifying numbers sewn on the back of their player uniforms."[1] The Giants played the St. Louis Cardinals at home. Sporting number 11, Freddie Fitzsimmons was the victor, 6–1.

Hoyt, 5–7 with the Giants, did not contribute as Terry had hoped, however. The former World Series hero was released by New York two months after the end of the 1932 season.

Prior to cutting his losses with Hoyt, Terry shored up his outfield depth by plucking 30-year-old Homer Peel away from the St. Louis Cardinals, as a Rule 5 draftee. This occurred on September 27, two days after the season's last pitch was thrown in New York.

On October 10, the proactive Giants skipper traded underachieving pitchers Jim Mooney and Bill Walker, along with a past-his-prime Bob O'Farrell and back-up outfielder Ethan Allen, to St. Louis, for catcher Gus Mancuso and unproven pitcher Ray Starr. In a deal that could easily be viewed as one of "addition by subtraction," Terry rid himself of two starters, in Mooney and Walker, who were a combined 14–22. The six-player exchange with the Cardinals primarily cleared the way for young pitchers Hal Schumacher and Roy Parmelee to become frontline starters, and both hurlers would rise to the challenge, especially Schumacher. The Giants clearly were intent on making changes in the receiving corps. In the middle of September, the front office had purchased Paul Richards from the American Association's Minneapolis Millers. Richards turned out to be the number two catcher for Terry's Giants the following season.

Four days before the end of October, a pending arrangement between the Giants and another organization was settled. On September 8, the Giants had acquired 27-year-old infielder Bernie James from Dallas in the Texas League for two players to be named at a later date. Terry eventually parted with infield fill-in and five-year-older Eddie Moore to complete the deal on October 27. A sum of $8,500 was substituted for the proposed second player. James would not see action with his new team until 1933.

After a brief lull, on December 1, utility infielder Gil English and some cash was sent to Portland's Pacific Coast League team for pitcher Joe Bowman. The Portland Beavers hurler did not make the Giants squad until 1934.

On December 12, Terry's biggest shakeup occurred, when he sent Freddie Lindstrom packing, along with semi-regular outfielder Chick Fullis. The trade desired by Lindstrom netted the Giants pitcher Glenn Spencer and outfielder Kiddo Davis. Occupying a roster spot for the entire 1933 season, Spencer did not contribute measurably to his new team. But Davis became the starting center fielder for the National League champions.

The prudent Terry also picked up back-up help at shortstop. As insurance for Travis Jackson's bad knees, Memphis Bill acquired John "Blondy" Ryan from the Buffalo Bisons of the International League in exchange for Jackson's 1932, injury-forced replacement Doc Marshall and cash. Marshall

5. The Championship Season—First Half

A formidable foursome of hitters and an intrinsic part of New York's offense in 1933. Left to right, Bill Terry, and outfielders Mel Ott, Jo-Jo Moore and Lefty O'Doul.

had been severely beaned early in September at Brooklyn. Marshall "got his skull in the way,"[2] as one hardened New York newspaperman put it, of a Van Mungo fastball and was knocked temporarily unconscious. The groggy player was carried off the field, sitting upright in the arms of teammates, and taken to a nearby hospital for examination. The 26-year-old shortstop missed the remaining three weeks of the Giants' season and never played another game in the major leagues.

The Ryan transaction took place on December 14, but did not quite end Terry's wheeling and dealing. Making room for Mancuso, Terry cut loose the Giants' starting catcher for the past five seasons. On December 29, Shanty Hogan was sold to the Boston Braves for the sizable sum of $25,000. Mancuso, with fewer major league seasons on his resume than Hogan, was thought by Terry to be more on the upswing than the overweight Hogan, who was a liability on the base paths. *United Press* correspondent George H. Beale unsympathetically described Hogan as weighing "a bit more than a man should and bit less than an elephant does."[3] Mancuso, entering his age 27 season, was actually a few months older than Hogan. At 5'10", he was three inches shorter than Hogan but at least 60 pounds lighter, tipping the scale at 185 pounds.

Terry, with his trades and changes in six months' time as manager, had turned over more than 50 percent of the team he had inherited from McGraw, and had replaced four of the starting eight players. Gone were Hogan, behind the plate, and Marshall, at shortstop, as well as two-thirds of the outfield in Lindstrom and the left field combination of Len Koenecke and Chick Fullis.

On January 16, 1933, press secretary James Tierney announced that the team had mailed contracts to 37 players. A week later, Tierney confirmed that Terry's projected starting outfield of Davis, Moore and Ott had come to terms.

Bill Terry arrived in New York from Memphis on February 3, to attend the New York Chapter of the Baseball Writers' Association dinner in two days, which had John McGraw scheduled as guest of honor and speaker. Stopping in at the Giants' midtown Manhattan offices, the manager was, of course, asked about the team and any pennant aspirations he might be entertaining. "We've made a lot of changes to our club," Terry replied. "We've got a hustling young club. I figure Pittsburgh and Chicago will be tough, so I'll just say we'll be one of the first three."[4] Held at the Commodore Hotel, the dinner, attended by more than 500 guests, was a success. Herb Pennock was named outstanding New York player of the year by the writers. On vacation in Havana, McGraw flew out of the Cuban capital to Miami and traveled by rail the rest of the journey to attend. After receiving his "man of the year" recognition, McGraw uttered some kind words about his successor. "Bill Terry is fine young man and a great ball player," he said. "I can only wish for him as long a career and as great a measure of success and enjoyment as I experienced during my long term as manager of the Giants."[5]

Other guests speakers were Branch Rickey and Heywood Broun. Of historic side note, the columnist Broun, during his remarks, called out baseball owners over segregation. Broun had been inspired by a *New York Daily News* editorial espousing integration of the major leagues that appeared earlier that same week. With the Writers' Association's "traditional minstrel show producing blushes and laughter,"[6] as part of the evening's entertainment, Broun's words no doubt fell on many deaf ears.

Four days after President-elect Franklin Roosevelt survived unharmed an assassination attempt in Miami, Florida, on February 15, the California Limited, a transcontinental train, headed west to California with nine New York Giants hopefuls and 16 Chicago Cubs on board. Other Giants made their own travel arrangements, many arriving ahead of the transcontinental. Terry himself left for California on the evening of February 21. He was joined

5. The Championship Season—First Half

in Texarkana, Texas, by Travis Jackson and proceeded to the West Coast from there.

The Giants' train arrived on February 23; its disembarking members gathered for an informal workout. Terry arrived the next day and was kidded by some in the press for having arrived late as usual to spring camp. Terry pointed out that the first official workout was not until the 24th, for which he was duly present. After the Giants' first official workout, which included 24 players, half of them pitchers, Terry raved about the way Travis Jackson looked, a reference to how the player's operated-on knees responded to their first big test. "That's worry off my mind,"[7] the manager said.

But after a second exhibition game, it became evident that Jackson's knees had not fully recovered, and Terry publicly declared he was considering moving Jackson to third base. Jackson was seen working more and more at shortstop with Blondy Ryan, the insurance policy player Terry had acquired over the winter. "Blondy Ryan got his baseball prepping at the hands of Jack Barry at Holy Cross," read one short bio of the player. "He is 25 [27 in actuality], weighs 178, and is an inch over six feet in height."[8]

During this traditional time of supreme optimism, Terry expressed no hints to the contrary in early assessments of his squad. "I think we're going to make the other clubs sit up and take notice this year. The club didn't seem to hustle enough last year. I was as much to blame as any one else. We lost too many games by one run, but the boys are all set for a big year now. They are all signed and satisfied, and that's half the battle, you know."[9] Indeed, there had been no contract issues on the Giants, under the apparently fairer Terry, with new recruit Gus Mancuso being one of the last players to come to terms, on January 30.

Practices were conducted at Wrigley Field and closed to the public. (The Pacific Coast League's Los Angeles Angels trained in San Bernardino for a second year in a row.) "I've never seen a better conditioned group of men for this time in the season," Terry stated as the team began two-a-day workouts. "There's only one man now that I would call overweight. I'll make no effort to hide his name. It's Bill Terry, but I'll tend to his case in a very short time."[10]

The remaining members of the team arrived by March 1. Among those reporting that day were starters Hughie Critz, Jo-Jo Moore and Mel Ott. The Giants played their first exhibition game three days later, at Avalon on Catalina Island, against the Chicago Cubs. New York was beaten, 10–2. Hal Schumacher and Roy Parmelee gave up four runs each. The Giants had committed to pre-season games with the Cubs, Chicago White Sox, and Pittsburgh Pirates, who were also training on the West Coast. The Hollywood Stars, Los

Angeles Angels and Seattle Indians were the other clubs listed on the spring docket as competition for Bill Terry's team.

Threatening to interrupt the spring exhibitions, a deadly earthquake struck Southern California on Friday, March 10, beginning with initial shock waves a few minutes before 6:00 p.m. The violent earth movements stretched from Santa Ana to Long Beach and Los Angeles, and were felt as far south as San Diego. The first major earthquake to hit Southern California since it became a population center left 120 dead, thousands injured and tens of millions in property damage. The Giants, staying at the swanky Biltmore Hotel, were not immune. Players and other guests evacuated the premises during the scary incident. Aftershocks and tremors continued for the remainder of the night and most of the next day. The Giants forged ahead with their scheduled home game the next day against the Chicago Cubs, in front of a sparse crowd, and, as one writer put it, "with one eye on the ball and another on the flag pole in centerfield, to see if the old girl had another convulsion on tap."[11]

Peter Williams related in his 1930s New York Giants chronicle that Terry was very close to uprooting the squad and moving them to Phoenix, Arizona, for the duration of spring camp, stating that his men were unable to sleep because of the persistent terrestrial rumblings that lingered afterward. The Giants were able to send a contingent to play the Seattle Indians in Santa Cruz as scheduled two days after the quake, while the other half of their team finished the three-game weekend set with the Cubs.

Prior to the Giants' March 12 game, Terry had this comment about the Long Beach Earthquake: "California is a great place to train a ball club so far as getting the players into physical condition is concerned, but it certainly raises a rumpus with the nervous system."[12] As a player that day, he seemed unaffected, hitting a game-winning, three-run home run in the bottom of the ninth inning to elevate New York to a 10–7 win over Chicago.

The Giants were forced to postpone their game with the Hollywood Stars in Long Beach on March 13.

Midway through camp, Terry appeared satisfied with the way his team was shaping up. The biggest questions pertained to his pitching staff. Who would supplement Hubbell and Fitzsimmons? The manager responded to speculation that one auxiliary hurler would be 25-year-old Al Smith, a 17-game winner in the Piedmont League last season. "Unless I'm greatly mistaken," said Terry, "the boy [Smith] will be one of the nine pitchers I'll carry through the new season."[13] Smith, however, would not make the club until 1934. Another pitcher, also named Al Smith, in fact, would be one of the pitchers to break camp with the Giants in lieu of the 17-game minor league victor.

5. The Championship Season—First Half

On March 24, Babe Ruth ended his protracted holdout and came to contract terms with Jacob Ruppert for a cut in salary to $52,000. "There will never be another $80,000 ball player,"[14] proclaimed Yankees business manager Ed Barrow, referring to Ruth's salary peak of a few years earlier. The same day, the Giants played their final California exhibition game. Gus Mancuso's RBI single in the bottom of the ninth inning delivered a 6–5 win over the Pittsburgh Pirates. The Giants headed to Arizona and then to Texas, playing games in both states, before continuing east in an exhibition tour that was to bring them to New York just before the start of the season.

John McGraw's coaches in 1932 were Dave Bancroft, Tommy Clarke and Ivy Olson. Clarke was the only hold-over in 1933. Along with 1932 mid-season appointee Mitchell as pitching coach, Terry brought in Billy Southworth, who had been Terry's first roommate with the Giants, and a bit of a mentor to him, helping him acclimate to the major league scene as a rookie. However, Southworth, who had been managing in the minor leagues, suddenly retired on April 1. The reason given was a knee injury. Terry hired Frank Snyder, a catcher with the Giants during the previous decade, to replace his former roomie.

On April 3, Bill Terry Day was observed in Memphis. Rain spoiled a parade that Chamber of Commerce officials had prepared for their hometown star, and kept attendance to 400 for an exhibition game between Terry's squad and the Memphis Chicks. The Giants defeated the Chicks, 10–2, on a muddy field, behind Carl Hubbell and Bill Shores. (The previous day, more than 8,000 fans had turned out to see a contest between the New York Yankees and Chicks.)

The Giants played the Birmingham Barons on April 4 and the Chattanooga Lookouts on April 5, in those minor league teams' home parks. Terry's club met up with the Detroit Tigers in Norfolk, Virginia, on April 7. Kiddo Davis hit two home runs, and Terry and Hank Leiber one each, in the Giants' 17–7 victory over the Tigers. Hal Schumacher won a starting job on the pitching staff with the complete game win. He could have legally celebrated afterwards with an alcoholic beverage, as beer and wine sales were permitted that day in the United States for the first time since 1920. All three New York clubs, as well as those in Chicago, added beer to their ballpark concessions menus that year. But teams in smaller markets did not follow suit, preferring to continue the previous temperate atmosphere within their pastoral confines.

The Giants, with a spring exhibition record of 19–9, reached New York on Saturday, April 8, completing what had been a more than 7,000-mile, cross-country trek begun nearly two months earlier. The well-traveled club played the Tigers again, at the Polo Grounds, followed by the Fordham Rams, before heading to Boston, intending to commence the season on Wednesday, April 12. This was the successful New York Giants roster that prepared to do battle in the National League: Mancuso (C), Terry (1B), Critz (2B), Vergez (3B), Ryan (SS), Davis (LF), Moore (CF), Ott (RF), Richards (C), Leslie (1B), Jackson (3B/SS), James (INF), Leiber (OF), Peel (OF), Hubbell (P), Fitzsimmons (P), Schumacher (P), Parmelee (P), Spencer (P), Starr (P), Shores (P), Smith (P), Luque (RP), and Bell (RP).

But the opener was rained out, and then snowed out for three more days, following a four-inch snowstorm that hit the Boston area. Because of the bad weather, the Giants did not play for five days (since their April 10 encounter with Fordham). An April 16 meeting, therefore, with Brooklyn became the team's first engagement of 1933. In their 3:00 p.m. season opener against the Dodgers at Ebbets Field, Carl Hubbell displayed the kind of exceptional pitching that he would spoil Giants fans with all season long. On a damp, overcast day, Hubbell threw 11 innings of one-run baseball, allowing eight hits. His mound opponent, Joe Shaute, matched him on nearly even terms for the same number of innings, permitting an equal number of safeties and yielding one unearned run. The game ended in a 1–1 tie, called after 14 innings because of darkness. Terry indicated right off who his primary bullpen men would be, calling in Adolfo Luque to replace Hubbell for two innings and Hi Bell for the other. The two spring training "surprises," outfielder Hank Leiber and shortstop Blondy Ryan, collected a pair of hits apiece. The right-handed batting Leiber had impressed Terry enough to win a platoon job in left with the left-handed swinging Jo-Jo Moore. Following the removal of the southpaw Shaute, Moore substituted for the 22-year-old Leiber, who had come up through the former Giants affiliate in Winston-Salem.

As far as Ryan was concerned, the following partial evaluation by a member of the New York press corps, printed during the first week of the season, made it clear the shortstop's job belonged to the former Jesuit college player for the foreseeable future: "It isn't by decree that Ryan is at shortstop. Travis Jackson would have been Terry's choice to guard that crescent of dirt, but the Arkansas traveler has a pair of knees that are giving him more trouble than a skinny chorus girl's and it's doubtful if Stonewall will play many ball games this year."[15]

As spiffy as their pitching was on Opening Day, the Giants showed off new uniforms for the initial time in a regular season game. In a first since the early years of the franchise, NEW YORK was printed across their road uniforms, with black and orange trim as new team colors. The Giants wore black caps for the first time in two decades, with matching undershirt and stirrups with orange piping. The home regalia differed only with having GIANTS emblazoned across the chest, instead of NEW YORK, and a whiter flannel base. The *Brooklyn Daily Eagle* made a reference to the new garb as "those Princetonish traveling uniforms of the Giants."[16]

Rain washed out the Giants' next game, on April 17 in Philadelphia. In the same city on April 18, Terry picked up his first win as full-term manager. Looking to reverse a noxious trend from last season, the focused pilot pulled what may have been considered an extreme move to attain a 3–2 victory over the Phillies. Terry called on the one-day-rested Hubbell to secure the final two outs of the game, in relief of Luque, who had come in from the bullpen with two outs in the eighth inning after the Phillies scored both of their runs. With the tying run on second base, Hubbell struck out Al Todd and retired Eddie Delker, both right-handed pinch-hitters. Todd had substituted for announced pinch-hitter Harry McCurdy, a left-handed batter summoned to face the righty Luque. Phillies manager Burt Shotton may have outsmarted himself with the moves, playing into Hubbell's deceptive screwball, which broke *away* from right-handed hitters. Center fielder Kiddo Davis clocked the inaugural home run for the Giants, a solo blast to open the scoring in the third inning, and also scored the decisive run on a Terry RBI single in the top of the eighth. Freddie Fitzsimmons started the contest for New York and received the win.

The following day, a second postponement due to wet grounds kept the intended three-game series to a single affair.

Hubbell was back on the mound for the third time in five days on April 20, for the Polo Grounds season inaugural, and he was brilliant. The left-hander stymied the Boston Braves, 1–0, on four hits with 13 strikeouts. Kiddo Davis scored the only run after tripling in the sixth inning. Second baseman Hughie Critz delivered the run-soring single. "Bill Terry had the boys dressed to kill in white suits, black windbreakers and caps with orange trim," wrote a beat writer, depicting the pre-game activity around the Giants' home opener. "The Manhattan College Band lent a college color to the occasion and the Polo Grounds glistened in new flags and fresh paint. John J. McGraw was a graceful reminder of the past as he marched to the flagpole with Mayor John P. O'Brien."[17]

The next day, Hal Schumacher made his first start of the season. A three-run fourth inning, in which he surrendered three walks, two wild pitches and a pair of hits, did the pitcher in. The Braves evened the three-game series with a 3–1 win. In the rubber game, Ray Starr, the unproven young pitcher, failed his first test, giving up five runs in two-plus innings. The Giants dropped to 2–2 with the 7–3 loss.

The following day, April 23, Freddie Fitzsimmons, the winner in the second game of the season over Philadelphia, faced the Phillies again in a one-game Polo Grounds stopover for the Phils. Fitzsimmons scored his second victory, pitching all the way in a 3–1 decision. He helped his own cause with a solo home run. A crowd of 20,000 was on hand for the first Sunday home game.

Brooklyn and Joe Shaute paid a visit to upper Manhattan on April 24 and drew Hubbell again. This time Shaute was no match for the screwballer. Hubbell tossed his second consecutive shutout, downing the Dodgers, 4–0. A Giant casualty, literally and figuratively speaking, was Bill Terry. The first baseman suffered a fracture of the ulna bone when hit on the wrist by one of Shaute's pitches. Terry, who had played in at least 149 games in each of the past six seasons, including 468 in a row, was sidelined for a month. Away from the diamond the same day, the Giants picked up pitcher George Uhle from the Detroit Tigers for the waiver price of $7,500. The Giants roster now contained a maximum 25 players, one more than on Opening Day.

On April 25, Schumacher rebounded nicely from his disconcerting start on the 21st and defeated the Dodgers, 8–2, in a complete game. The Giants took a 7–0 lead after two innings and never looked back. Mel Ott hit his first home run of the season, a three-run "rocket against the green roof of the right field grandstand."[18] Bill Terry's understudy for the past two years, Sam Leslie, went 1-for-3. He scored a run and drove in one in his first game at first base. Roy Parmelee, whose colorful sobriquet was "Tarzan," followed Schumacher with a season debut that was near-historic. The hard-throwing young pitcher tossed a one-hitter against the visiting Philadelphia Phillies on April 26. A third-inning smash hit through Johnny Vergez at third base that went for a double was the Phillies' sole safety. Parmelee's own wild pitch spoiled his shutout in the same inning. The wild toss may be an example for the genesis of Parmelee's more evocative nickname, as this contemporary report confirmed: "The big Michigan right-hander's nickname was hung on him because of his propensity for getting himself 'out on a limb' while doing mound duty. He is addicted to streaks of extreme wildness on no notice or slight provocation."[19] Only six balls were hit out of the infield against the Giants' right-hander, who struck out six and walked four in the 3–1 final.

Hoping to take a page from Schumacher's book, Ray Starr made his second start on April 27. Starr threw a fine six innings, allowing the Phillies two runs, one earned, before he was removed for a pinch-hitter with the score tied, 2–2. Terry then called on Hubbell. The left-hander with two days' rest pitched three scoreless innings, extending a scoreless streak to 26 frames; he picked up a 5–2 win when the Giants plated three runs in the eighth inning.

Hubbell doubled in the last of the runs. Blondy Ryan and Gus Mancuso collected run-scoring, extra-base hits in the inning.

After an off-day, the Giants made it six wins in a row, defeating the Dodgers at Ebbets Field, 2–1. Freddie Fitzsimmons won his third game in as many starts, while sweating out the game's final out in the dugout. Clinging to his one-run lead, Fitzsimmons left the tight contest with the bases loaded and two outs in the ninth inning. Adolfo Luque, his reliever, retired Brooklyn's Joe Stripp—throwing a 3–2 pitch with 25,000 fans roaring against him—on a pop-up to first baseman Sam Leslie.

On the last day of the month, the Giants visited Braves Field and dropped both ends of a doubleheader. (Originally scheduled as single game, one of the four rain/snowouts from the opening week was made up here.) In the curtain raiser, Hubbell, making his sixth appearance in the Giants' first 12 games, and having allowed only one run in 32⅔ innings, was solved for three runs in eight innings by the Braves; he suffered a 3–0 defeat as his teammates failed to muster any support. In the second game, Glenn Spencer, making one of his three starts on the season, pitched well, permitting two runs in six innings. But the main bullpen men, Bell and then Luque, fell apart and conceded six runs between them. The Braves were victorious, 8–4, doubly pleasing a throng of 35,000, "the largest gathering in a Boston ball park in April for many years."[20]

The Giants finished April with an 8–4 record, 1½ games out of first place.

After an off-day on Monday, Schumacher took a temporary step backward on May 2, the beginning of an 11-game homestand. The right-hander was tagged for eight hits and four runs in 5⅓ innings. The Giants endured their second shutout in three games, 11–0, at the hands of the Chicago Cubs. Travis Jackson made his first start of the season at shortstop. He registered six assists and six putouts but was hitless at the plate. George Uhle saw his first action for the team as a pitcher and gave up six runs in less than three innings.

A rainout the next day prompted the teams to play two games on May 4. Fitzsimmons proved a stalwart again, winning the first game, 2–1. Though he allowed eight hits and six walks, Fitzsimmons, whose ERA dropped to 1.05 with the complete game, was able to minimize damage by his opponents. He recorded six assists and knocked in the Giants' first run in the fifth inning. Kiddo Davis singled home the decisive run in the next inning. In the nightcap, Parmelee earned a permanent spot in the starting rotation, hurling eight strong frames. He was touched for four runs but only two were earned. He left with a 5–4 lead, and Terry trusted no one but Hubbell to obtain the final three outs, which the left-hander accomplished in 1-2-3 fashion.

The Cincinnati Reds opened a three-game set with the Terrymen on May 5. Spencer recorded a shaky start and was the losing pitcher, 8–5. His two hits on Opening Day notwithstanding, Blondy Ryan had gotten off to a slow start with the bat. As a consequence, Travis Jackson started his fourth consecutive game at shortstop. It would be Jackson's last start for two months, as his troublesome knees relegated him to pinch-hitting and late-game defensive substitution duties until then. The unsettled issue at shortstop attracted more attention. The *New York Sun* published a story of a proposed trade Bill Terry had in the works to send Sam Leslie to the Chicago Cubs for shortstop Billy Jurges and an unnamed pitcher.

Rain washed away the next day's game, forcing a twin engagement on May 7. The Giants managed only two hits in the first game, one of them a home run by Leslie, his first of the season. It was the only run of the game, as Hubbell once more lathered up his whitewash brush and blanked the Reds on five hits. The 4–1 Hubbell's third shutout in five starts lowered his ERA to 0.71. In the second game, Schumacher made his case as a regular starter by keeping the visitors off the board, winning 5–0 and evening his record at 2–2. He allowed two hits and two walks and struck out a pair. Johnny Vergez hit his second home run and drove in two runs. A big Sunday crowd of 40,000 was happily entertained throughout the sun-filled afternoon.

Baseball owners had launched what could be called a counter-offensive against the steep drop in attendance over the past two seasons. The following news brief in *The Sporting News* explained the magnates' initiative: "The New York Giants have made available many additional seats at bleacher prices by setting aside a portion of the right field stands for that purpose and other clubs have done likewise. It has been proved by the New York Yankees and Brooklyn Dodgers that increasing the accommodations at bleacher prices attracts fans who are not able to pay the toll for the more desirable seats."[21]

On May 8, the St. Louis Cardinals crossed over from Brooklyn, where they had been engaging the Dodgers, and handed Fitzsimmons his first setback, 4–3. Tex Carleton was the Redbirds' winner and Dizzy Dean recorded a ninth-inning save, striking out two batters. Home runs accounted for all of the scoring. For the Cardinals, Ducky Medwick and Frankie Frisch homered, with Frisch's coming with two men on base. Sam Leslie drove one out the park for home club. For the second series in a row, thanks to a scheduling happenstance, Leo Durocher was the starting shortstop in a series-opening game for the visiting team at the Polo Grounds. Durocher, who scored two runs in the Reds' May 5 loss to the Giants, had been traded by the Reds to the Cardinals in a six-player deal on May 7. In the May 8 Cardinals victory over Fitzsimmons, he went 0-for-2 with a run scored.

5. The Championship Season—First Half

Rain washed out the final two games of the Cardinals series. During the downtime, Terry optioned Hank Leiber, the starting left fielder on Opening Day, to Jersey City. Leiber had appeared in only five more games since then, all as a pinch-hitter, and was caught in the cross-hairs of Terry's administrative aim to cut the roster to 23 players by May 15. The aim was reached with Terry presently on the inactive list.

Following the two unplanned days off, Terry, who was managing in civilian suit and tie, bypassed Parmelee to pitch Hubbell, on normal three days' rest, against the first-place Pittsburgh Pirates on May 11. Earlier in the season, Hubbell had been sought for an opinion on the baseball's material composition this year. His response downplayed the ball's makeup and placed the onus on himself and his pitching brethren. "If the ball is lively," said Hubbell, "the batters will pop them up just a little higher, that is, if they are popping them up and not lining out drives. Bad timing is what dumps a hitter into a slump."[22] The Pirates came out measuring Hubbell's slants like no other previous team, with an output of 12 hits and seven runs (six earned). Though he hit a home run, Hubbell suffered his second setback, 7–6.

Schumacher received his fifth start in the second game of the series on May 12. The pitcher benefited from the Giants' biggest offensive production so far, cruising to an 11–3 win. Leslie drove in three runs on three hits as he continued his strong hitting in place of Terry. The weak-hitting Blondy Ryan clocked his first home run with two men aboard. The next day, the Giants made it two in a row over the Pirates, winning an extra-inning contest, 2–1. The Giants tied the game in the ninth on an infield single by Sam Leslie. In the 11th frame, with the bases loaded and two outs, Travis Jackson was called out of the first base coaching box to pinch-hit for Adolfo Luque. Jackson delivered a drive that would have easily gone for two bases, to win the game on an official single. Fitzsimmons had pitched the first eight innings, followed by Hi Bell for two more stanzas, before he yielded the 11th to Luque, the winning hurler. Pirates pitcher Larry French absorbed the tough-luck, complete-game loss, with both runs unearned.

Terry's team beat the Pirates the next day and tied the Bucs for first place with identical 15–8 records. Terry had decided to bring Roy Parmelee along slowly. Enlisting a repeat Hubbell-Fitzsimmons-Schumacher starting rotation with a previous spot start from Glenn Spencer, Terry had not called on Parmelee in ten days. But on May 14, the right-hander won for the third time in as many starts, 5–1. He was touched for six hits, walked four and struck out six Pirates.

The broad-shouldered hurler credited his early success to a tip given to him by his manager and the work he did in the minor leagues the prior season, as well as assuming a more relaxed approach on the mound.

Bill Terry has been teaching me how to overcome my wildness. He has told me to lengthen my stride in the box and it's working out fine. Perhaps my chief trouble when I was up here before was that I didn't get enough work. I did more pitching in the [American] Association and my control was better. Then too, I might have been bearing down too much up here. I've overcome that tendency, too.[23]

The Giants, having concluded a 7–4 homestand, embarked on a nearly two week-long road trip. It began in Chicago on May 16 on a positive note, thanks to the club's top pitcher. Carl Hubbell defeated the Cubs, 4–1, for the Giants' fourth straight win. In control all the way, he scattered eight hits, struck out five and walked one, and the run he allowed was unearned. Four Giants drove in runs. Rain postponed the middle game of the three-game set, causing a doubleheader on May 18. In the first game, Schumacher continued to show tip-top form, tossing a six-hit shutout. The road team scored three runs, one of them on catcher Gus Mancuso's first home run. The Giants' five-game winning streak was halted in the afterpiece. Freddie Fitzsimmons was knocked from the box in the fifth inning after being pasted for seven runs. Glenn Spencer and Ray Starr participated in mop-up chores in the 10–1 defeat.

As the Giants left town the same day, a national buzz began circulating around baseball when it was announced that an inter-league clash between the top talent of each major circuit would take place in Chicago on July 6.

A four-game weekend set in St. Louis started badly and ended worse. The fifth-place Cardinals beat the Giants four straight games, including a Sunday doubleheader on May 21. In the Friday opener, Parmelee and Hubbell, in relief, lost a 7–2, eighth-inning lead, as the Cardinals tied the contest in the frame. In the bottom of the tenth, the Cardinals' Pat Crawford singled in the winning run, sinking loser Adolfo Luque in the 8–7 decision. A Mel Ott grand slam went for naught. On May 20, Dizzy Dean beat Hi Bell, who was given a spot start, 4–1, in what would have been Hubbell's normal turn had Terry not used him for an inning and two-thirds the prior day. Hubbell started on May 21 and was outdueled by Bill Hallahan in the lidlifter of the Sunday duet, 2–1. In the nightcap, on short rest after the rough outing two days earlier, Fitzsimmons was hit hard again, losing 8–4. Spencer and Starr repeated previous cleanup duties for the same starter.

The lost weekend dropped the 17–13 Giants into second place, three games in back of the Pittsburgh Pirates. Schumacher righted things with his fourth straight complete-game win and third shutout, humbling the Cincinnati Reds, 9–0, at Redland Field on May 22. Ott drove in three runs and Leslie went 4-for-4, as the Giants pounded out 16 hits.

Parmelee upped his record to 4–0, with a big assist from Luque, the next day. Reviving some of his past glories at Redland Field, the veteran hurled four innings of shutout relief to preserve Parmelee's 6–4 win. Parmelee helped himself too, clubbing a three-run home run (the first of his career) in the second inning. After the game, the Giants optioned pitcher Bill Shores to the Kansas City Blues of the American Association and activated one William Terry.

The Reds avoided the sweep the following day, defeating George Uhle in his first start for the Giants, 3–1. The former American League ace lasted only two and 2/3 innings, allowing five hits and three walks. Bell and Starr held the home club scoreless afterward. His wrist healed, Bill Terry returned to action as a pinch-hitter and reached on an error. The youthful pilot was now facing the decision of whether to replace Leslie, who was currently hitting .317, slugging well over .500, and fielding his position well. Leslie would continue to play—for now. The "Terryless" Giants had gone 15–11 during their manager's playing absence.

The Giants had two games postponed by rain in Pittsburgh, their next road stop. In the one game squeezed in amid the unrepentant showers, on May 26, Hi Bell picked up his first win of the season. In relief of Fitzsimmons, Bell kept the Pirates from scoring for the final four innings of the game, while his team rallied for a 6–5 win. Catcher Mancuso's solo home run in the eighth inning provided the winning tally. "A circus catch by Blondy Ryan," specified one news brief, "saved the game for the Terrymen, halting a Pirate rally in the fifth."[24] The bases were loaded at the time of Ryan's grab. Pinch-hitting for the ineffective Fitzsimmons, Terry singled in the tying run for the winners in the sixth inning.

The New Yorkers headed back east after the final game of their proposed three-game series in Pittsburgh was canceled by rain on May 27. The team met Brooklyn the following day at Ebbets Field.

Early fan voting for the "feature of the World's Fair sports program" was released the prior day. Though not back as a regular yet and hitting .226 (7-for-31), Terry was the National League fans' overwhelming choice to start at first base. Also by wide margins, Frankie Frisch and Pie Traynor outdistanced all second and third basemen. Phillies shortstop Dick Bartell held a slim voting margin over Pittsburgh's Arky Vaughan. Another Phillie, Chuck Klein, was by far the leading vote-getter in the outfield. Paul Waner of the Pirates and Brooklyn's Lefty O'Doul held comfortable leads over other recognized flychasers. Hubbell placed behind Chicago's Lon Warneke as the most desired pitcher.

Hubbell did not elevate his cause with the fans in his outing against the Dodgers at Ebbets Field on May 28. His record slipping to 5–4, he lasted only five innings and was cuffed for ten hits and four runs. The Giants were defeated by their inter-borough rivals, 5–4.

Charles Stoneham used an off-day on Monday, May 29, to submit an initiative to his fellow owners to nominate John McGraw as National League manager for the upcoming All-Star gala in Chicago.

Most teams in both circuits played doubleheaders as part of a Decoration Day celebration on May 30. The Polo Grounds hosted its first games since May 14. Max Carey's Dodgers were the Giants' opponents; only 15,000 fans turned out to see the teams break even on the day. Two late-inning home runs by the Giants in the opener lifted them to a 2–1 win. Terry pinch-hit a home run in the eighth inning and Bernie James, filling in for an ailing Hughie Critz, surprisingly hit a walk-off shot in the ninth. (It was James' only major league home run.) With a scoreless last inning of work, Luque picked up his second win. Van Mungo absorbed the complete-game loss for Brooklyn. In the nightcap, Walter "Boom-Boom" Beck subdued the Giants, 3–1, on four hits. Parmelee suffered his first loss, hurling eight innings and giving up a decisive two-run homer to Tony Cuccinello. Wet grounds prohibited the Dodgers and Giants from playing the next day.

The Manhattanites departed from Penn Station for Philadelphia the next morning with a 21–16 record. After the season's first six weeks, the New York Giants were two games behind two teams which were tied for first place, Pittsburgh and St. Louis, the Cardinals having recently come on strong in the standings. Before leaving for their game later that afternoon, Terry told a newspaperman that so far he was pleased with his pitching and the performance of other players, in particular, his shortstop. "I'm mighty proud of my staff," Terry remarked. "All Ryan lacks to be just as good as Charlie Gelbert or Leo Durocher is experience. Of course I looked for Travis Jackson to return long ago, but I want him to rest his knees up a little longer and not be in too much of a hurry to return to the game, [though] we miss his bat."[25]

The Giants took three out of four games from Philadelphia from June 1–3, with Fitzsimmons, Hubbell and Bell tossing complete game victories at the Baker Bowl. Bell's was a five-hit shutout on June 3. The second game of a doubleheader, the contest was a make-up for one of the April rainouts endured by the Giants in the Quaker City. The game marked the return to the starting lineup of the Giants' future Hall of Fame first baseman. He homered in the 5–0 win, as did Gus Mancuso.

The Giants swapped out a new 23rd man during this time. The day before Bell's shutout win, Jack Salveson, a right-handed pitcher, was obtained from the Dallas club in the Texas League. The roster limit was not exceeded with the designating of former Villanova pitcher Al Smith (no relation to the

5. The Championship Season—First Half

Piedmont League hurler) to the inactive coaching staff. The carrying of Smith as a player and then his appointment as a coach may have been an unreported act of charity on the part of Terry. Smith, who had not participated in a single game, was a "one game and done" major leaguer with the Giants in 1926 and never coached again at the big league level after this season. (Smith was voted a full World Series share.)

The next day, June 4, at Ebbets Field, two Giants pitchers held the second-division Dodgers to eight hits combined in a doubleheader won by the visitors, 2–0 and 6–1. Schumacher tied Hubbell for most wins on the club with six in hurling his fourth shutout. In the back end of the Sunday affair—attended by 32,000 fans—Fitzsimmons, pitching on two days' rest, improved to 6–3 with a five-hitter.

Gus Mancuso caught every pitch of both games for the second day in row. The Mancuso trade was working out fine for the Giants, especially as a steadying influence for the mound corps. "Mancuso has been a great player for me," said the manager who traded for him eight months earlier. "He is as popular with the players as any man in the club and he has helped greatly in the development of the pitchers. He is an iron man and can catch every day. I'd be perfectly satisfied if I had a whole squad of Mancusos."[26]

After the back-to-back road twin bills, the Giants welcomed the usual Monday off-day before resuming the series with Brooklyn on June 6. Hubbell won his seventh game, 7–2, tossing an eight-hitter and not permitting any free passes. Ott hit his sixth home run. He and Blondy Ryan each knocked in a pair of runs.

The schedule-makers gave New York another day of rest on June 7, as they waited for their next opponents, the last-place Philadelphia Phillies, to finish a series in Boston. The following day, the 27–17 Giants commenced their longest homestand of the season, 25 games. The Polo Grounders had climbed into first place, percentage points ahead of the St. Louis Cardinals.

The extended homestand did not start well for Roy Parmelee. In the June 8 opener, he was knocked from the box in the second inning—but not all by the Phillies' hitters' doing. He deserved a far better fate as the six runs he gave up, on four hits and a walk, were all unearned. Critz, Ott and Mancuso all committed errors that contributed to the Phillies' undeserved scoring. Hi Bell pitched 3⅓ innings of scoreless middle relief. New York experienced record-setting temperatures that day, and Bell was overcome by the heat and forced to retire after the Giants had come back from a five-run deficit to take the lead, 7–6, on Ott's solo home run in the fifth frame. Homer Peel, receiving a start in the outfield, clubbed a grand slam. Terry also homered. After Ott's blast, a perhaps overly excited Terry summoned Hubbell, on one day's rest.

The Giants did not score the remainder of the game, and Terry let Hubbell pitch the last four innings. He did so, providing four shutout stanzas. Though Bell was the pitcher of record, the official scorer awarded Hubbell the win, presumably because of his slightly better pitching line. It was Hubbell's eighth victory. A sparse crowd of 4,000 people turned out to see their first-place club.

In the series' second game, played on June 10, a two-run double by Ott and a two-run homer by Johnny Vergez in the first inning propelled the Giants to their ninth win in ten games versus the lowly Philadelphians. Fitzsimmons won his third in a row, 5–2. Permitting both runs, he went seven innings, relieved by Adolfo Luque for the final two innings. Vergez hit two more home runs the next day, his fourth and fifth, but Schumacher (6–3) was not sharp and the Giants were beaten, 7–5, as Philadelphia avoided the sweep. The Sunday matinee attracted 12,000 spectators.

The Giants spent their Monday, June 12 off-day in anything but idleness. The team traveled to Canton, New York, to play an exhibition game and attend a graduation ceremony for one of their teammates. "For the first time in baseball history," summarized one report of the proceedings, "a major league player today received a college degree during the championship season when Hal Schumacher, pitcher of the New York Giants, was graduated from St. Lawrence University."[27] The entire club was present for the occasion, in which Schumacher received a Bachelor of Science diploma. The college grad then changed out of his cap and gown in order to hurl the first two (scoreless) innings of the exhibition game between the Giants and his former St. Lawrence Larries team. The Giants won handily, 12–4. Terry, Leslie and Ott homered for the winners.

The pace-setting Giants were one game ahead of the St. Louis Cardinals when they came back home to face the sixth-place Boston Braves on June 13. Carl Hubbell (9–4) kept the club in its precarious perch by pitching past *seven* errors, three by Johnny Vergez, to win, 6–3. In the series' next contest, Parmelee was stung early and often by wildness. He walked five of the first six batters he faced before he was pulled in the first inning. All five baserunners ended up scoring, but the Braves could not dent the plate after that and the Giants rallied for an 8–5 victory. Ott contributed to the offense with his eighth home run. Allowing only two hits and no walks, Luque pitched the last seven shutout innings for the much-deserved win, his third. The Braves denied Fitzsimmons a chance at his eighth win the following day, rocking the husky pitcher for six hits and six runs in 3⅓ innings. Bill McKechnie's Braves escaped town with a 7–4 win.

On the June 15 trading deadline day, Terry cashed in a bargaining chip

5. The Championship Season—First Half

that had increased significantly in value while the manager was on the shelf with his broken wrist. Terry traded Sam Leslie to Brooklyn—in desperate need of a first baseman—for Lefty O'Doul and Watty Clark. O'Doul, the defending batting champion of the National League, had slumped badly and was hitting only .252. Clark, a 20-game winner in 1932, was currently a sub-.500 pitcher at 2–4. Though the two Brooklyn teammates were over 30, the trade reflected the constant pressure to produce that ballplayers lived under from a prevailing front office mindset that had little patience for underperforming athletes. A few hours later, the Giants sold Ray Starr to the Boston Braves in order to reach the 23-man roster limit.

Leslie was naturally in the starting lineup when the men from Flatbush revisited the Polo Grounds on June 16. The former back-up first baseman homered and drove in two runs in the Dodgers' 3–1 victory. Van Mungo pitched an eight-hitter for Brooklyn. Permitting two runs, Schumacher (6–4) suffered the loss. The next day, the May 31 "wet grounds" postponement was made up as part of a twin bill. In the first game, the Dodgers deciphered Hubbell, but the Giants pitcher received strong enough offensive support to spare him a potential defeat. The Giants came out on top, 8–7, with Hi Bell getting the victory in relief. Lefty O'Doul, in his second game as a Giant, provided a game-deciding, two-RBI hit in the eighth inning. The nightcap was called because of darkness after 11 innings, tied 3–3. Watty Clark delivered four scoreless inning in relief of Freddie Fitzsimmons. A throng of 35,000 fans delivered partisan cheering for the Giants throughout the day.

Fifteen thousand fewer followers turned out the following day, Sunday, June 18, to see Roy Parmelee hurl his first major league shutout. The change in visitors may have had something to do with the drop in attendance. Parmelee outdueled Chicago Cubs eight-game winner Lon Warneke, 2–0. The 26-year-old hurler allowed eight hits but walked none, which must have been as satisfying as the shutout for the pitcher who was prone to wildness. One day hence, Schumacher followed with his fifth shutout and the Giants' major league-leading tenth of the season, a 3–0 decision over Charlie Root. O'Doul, playing left field, had three singles. (O'Doul became the Giants' regular left fielder for the next month, until his average began to slip.) The Cubs then beat a combination of Hi Bell and Glenn Spencer, 5–3, on June 20. Curiously, Terry brought in Hubbell to pitch the final two innings, though the Giants were behind by their two-run margin of defeat.

Meanwhile, the pre–Decoration Day proposal of Charles Stoneham for appointing John McGraw as National League manager in the special All-Star exhibition game was approved by the other owners.

The Giants used another well-pitched game, this time by Fitzsimmons, to win the third of four scheduled games versus Charlie Grimm's boys, on June 21. Fitzsimmons (8–4) did not walk a batter and yielded only three singles in the 3–1 win. Because of two double plays, one of which scored the Cubs' lone run, no Chicago batter was left on base over nine innings.

Fifth-place Cincinnati came into town to begin a five-game weekend set on June 22, and Hubbell greeted them with the Giants' third shutout in five games. Johnny Vergez's seventh home run and two RBI backed Hubbell's 4–0 win, number ten on the season.

After Watty Clark was outdueled by the Reds' Eppa Rixey, 2–1, one day later, the Giants won the three remaining games. In the third meeting, benefitting from a well-balanced 12-hit attack by his teammates, Parmelee (6–2) tossed his second straight walkless complete game, winning 5–2. Terry did not have to use the bullpen in a doubleheader triumph on June 25, as Schumacher and Fitzsimmons proficiently took care of business, hurling 7–1 and 6–3 wins, respectively. Vergez drove in six runs, on four hits, in the two games. Another 35,000 rooters were present to support their excelling club, now with a three-game lead atop the National League.

Because all four "western clubs" were visiting their eastern counterparts, Monday, June 26 dawned with a full slate of action on tap. But rain in the northeast postponed the entire National League schedule. The Giants and Pittsburgh Pirates, the new team in town, hoped to play two the following day, but wet grounds precluded the attempt. When the weather and field finally cooperated on June 28, the teams salvaged one of the rainouts by playing a doubleheader. In the first game, Pittsburgh reached Hubbell for ten hits and four runs in 7⅓ innings. It was enough to hand the southpaw his fifth defeat, 5–2. In the vesper affair, the Giants used clutch long ball excitement to pull out a victory. With one out in the bottom of the ninth inning, Hughie Critz hit a two-run circuit clout, his first of the campaign, to tie the contest at four runs apiece. In the tenth, Gus Mancuso put a charge into one with two men on to give the Giants the ball game, 7–4. It was the catcher's first walk-off home run as a big leaguer, one of two he would hit in his career.

The last four days of the 25-game homestand were occupied with the visit of the St. Louis Cardinals, starting on Thursday, June 29. Due to the recent successes of New York, the Cardinals had slipped 4½ games behind the Giants. Third-place Pittsburgh was six games behind and the Chicago Cubs, eight games in arrears, rounded out the first division. In the five-game set, the Cardinals made early, attention-grabbing statements, winning the first two games and stretching to seven their winning streak over the Giants on the season. Tex Carleton defeated Watty Clark, 7–3, and Dizzy Dean edged Hal Schumacher, 1–0, in a classic pitcher's duel on June 30. Ducky Medwick's four-bagger in the ninth inning decided the contest. In Carleton's win, Cards outfielder Ethan Allen smacked an inside-the-park home run, which was nullified when the attentive Terry noticed that Allen had batted out of order. Medwick, who should have hit, was called out and Allen batted again, only to ground out.

The Giants widened their lead back to 3½ games, easily winning game three, 11–1. Kiddo Davis hit a three-run home run, as everyone in the starting lineup recorded at least one hit. Freddie Fitzsimmons became a ten-game winner. Not taking any chances, Terry removed his starter with two outs and two men on base in the sixth inning. The Giants were leading, 6–1. Hi Bell came in and finished the task exceptionally.

If 1931 was the year that the Depression truly became "Great," then 1933 was the year that made Carl Hubbell truly great, and no game better defined that greatness than the one he pitched on July 2, 1933. In the first game of a doubleheader, Hubbell tied moundmate Schumacher for most shutouts in the league with five—and what a shutout it was! "With 45,000 fans cheering him on," read one of the many glowing accounts of the day, "Carl Hubbell blanked the St. Louis Cardinals for 18 innings, the longest major league game played so far this season. Hubbell gave up only six hits in his prolonged duel and did not issue a free pass."[28] The Giants' ace struck out 12 and permitted only one batter to reach third base. Masterfully, he retired the side in order in 12 of the 18 innings.

Leading off the bottom of the 18th inning, Jo-Jo Moore walked, and Mancuso sacrificed him to second. Pinch-hitting for Ryan, Travis Jackson was walked intentionally. Batting for himself (which indicated he would have come out to pitch the 19th inning), Hubbell moved both runners along with a ground out to the right side of the infield. The leadoff batter, Hughie Critz—in his ninth at-bat of the game—singled up the middle and brought home Moore. An all-time diamond classic, the low-scoring battle lasted four hours and three minutes.

"I never found myself tired," Hubbell remarkably said after his masterpiece. "There was only a pitch or two that wasn't just about where I wanted it."[29] In an interview with a national baseball publication nearly four decades later, Hubbell put his immense endeavor in perspective:

> It wasn't the most important game I ever pitched or won, but it was probably the best. I remember that Frisch hit a couple of long fouls that were almost home runs because of the short fences and Medwick just missed one, too. I didn't notice the physical strain because it was a gray, muggy day. I guess all the tension builds up nervous energy. But I was sure glad to see Critz's ball go through because I thought it would never end. And about an hour after the game ended, I was completely washed out.[30]

Tex Carleton, who had opened the series three days earlier, stoutheartedly pitched 16 innings for the Cardinals prior to being removed for a pinch-hitter. Jesse Haines was the loser in relief.

The Cardinals were also helpless against Roy Parmelee in the nightcap, falling 1–0. The game was an added attraction due to one of the rainouts from the Cardinals' initial New York trip in May. Johnny Vergez's eighth home run (second on the team behind Ott) in the fourth inning was all the scoring in the game, finished in descending darkness. Parmelee fanned 13 and walked no one, but was overshadowed by Hubbell. Cardinals manager Gabby Street enlisted Dizzy Dean—on one day's rest—to oppose Parmelee. Dean allowed five hits, one more than his counterpart, in absorbing the hard-luck loss. Dean's pitching line in his two games, over three days, amounted to 17 innings, 11 hits, three walks, ten strikeouts, and one run; his record was 1–1.

Parenthetically, Giants shortstop Blondy Ryan was spiked in the second game and had to be removed, while catcher Gus Mancuso caught both games of the pitching-rich doubleheader, all 27 innings. Ryan would be out for ten days. Mancuso's arduous day would consist of 15 putouts and two assists in Parmelee's gem, and 13 putouts and an assist in Hubbell's tour de force. He had a hit in each game.

Brandishing the doubleheader sweep, the Giants concluded their long home stay with 16 wins and 8 losses. The team then headed to Boston, where it dropped two out of three to the Braves. Both clubs bypassed their Monday off-day to make up another of the canceled games from the start of the season. On July 3, Schumacher (9–5) continued to shine with a 5–2 triumph. He pitched a seven-hitter and lost his shutout in the ninth, giving up only one earned run. The Giants were shut out for the fourth time on the season, in the first game of a holiday doubleheader. Braves right-hander Ben Cantwell achieved the deed, 3–0, over Fitzsimmons, who allowed only one earned run. Hi Bell could not put anything over on the home team in the second encounter and dropped an 8–5 decision.

Ten teams in both leagues continued on with their schedule on July 5. The Giants were not one of them. The following day, the "dream game of baseball" took place.

Bill Terry's Giants stood with a record of 44–27, clutching a first-place lead of 5½ games over the St. Louis Cardinals.

6

"The Game of the Century"

The indomitable spirit of the United States and its people was no better represented in the 1930s than with the World's Fair opening in Chicago on May 27, 1933. With 400 banks failing in January and February alone and more than one-third of all lending institutions in the country shuttered; with unemployment peaking at 24.5 percent during the year; with its fruited plains now barren and cracking from a depressed agricultural environment and calamitous drought, America presented to the world not only a symbolic beacon of hope but a tangible representation of better times ahead with the Chicago World's Fair.

Chicago, the fourth-largest city on earth at the time, and celebrating its 100th anniversary, called its exposition "A Century of Progress." Spread out along more than 400 acres of prime Lake Michigan waterfront, the Fair's most popular outdoor attraction was the Sky Ride, "[an] engineering masterpiece featuring two 625-foot towers, which provided a panoramic view of the fair and neighboring states."[1] An electronic exhibit in the General Electric building amazed visitors by popping kernels of corn without wired connections, using only "microwave" emissions. Just as wowing, at least for adult male fairgoers, was the "Sensational Sally Rand's" *exhibitions*. The sensational—or scandalous, depending on one's point of view—Miss Rand left little to the imagination with her strip-tease routines, which took place, appropriately enough, within the "Streets of Paris" concession.

Against this backdrop and extensively much more, Arch Ward had proposed bringing baseball's brightest stars together for one day to play an exhibition game for the glory of their respective leagues. Ward was the *Chicago Tribune's* sportswriter-promoter of the event who had convinced baseball's hierarchy that such a game would not only be feasible but also profitable. Ward smartly reached out to the baseball public, enlisting a regiment of newspapers around the country to enable fans to vote for the starting players of each squad. From the start, the idea was met with overwhelming public approval. Over half a million ballots were cast, with Philadelphia A's outfielder

Al Simmons receiving the most votes, 346,291—roughly 25,000 more than Babe Ruth. The game would be played Thursday, July 6, 1933, at Comiskey Park rather than Wrigley Field because of Comiskey's larger seating capacity. "The fans' dream for years—a game between the best players in the two major leagues is about to come true," trumpeted a *Sporting News* article that provided supplemental details.

> The umpires selected for the game are Bill McGowan and Bill Dinneen for the American League and Bill Klem and Cy Rigler for the National League. The two national radio stations [CBS and NBC] will broadcast the game, play by play. Tarpaulins from Comiskey Park, Wrigley Field and Soldier's Field will cover the diamond, insuring its perfect playing condition, and the game will be played unless there is a downpour at playing time.[2]

Nearly all of Comiskey Park's available tickets were sold to eager fans. Perhaps no greater example of that public hunger involved the 2,500 bleacher seats that were purposely held back and went on sale July 2. Their pocketbook-friendly 55-cent selling price was equal to a regular season game at Comiskey. All were swooped up in 45 minutes. Ticket hawkers resold box seats to the more well-heeled fans for $10.00, high above their original retail offering of $1.65. The next price-level seats of $1.10 were commanding $5.00 each. The official attendance was 47,595, shy of Comiskey's 52,000-seat capacity. Ticket sales generated a gross of more than $56,000, with the net profits of $45,000 turned over to the Association of Professional Baseball Players of America, an eight-year-old organization benefitting needy, retired players and umpires.

On the day of the All-Star Game, where the "panorama of stars" in Comiskey Park rivaled anything seen on Oscar Night in Hollywood, news came from Tinseltown that America's once and longtime sweethearts, Mary Pickford and Douglas Fairbanks, were separating and putting up for sale their famous "Pickfair" residence.

Not one to be separated any time soon from his love of managing, Connie Mack had been chosen to be John McGraw's inaugural game counterpart. The longtime American League field director had expressed surprise and regret when told of the retirement of the Giants pilot a year earlier. He and the 60-year-old McGraw had spent a century combined in the game and had managed over 9,000 games between them. The 70-year-old Mack would continue to guide the Philadelphia Athletics for 17 more years and become the winningest manager of all time with 3,731 victories. Cornelius McGillicuddy perpetually directed his team's ball games while wearing a jacket and tie with a high, stiff collar. In the more than 7,600 games he managed, the soft-spoken Mack was ejected only once—as a player-manager in 1895.

McGraw, in recent years, had almost exclusively adopted the same sartorial approach as Mack. For the initial All-Star Game, he chose not to sport

6. "The Game of the Century" 139

the league's specially designed uniforms inscribed with the words NATIONAL LEAGUE on the front. Instead, McGraw mimicked Mack's preferred style of dress, opting for a brown suit and white sailor's hat in the dugout.

It was announced beforehand that each team would use three pitchers for the game. Lon Warneke had been the top vote-getter among pitchers in the National League, and Lefty Grove was the most popular choice for the Junior Circuit fans. (Grove received the most votes of any hurler, 327,242.) But neither fan favorite ended up starting the game. McGraw decided to open with Hubbell. A day prior to the game, reporters inquired whether Hubbell's intended start was etched in stone due to his laborious, 18-inning masterpiece a few days earlier. A rumor had circulated that Hubbell—on the advice of Bill Terry—had asked out of the game completely. "I have picked Hubbell to pitch the first three innings," answered McGraw, "and unless his arm bothers him, we'll stick to that plan."[3]

But the plan was altered by McGraw, who started St. Louis Cardinals left-hander Bill Hallahan in Hubbell's stead. The decision was apparently made after McGraw met with his coaches, Max Carey of Brooklyn and Bill McKechnie of Boston, on the morning of the nearly sold-out contest. Bill Terry had subtly lobbied, in the press, that Hubbell should not start the game. With the marathon game against the Cardinals obviously weighing on him, Terry would have preferred that Hubbell not pitch at all. It leaves one to wonder whether the once intransigent McGraw had acceded to Terry's desire for placing the player and the player's team ahead of the exhibition game—something that endures to this day in the now grand-scale exhibition classic. McGraw never admitted that was the case.

Mack himself made a last-minute switch in starters to Lefty Gómez of the New York Yankees. The first pitch was scheduled for 1:30 Central Standard Time, and was eventually delivered under a cloudless, blue sky. Chicago mayor Ed Kelly and baseball commissioner Landis were among the dignitaries on hand. Contingent plans in place to play the game starting at 11:00 a.m. the next morning, in case of rain, were long forgotten by then.

Both teams brought 18 players. The National League carried one fewer pitcher than the American League's five. The NL opted to take an extra infielder over the AL's two surplus infield men. The visitors brought a backup at every infield position but first base (Terry), while the home team carried no substitutes for hometown starter Jimmy Dykes, at third base, and shortstop Joe Cronin. There were five outfielders and two catchers per squad.

Gómez took the mound wearing his home Yankees pinstripes, as all American League players sported their home uniforms. Pepper Martin was the first All-Star batter for posterity. He grounded out to Cronin. The Washington Senator was one of six playing managers in the major leagues that season and one of two in this game. (Lew Fonseca of the White Sox, Marty McManus of the Red Sox and Charlie Grimm of the Cubs were the others. Frankie Frisch would join the ranks shortly.) Cronin was involved in all three orderly outs of the half-inning. He threw out the next batter, Frisch, and recorded a putout on third-place hitter Chuck Klein's liner.

Gómez was tossing to Red Sox catcher Rick Ferrell. At first base was stationed Gómez's teammate Lou Gehrig; the second baseman was Charlie Gehringer of Detroit. The White Sox's own Jimmy Dykes had been selected for third base, in perhaps the first questionable voting result in the game's history. Pinky Higgins of the Athletics was out-hitting Dykes by more than 50 points. It would be more difficult to question the starting outfield of speedy left fielder Ben Chapman, slugging center fielder Al Simmons, and the star of stars, Babe Ruth.

Hallahan, a 19-game winner in 1931, benefitted from his 8–2 record on the season to receive his only All-Star appointment. He threw his first offering to his Cardinals batterymate, Jimmie Wilson. Two other familiar St. Louis players backed him on defense, third baseman Pepper Martin and second sacker Frankie Frisch. At shortstop was Dick Bartell of the Phillies, with Bill Terry rounding out the infield. In the outfield pastures, the Reds' Chick Hafey in left, the Braves' Wally Berger in center, and Phillies masher Chuck Klein were the other starters. In the first inning, after issuing a one-out walk, Hallahan struck out Babe Ruth after falling behind him 3–0, the last pitch a called strike. Lou Gehrig grounded out to end the inning.

The National League threatened in the second inning, following singles by Hafey and Terry to open the frame. But Wally Berger bounced into a twin killing and Bartell struck out to squash the threat. In the American League's turn, Hallahan, living up to his "Wild Bill" cognomen, issued back-to-back walks with one out. After the second walk, Hallahan's third of the game, the entire infield gathered around the mound to try and settle down the lefthander. He retired catcher Ferrell on a fly out, with both runners holding, but then yielded his first hit—to his weak-hitting mound opponent. Gómez's single knocked home Jimmy Dykes from second with the first run of the game. It was all the scoring in the inning for the Junior Circuit as the next hitter, Chapman, grounded into a force play.

Gómez retired the side in order in the third, his last inning of work. Hallahan's third trip to the mound was not nearly as efficient. He opened the inning by surrendering his fourth walk. Then he served up a home run to Babe Ruth—"a wallop into the lower section of the right field grandstand."[4] The AL took a 3–0 lead on the Babe's two-run drive to right. Following Ruth's homer, Hallahan issued another base on balls, to Lou Gehrig. John McGraw made all of his decisions and pitching moves ensconced in the first base visitors' dugout. After Hallahan had walked Joe Cronin in the second inning, he had ordered two pitchers to begin warming up in the bullpen. Following the fifth free pass to Gehrig, McGraw signaled from the dugout to first baseman Terry to take Hallahan out and bring in Cubs pitcher Lon Warneke. Known as the "Pride of the Ozarks," Warneke induced a double play from the first batter he faced, Al Simmons. After a single by Jimmie Dykes, Warneke retired Cronin without any further scoring on the AL's part. McGraw let Warneke hurl three additional innings for the National League.

Taking over mound duties for the American League in the fourth inning was Alvin "General" Crowder. The Washington Senators hurler held the NL scoreless for two more frames, retiring six men in a row.

It was during Warneke's time on the mound that a change in baseballs was introduced. During the first four and one-half innings, the American League's official ball was used. Afterward, the NL baseball was put into play. The umpires also switched base assignments at this point. After five fruitless innings, the National League finally dented the plate in the sixth against Crowder, in his third inning of work. McGraw made his second substitution of the game to open the frame, when he sent in Giants outfielder Lefty O'Doul to bat for catcher Jimmie Wilson. O'Doul grounded out. McGraw let Warneke, who had thrown three full innings, hit, and the pitcher tripled. He came home with the NL's first run on an infield ground out by Martin. McGraw's old, pride-wounded pepper-pot, Frankie Frisch, hit a home run to right field to bring the elite visitors to within one run, 3–2. Klein followed with a single, but Hafey ended the threat with a ground out. In the bottom of the inning, Cubs catcher Gabby Hartnett took Wilson's spot behind the plate.

McGraw's dugout equivalent was virtually inactive during the game. Mack did not use his own A's slugger Jimmie Foxx at all. The major league leader in home runs, Foxx remained on the AL bench while Lou Gehrig played all nine innings for the American Leaguers. Apart from removing Ruth in the top of the ninth inning and realigning the outfield so that Ruth's replacement, Sam West, could play center field, Mack made only one other lineup change. He pinch-hit the Cleveland Indians' Earl Averill for General Crowder in the bottom of the sixth inning. All of Mack's non-pitching starters—except Ruth—played the entire game. The venerable baseball sages, with their sparse substitutions, set the tone for future All-Star Games, where first-stringers regularly played through most of and often the entire game, with winning, of course, as the sole objective.

The Averill substitution by Mack was a good one. The Indians outfielder delivered a run-scoring single, plating Cronin, who had opened the home half of the sixth inning with a hit and moved up a base on a sacrifice by catcher Ferrell. The run doubled the American League's lead and was the last scoring of the game. Following Averill's RBI hit, leadoff hitter Chapman advanced the pinch-hitter to second with a bunt single. Warneke dug in and obtained a foul fly out to right from Charlie Gehringer as Averill proceeded to third. Ruth came up with runners on first and third. Warneke struck out Ruth to choke off any further scoring.

Lefty Grove replaced Crowder in the top of the seventh inning. Grove allowed a single to the first batter he faced—Terry. The next hitter, Berger, was not as successful, forcing Terry at second base. Trailing 4–2, with one out and a man on first base, McGraw made another move to try and kick-start the offense. He pinch-hit Pie Traynor for the seventh man in the order, shortstop Bartell. Traynor doubled, putting men on second and third with one out. One can imagine McGraw's old baseball juices flowing at this point, seeking to get the Nationals back in the game and one-upping his former World Series adversary across the way. But the eighth-place hitter, Gabby Hartnett, struck out. McGraw then called on Chicago Cubs infielder Woody English to pinch-hit for Warneke. The strategic move did not pay off. English flied out to end the inning, suppressing whatever internal excitement the old man still had flowing through him. English took over at shortstop for starter Bartell.

At this point as well, McGraw brought in Hubbell, who pitched the final two innings for the elder loop without allowing a run. Hubbell did have some trouble in the seventh, however. He left two runners on base, following a walk to Lou Gehrig and a single by Jimmy Dykes.

In the top of the eighth, Grove and his team were bailed out by a sparkling defensive play in deep right field by Babe Ruth. Though past his prime, the great all-around player raced back to make a leaping one-handed stab of a potential home run drive hit by Chick Hafey. Ruth, who had earlier misplayed Warneke's drive into a triple, saved the American League's bacon. The splendidly recorded out, with a runner on base, was the last out of the inning.

In the lower half of the eighth, McGraw gave Paul Waner a defensive taste of the game, putting him in right field for Chuck Klein. Waner was inactive as the AL went down in order to Hubbell.

Terry, hitting fifth in the lineup, grounded out to open the ninth against Grove. Berger lined out to Chapman, now playing in right. The game's losing manager then employed his fourth and final emergency hitter. Batting for Hubbell, Tony Cuccinello struck out to end the game.

After the contest, McGraw made his way to the victors' locker room to extend his congratulations to the winning manager. The two men who had bridged the developing 19th century game to the established modern pastime chatted for about a minute.

"It was a splendid game, wasn't it?" McGraw asked rhetorically of the gathered press. "Hallahan is either good or bad—and today he was bad." McGraw continued a completely softened stance on what was once his disagreeable opinion of the game's greatest home run hitter. "Babe Ruth checked one of our [scoring] spots when he went to the wall to grab Hafey's long fly. I thought sure it was a home run. He was marvelous. That old boy certainly came through when they needed him."[5]

Players from both sides entreated autographs on souvenir baseballs from both Mack and McGraw in the clubhouses. McGraw made it clear he had no desire to return to the game.

"I'm through with it," he said. "I have quit."[6]

7

The Championship Season—Second Half

"We've been getting fine pitching and timely hitting,"[1] said Bill Terry a few weeks before the All-Star Game interruption. As part of an overall team assessment, the manager also pointed to individual players who had played a part in the team's improvement.

> You can put your finger on two vital spots in our infield and find the reason for most of our improvement over last year. The first is Johnny Vergez, a great third baseman again. The other is Hughie Critz. They've both come back after tough seasons. Joe Moore in left field is playing marvelous ball. Gus Mancuso has handled the catching in marvelous style. He has been responsible for a lot of our good pitching. The defense, but for a couple of bad days, has been great. Add to those things the finest morale of any club in baseball and you've got the reasons the Giants are in first place.[2]

The Giants' fine pitching continued in the games following the All-Star Game, but the offense failed to provide support. Another ten teams played on the day after the inaugural star-studded game, the Giants included. After the July 4 doubleheader defeat in Boston, Terry's club picked up the season on July 7. Conveniently for Terry, Hubbell, O'Doul and Schumacher, the Giants' All-Star representatives, the team began a four-game set with the Cubs in Chicago.

In the first encounter, Roy Parmelee started well, but a shaky fourth inning prompted Terry to remove him in favor of Adolfo Luque. The battle-tested reliever escaped the inning holding a 5–2 lead, but could not close out the game. The Cubs reached him for three tying runs in the eighth inning. In the tenth, Travis Jackson committed an error allowing the Cubs to score a win, 6–5. Watty Clark was the loser, in relief of Luque.

Hal Schumacher was defeated the next day, 2–1, by Guy Bush. The same day, the Giants released George Uhle. Terry would later say the $7,500 purchase of the worn-out pitcher was his worst mistake of the season.

Through both games of a July 9 doubleheader, the Giants scored only one run. Predictably they dropped both contests. Hubbell accepted a 4–0 loss to Lon Warneke in the opener, and the Cubs' Bud Tinning outpitched Freddie Fitzsimmons, 2–1, in the nightcap.

Now mired in their longest losing spell of the campaign, the Giants rolled into St. Louis for another quartet of games against the second-place Cardinals. An off-day did not help right the team, as Dizzy Dean sustained his recent masterful hurling against the Giants, winning 2–1 on July 11. Both St. Louis runs off Giants starter Parmelee were unearned. The seventh-inning runs were the first scored by Gabby Street's club in the last 36 innings against Giants pitching. Terry's squad committed five errors, one by Parmelee himself. Travis Jackson, who had been filling in for the spiked Blondy Ryan, had a particularly tough day with two miscues. It was the last game Jackson would play for three weeks, as his knees loudly rebelled against his recent everyday playing again and his manager coincidingly received an encouraging telegram from a rehabbing Ryan, reading *"They cannot beat us. En Route.—Signed J.C. Ryan."*[3]

With the Cardinals now within 2½ games of his ballclub, and the team in the throes of its longest losing streak of the season, seven games, Schumacher stepped up the next afternoon and delivered his sixth shutout, snapping the bad string. Suffering the 3–0 defeat was Bill Hallahan. Terry contributed a two-run single. Bernie James filled in at shortstop more than adequately. "Ryan's loss was our hardest blow," said Terry, prior to Schumacher breaking the slide. "I was forced to send in Jackson, who had a bad knee, to short."[4]

While the Giants were anticipating Ryan's imminent return, someone the Cardinals could not have been looking forward to seeing—Carl Hubbell— toed the rubber the following day, July 13. Johnny Vergez again came through with a clutch hit—a ninth-inning solo home run, to put Hubbell (12–6) and the Giants over the top, 3–2. Tex Carleton delivered the home run pitch. Ryan, fitted with a fiber shin splint, was back in the field and steadily registered four putouts and an equal number of assists. In all, Ryan missed nine games following his injury on July 2.

Gabby Street once again burdened Jay Hanna Dean and brought him back on two days' rest to face the Giants in the series finale on July 14. Dean not only did not have it, he suffered his worst outing of the season. The Giants routed the Cardinals' emerging ace, who did not make it out of the fifth inning, having yielded nine runs, eight earned. In the 12–7 Giants win, Terry collected a trio of hits, runs and RBI. Watty Clark picked up the win in relief of an ineffective Fitzsimmons. The three consecutive defeats knocked the starch out of the Cardinals, as the club slipped into fourth place, 5½ games off the pace. (This was the start of a Cardinals team slide that eventually cost Gabby Street his job. He was fired and replaced by Frankie Frisch on July 23. The 46–45 Cardinals were in fifth place, eight games out of the running, at the time.)

The series in St. Louis has to be considered as a pivotal point in the season for the Giants. After taking their lumps against the Cubs and losing the first game to the Cardinals, Terry rallied his team to not only halt their losing ways but carry through to win the series at Sportsman's Park.

Feeling good about their St. Louis stand, the Giants journeyed to Cincinnati, where the club took two out of three from the last-place Reds. The opening contest of an anticipated four-game series was called off due to rain on July 15. In a scheduled July 16 doubleheader, the Giants again had difficulties scoring throughout the day. Plating only one run over two games, the team fortunately won one of the contests. Yielding eight hits and no bases on balls, and pitching on two days' rest, Carl Hubbell shut out the Reds, 1–0, in the second game. Terry, hitting in his 13th straight game, scored the decisive run on a Johnny Vergez single. Hubbell pitched out of a bases-loaded, no-out jam in the ninth inning to record his 13th victory. In the first game, the Reds' Red Lucas was magnificent, blanking the Giants, 1–0, in 15 innings. Nearly as magnificent was Roy Parmelee, who suffered the heartbreaking defeat, allowing a run-scoring single by Rollie Hemsley with one out in the final inning.

The Giants and/or Reds opted not to make up the July 15 rainout on the Monday off-day. On Tuesday, July 18, the Giants concluded their curtailed Ohio engagement with an easy 14–1 whipping of the home team. Schumacher (11–6) cruised to the complete game win. Vergez clubbed his tenth homer, a grand slam, and knocked home five runs. The Giants headed to Pittsburgh with a 3½-game advantage over the Cubs and four over the Pirates.

In the Steel City, the league leaders crammed six games into a four-day encampment, making up the two rainouts suffered during the New Yorkers' first trip into Pittsburgh in May. (This may be why the Giants preferred to keep the day off on Monday.) The Giants split the half-dozen games with the Bucs. In the twin bill opener, July 19, the Pirates' Larry French bested Fitzsimmons, 4–1. In the afterpiece, Hubbell hurled 8⅓ innings for a 7–3 win. The effort, on two days' rest again, came in relief of starter Watty Clark, whom Terry replaced in the first inning after nearly surrendering the four-run lead the Giants had established in their first trip to bat. Mel Ott scored three runs; Vergez had three hits and scored two runs. A day later, Adolfo Luque absorbed his second loss when he was touched for two runs in the bottom of the eighth inning, hanging the Giants with a 6–5 loss. Parmelee pitched the first five innings. Half of the Pirates' runs were unearned.

7. The Championship Season—Second Half   147

New York avoided a third setback in the series, scoring twice in the top of the ninth inning to register a 6–5 win on July 21. Hi Bell provided fine middle-inning relief. Clark picked up his second relief win in six days, when Mel Ott delivered the key bases-loaded single to plate a pair of runs. Jo-Jo Moore slashed five hits (all on the first pitch), and Terry extended his hitting streak to 18 games. The next day, Terry called on both Hubbell and Parmelee on short rest for the series-closing twin engagement. Hubbell, with another 1–0 dazzler, outshined Larry French, who like his counterpart was pitching with only two days between assignments. For Hubbell, it was his third 1–0 whitewash of the month, tying Dick Rudolph's August 1916 record for most 1–0 shutout victories in one month. (A third pitcher, Félix Hernández, equaled the rare achievement in August 2012.) Terry had his hitting streak snapped at 18 games in the grand Hubbell opener.

Having thrown five innings in a no-decision just two days earlier and less than a week removed from his 14⅓-inning laborious effort, Parmelee, not surprisingly, experienced a short outing in the nightcap. The Giants went down to defeat, 7–2.

Following the loss, the Giants returned to New York that evening, holding a slim 2½-game lead over the Cubs. A Sunday Ebbets Field confrontation with the floundering 37–49 Brooklyn Dodgers awaited them the next day, July 23. Erupting for seven runs in their last at-bat, the Giants spoiled a Flatbush celebration by earning an 8–5 victory. Vergez's three-run double was the big blow. Luque (4–2) was the victor with two innings of late relief. In one of two relief appearances on the season, Schumacher pitched a scoreless bottom of the ninth.

Following their road journeys, the Giants enjoyed two days off. The team played its first home game in more than three weeks on July 26. The Dodgers were their foes—or foils—as the Brooklynites were swept a pair of games by their inter-city rivals. The second game was as a replay of the June 17 encounter that had ended unresolved, 3–3. The Giants hit three home runs in the opener: Kiddo Davis, his fourth, Vergez, number 11, and Melvin Ott, his tenth. Ott's blast came in the bottom of the ninth, with his manager on board, and gave the Giants a 5–3 triumph. Hi Bell evened his record at 4–4, pitching a scoreless ninth in relief of starter Schumacher. In the second game, Vergez was knocked unconscious for several minutes, following a beaning, and had to be removed from the game. Bernie James replaced him and enjoyed a closer view of Parmelee turning back Brooklyn, 4–3. Picking up his first win in over three weeks (despite pitching well), Parmelee (8–5) permitted six hits and struck out ten.

The next day, after four days off, which must have seemed like a vacation to him in light of his pitching workload over the past few weeks, Hubbell (16–6) authored his fourth shutout of the month—and eighth of the season—defeating Brooklyn, 2–0. The blanking extended to 38⅓ innings a scoreless streak by Hubbell, who lowered his league-best ERA to 1.53. Spelling Ott in right field, Lefty O'Doul collected three hits, including two doubles, and an RBI. The winning pitcher knocked in the other run.

As Brooklyn left the Polo Grounds, licking their wounds, the Giants waited for the second-division Boston Braves to arrive from Philadelphia. In the teams' initial encounter, on July 29, Bill Terry's troupe moved a season-high 21 games over .500 (57–36) with an exciting triumph. The manager provided the biggest thrill. "Bill Terry put a dramatic finish on a close game today," amplified one widely circulated report, "by walloping a home run with two outs in the ninth inning to give the Giants a 6 to 5 triumph over the Boston Braves."[5] It was the Giants' fifth straight win and third in their last at-bat. In most official records, Freddie Fitzsimmons has been given an undeserved victory in the game, though he was removed in the seventh inning. The actual pitcher of record, Hi Bell, was denied the rightful victory.

In the next two games, Schumacher, 5–3, and Hubbell, 3–1, were defeated by the plucky Braves, as the Giants lost their first series since being swept by the Cubs immediately after the All-Star Game. In Schumacher's start on July 30, Hubbell was questionably used by Terry again for two (scoreless) innings with his team down by the two-run, final margin of defeat. The Giants were then presented with their fourth scheduled off-day in eight days on Monday, July 31.

On August 1, Hubbell pitched six innings and yielded two runs. He did not walk anyone and allowed five hits. Hubbell stretched his scoreless innings streak to 45⅓, until he gave up his first run to the Braves in the sixth frame. The mark established a then-National League record. Terry removed his top pitcher for a pinch-hitter with the score 2–1. Reliever Luque gave up the visitors' third run. In obtaining the win, Braves pitcher Walter "Huck" Betts pitched one of his best games of the season, although he walked five men.

Over the same weekend, the Giants' front office filled the available roster spot, following the release of Uhle, by readdressing what could be categorized as an ethnic sticking point for the club. "The Giants, who for years have been trying to acquire a Jewish ball player of major league caliber," attested one wire report, "believe now they have their man in Harry Danning, rangy young catcher. Danning, who has trained with the club for the last three springs, has been recalled from Buffalo to assist Gus Mancuso with the catching chores and to act as a pinch-hitter."[6] Danning would enter only three games over

7. The Championship Season—Second Half

the remainder of the season, as the third-string backstop behind Mancuso and Paul Richards. He was given George Uhle's former number 28.

The top-seated Giants (57-37) began August with a 3½-game advantage over second-place Pittsburgh. The Cardinals and Cubs were 6½ games behind. Boston was fifth at 10½ games back. With little pennant aspirations, the Philadelphia Phillies slogged 16½ games in back of the Giants, while Brooklyn (17½) and Cincinnati (19) brought up the rear of the standings.

The Giants were back on the road on August 2, engaging the Philadelphia Phillies in a midweek doubleheader, the result of the rainout from April 19. The men from Gotham appeared to be caught off guard and were soundly beaten, 13-6, in the first game. Fitzsimmons was knocked out in the fourth inning, and two little-used pitchers, Jack Salveson and Glenn Spencer, saw mop-up action in the ambush. Mel Ott homered twice and drove in five runs in the losing cause. But in the nightcap, the Giants punitively responded with an 18-1 whipping of Philadelphia, pounding out two dozen hits and scoring in every inning but the sixth and eighth. Ott and Lefty O'Doul hit for the circuit. Jo-Jo Moore reaped his second five-hit game in two weeks. Parmelee pitched the distance in the laugher.

"Threatening weather" prevented the next day's game (it was made up on August 5). One day hence, August 4, the Giants continued to flex their hitting muscles at the cozy Baker Bowl, matching their biggest runs output with a repeat 18-1 victory. Moore, Ott and O'Doul raked four hits apiece. Ott collected his 1,000th career hit. At 24 years, five months and two days old, Ott became the second-youngest man in baseball history to reach the four-digit hit level (Ty Cobb, 24/4/25). Watty Clark was the starter and winner. Hubbell, his reliever, smacked a three-run double in a nine-run Giants eighth inning, which broke open the game.

In the remade doubleheader on August 5, the Giants plated 11 more runs in the opener, for a grand total of 47 in three games. The 11-3 decision was reeled in by Schumacher, now 12-7. Ott cracked a grand slam and Lefty O'Doul put two blasts over the wall. That gave Ott four home runs in as many games, as well as a 9-for-17 batting line, ten runs scored and 14 RBI.

Fitzsimmons had been 4-0 against Philadelphia before his defeat in the series' opener. In the second-game finale, Terry decided to start Fitzsimmons on two days' rest. He may have been forced into it by wastefully using Hubbell in relief the prior day, rather than pitching Hubbell in what would have been his regular turn in this contest. The Phillies once more got the better of Fitzsimmons, sinking him and the Giants, 7-3. Four Giants errors, two by the normally excellent fielding pitcher, contributed to five unearned runs. Ott went 2-for-4, with a run scored.

Terry may have wanted to hold Hubbell back for Brooklyn, the Giants' next opponent. Hubbell had pitched some fine games against the Dodgers in 1933, but twice had been hit hard by them. If that was the case, then both decisions—to use Fitzsimmons on short rest and hold back Hubbell—backfired on Mr. Terry. The Opening Day tie game was replayed as part of a Sunday diamond duet on August 6. In the first game, the Dodgers knocked around the National League's best pitcher, defeating him, 6–3, though only half of the runs were earned. Utility infielder Bernie James, playing in place of a sore-legged Hughie Critz, committed two errors, and Terry had one miscue. Terry drove in two runs in the second clash, as the Giants squeaked past the home team, 3–2. Adolfo Luque netted his fifth win with 3⅔ innings of air-tight relief of starter Roy Parmelee. More than 20,000 fans were hand for the Ebbets Field event.

After the usual off-day on Monday, the series resumed on August 8 and the Giants resumed an apparent weaker-hitting trend of the past few games. The team was held scoreless for 11 innings in a masterful effort by Dodgers hurler Ray Benge. Hal Schumacher, the 1–0 loser, had the misfortune of matching up with Benge on his best day of the season. It was Schumacher's second 1–0 defeat of the campaign.

The Giants headed back to Manhattan, their record 61–42, maintaining a three-game lead over the Pittsburgh Pirates and four-game advantage over the third-place Chicago Cubs. The Boston Braves and St. Louis Cardinals were tied for the fourth spot, 7½ games behind the Polo Grounders. The Giants would take advantage of a 17-game homestand to gain firmer footing in the team's claim for supremacy in the National League.

On Thursday, August 10, for the second time on the season, the Philadelphia Phillies opened an extended homestand against the Giants at the Polo Grounds. Roy Parmelee became a ten-game winner, hurling a 4–0 shutout and a league-best 18th shutout for the Giants' pitching staff. Parmelee permitted only two hits, one in the eighth inning and the other in the ninth. He struck out six and walked two. Kiddo Davis cranked a two-run home run.

After a scheduled off-day on Friday, the three-game series concluded over the weekend. On Saturday, Freddie Fitzsimmons, the only starter who had not spun a shutout, kept the Phillies off the board for nine innings and pocketed his 12th triumph against nine defeats. Hughie Critz contributed an RBI single and Lefty O'Doul smacked a solo home run in the 2–0 win.

On August 13, a disappointing Sunday crowd of 15,000 came out to see the league's best pitcher succumb to a pitcher named Phil Collins. A spot starter, Collins (5–11) outclassed Carl Hubbell, 2–1. Left-handed-hitting first baseman Don Hurst pulled two Hubbell offerings into the right field grandstand for solo home runs. Hubbell pitched eight innings before exiting for a pinch-hitter.

An 11th meeting between the Giants and Phillies at the Baker Bowl was rained out on August 14. Smack dab in the middle of the Giants' homestand, the date was a scheduling quirk in which teams routinely made one-game stopovers in cities of opposing regional teams. Because of future scheduling conflicts, the game would be lost to both clubs that season.

An off-day on August 15 opened the way for Terry to attend a planned get-together with a segment of hometown wordsmiths with whom he had encountered some disharmony. One newspaper announced the occasion in this manner: "Following printed reports of clashes between Bill Terry, manager of the New York Giants, and baseball writers, Terry is going to play good fellow with the scribes today. He will be host to the writers at a luncheon at a downtown restaurant and, over an attractive menu, the reported rift between the young manager and the reporters may be mended."[7]

Although the Giants, 63–43 at the time, held a 3½-game first-place lead, Terry had not escaped criticism in the press. The fault-finding stemmed mostly (as with all managers) from in-game decisions. To be fair, the second-year manager had also received—deservedly—a great deal of praise, both locally and nationally, for his work from the dugout. There was little else to bring disapproving sentiment on Terry's performance, as only two games ago he had been hitting over .350.

From one of those press box nonpartisans came the following peek into the sit-down, in which Terry sounded confident about his team and how it was approaching the final six and a half weeks of the season:

> Memphis Bill was wearing a linen suit and attacking a light snack of chicken livers on toast... "What's there to worry about?" he asked. "We're still up there.... But I don't let my players talk pennant. It isn't a good thing. We're just thinking about trying to win the day's game. That's the attitude of the players, I think. Today's the day to worry about. No good in worrying about tomorrow until it's today, if you know what I mean."[8]

Terry also revealed that the Giants had purchased Phil Weintraub, a left-handed-swinging outfielder, from the Birmingham Barons, with the purpose of his joining the big club during the September roster expansion. Weintraub's Jewish ethnicity was flagged in the press, in what had seemingly become a magnetizing topic.

A series with the Cincinnati Reds commenced on a good note for the home club, thanks to another exceptional outing by Schumacher. The pitcher five-hit the cellar dwellers, 5–0, August 16. It was his seventh and final shutout of the season. He collected three hits, drove in a run and scored one, in the overall enjoyable experience. Roy Parmelee pushed the Giants a season-high

22 games over .500 (65–43), the next day, with a 7–2 complete game win. Parmelee (11–5) pitched around a dozen surrendered hits in obtaining his fifth straight win. (In St. Louis, also on August 17, Lou Gehrig established a new major league record for playing in consecutive games. Breaking Everett Scott's record of 1,037, Gehrig finished the season with 1,350.)

One day later, Fitzsimmons showed he was not to be outdone, throwing the Giants' third straight complete game victory over the Reds, 4–1. Vergez hit a solo home run; Terry and Ott drove in the other runs. Fitzsimmons lost his shutout with two outs in the ninth when mound opponent Red Lucas singled in a run. The Reds gladly left town and were replaced on the Polo Grounds docket by the Chicago Cubs.

Because of the recent off-days and rainouts, Giants starters had been afforded a welcome breather between their outings. Carl Hubbell, for example, had not pitched in six days, since August 13, and only twice since August 6. On August 19, he turned back the Cubs, 8–4. Hubbell was removed in the eighth inning, after the Cubs mounted a comeback. Hi Bell recorded the final six outs. Mel Ott hit two home runs (16 and 17) and Lefty O'Doul one (12, seven with the Giants), as they drove in three runs apiece. In the fifth inning, Jo-Jo Moore was hit on the right arm by a pitched ball. He reached first base, but crumpled in pain at the bag from the after-effects of the blow. Cubs manager Charlie Grimm agreed to a courtesy runner in order to allow Moore to stay in the game. But Moore could not take the field at the end of the half-inning and was removed. He was not seriously hurt.

The next day, with a Sunday afternoon gathering of 30,000 at the Polo Grounds, including Hal Schumacher's father Andrew, his 22-year-old offspring subdued the Cubs on seven hits, 6–1. Four Cubs' errors eased the way for multiple Giants' scores, including two driven home by Schumacher. With their fifth straight win and seventh on the homestand, combined with an inopportune Pirates losing spell, the Giants had opened a 7½ game lead simultaneously over three clubs, Pittsburgh, Boston and St. Louis. The Cubs had slipped eight games back.

An uncommon Monday wrap-around game with the Cubs was postponed due to rain. A make-up doubleheader the next day, August 22, was also washed out. With Ethel Waters' *Stormy Weather* the number one song in the country for much of the summer, the Giants, with their numerous postponements, could have easily adopted the romantic ballad as their season-long theme song. The Cubs left New York in order to meet an engagement in Philadelphia. Since it was the Cubs' final trip into New York, the Giants would be forced to make up the two missed games on a subsequent trip to the Windy City. (Terry's club played 13 games at Wrigley Field in 1933 in lieu of the normal 11.)

7. The Championship Season—Second Half

No one in the press corps, or even on the Giants team, could have been faulted in the interim for entertaining presumptive World Series thoughts. Based on a quote Terry made the day of the Cubs' first rainout, the manager clearly had on eye on the brass ring. "So far we have not felt the strain," said the skipper. "The trick now is to stay loose, to be on our toes, to hustle but not tighten up. If we could just forget we are leading the league that would be great. But it is difficult, especially when you are approaching the end of the race and you are keyed up with expectations of winning."[9]

The evening the Cubs left town, the meteorological cause of the recent postponements arrived in full force. The Chesapeake-Potomac Hurricane, now a tropical storm but still maintaining hurricane-force wind gusts, passed through New York and its vicinity. The hurricane left tens of millions of dollars in damage and dozens dead in its wake. The Giants' game with the Pittsburgh Pirates on August 23 was unplayable. A rescheduled doubleheader the next day was called due to wet grounds. Ebbets Field must have had better drainage or a more resilient tarpaulin as the Dodgers and Reds played two games that August 24 afternoon.

The skies over New York finally cleared on the morning of August 25. The Giants' four-day inactivity cost them a game and a half in the standings, with the Boston Braves taking sole possession of second place, staring at a half-dozen-game shortfall. The Pirates' series was rescheduled over two days, with back-to-back doubleheaders on August 25 and 26. The four days of forced idleness did not seem to bother the Giants' strongest hitters. In the first game, Mel Ott slugged a game-tying three-run home run in the fifth inning and boss Terry slammed his second walk-off four-bagger of the campaign in the 11th, propelling the Giants to a thrilling 8–5 win. Fitzsimmons went the first ten-plus frames; Adolfo Luque pitched a 1-2-3 11th for the win, his sixth. In the afterpiece, Parmelee (12–5) maintained his top-notch pitching, tossing his fifth complete-game win in six starts (5–0 record). Ott homered again and so did Vergez, his 14th round-tripper. The Giants pleased an exceptional Friday crowd of 35,000 considerably. (Charles Stoneham's team would become the envy of National League owners at the box office as well, attracting more paying customers than any team, 604,471.)

In the initial game of August 26, the top-of-the-heap New Yorkers stretched their win streak to a season-high eight games, and 11 out of 13, with a 2–1 win. Carl Hubbell was most responsible for the triumph. Hurling his 17th complete game on the season, Hubbell won his 18th game against nine losses, and lowered his ERA to 1.71. The Giants fizzled in the second game, dropping a 7–2 decision. Watty Clark started and was pulled in the sixth inning, where the Pirates took a 4–1 lead as Luque permitted a three-run home run to pinch-hitter Hal Finney. A bigger turnout than the previous day was on hand, as it seemed Giants rooters were beginning to get infected with pennant fever. "One of the season's biggest crowd of leather-lunged citizens came out to whoop it up for the Giants," recounted one of the game's impartial observers, "some 50,000 spectators crowding hotly into all seats except those at the tip of the horseshoe."[10]

The Horseshoe was similarly packed for a third straight twin bill the following day. The new Polo Grounds invaders were the St. Louis Cardinals, presently ten games behind the league leaders. Because of the rainout from May 10, the teams planned to play five games over four days. The first day of the series, Sunday, August 27, was the natural fit for the make-up game and doubleheader. Dizzy Dean tamed Terry's crew for the fourth time on the season, 7–1. Schumacher was on the short end of the decision.

The second game, opened by Hi Bell, was called a 5–5 tie after eight innings, because of darkness. Fitzsimmons, in relief of Bell, cranked a game-tying home run in the final inning. A heavily overcast day conspired against the teams, as the capacity crowd was left dissatisfied. The nightcap produced a rhubarb involving Terry and two other Giants, precipitated by a close play at first base that went against the home favorites. Terry became so enraged over a safe call by first base umpire Ted McGrew, involving Frankie Frisch, that he twice chest-bumped McGrew. Mel Ott charged in from right field and, after a choice word or two, received the "heave ho" from the arbiter. Coach Tommy Clarke was also ejected. Terry, the most blatant offender, at least under more modern baseball sensibilities, received no on-field sanction. A replay of the undecided game was scheduled as a doubleheader two days later.

In game three of the series on August 28, Terry produced his most questionable pitching decision of the season, one that cost the Giants the ball game. The Giants rallied with three runs in the bottom of the eighth inning to take a 6–5 lead. Fighting through his poorest outing in more than two months, Parmelee tried to ride the rally home to victory. But when the first batter of the ninth singled, Terry prudently turned to the bullpen. Not so prudently, he brought in Schumacher, who had pitched seven innings *yesterday*. Schumacher promptly surrendered a two-run home run to the first batter he faced, Bob O'Farrell. He allowed a hit and walk to the next two batters, plus a run-scoring wild pitch, before being pulled. Watty Clark retired the Cardinals, but not before allowing four more runs to cross the plate (one charged to Schumacher). A one-day-rested Dizzy Dean recorded the last three outs for the Cardinals, though not without difficulty. He gave up two runs on three hits. The final was 12–8.

7. The Championship Season—Second Half

With the two wins, the fourth-place Cardinals had trimmed their deficit to eight games, while the second-seated Boston Braves stayed within six lengths of the front-runners. As had occurred all season long when the Giants seemed to be wavering, Hubbell provided the steadying elixir. The premier portsider blanked the Cardinals, 3–0, in the first of two games on August 29. In recording his 19th victory and ninth shutout, Hubbell struck out 12, including every man in the lineup at least once. The Giants manufactured their runs, on five hits and two walks, against seven-inning starter and loser Bill Hallahan. (In between games, Lefty O'Doul was paid tribute by a group of boys from the Brooklyn YMCA. O'Doul had become a fan club idol of the group the prior year and, following through on a pledge he had made, had personally outfitted their youth baseball team with uniforms and equipment this summer.) In the make-up game, former Giant Bill Walker turned in his best game of the season, besting Fitzsimmons, 2–0. Walker tossed a five-hitter and homered off Fitzsimmons for the Cardinals' first run. A Ladies Day crowd of 25,000 watched the mixed-result proceedings. It was the Giants' fourth doubleheader in five days. They had swept one, split two and lost a game, with one tie in the other (4–3–1).

In the Wednesday, August 30 finale, both Hal Schumacher and Dizzy Dean made their second starts and *third* appearances in the four-day series. Schumacher, walking half a dozen batters and permitting nine hits, gritted through to a 5–4 win. Equally gritty, Dean allowed six free passes and ten hits, the last of which—a single by Lefty O'Doul in the bottom of the ninth inning—delivered the winning run. The Giants' winning rally came after a Jo-Jo Moore double, a bunt single by Critz, and an intentional pass to Terry. Dean bore down and struck out Ott. But mid-season acquisition O'Doul followed with a hard bouncer that third baseman Pepper Martin could not make a play on. O'Doul had hammered a two-run home run earlier, as had Terry, accounting for all of the Giants' scoring until their final at-bat.

The Giants completed an 18-game homestand with a fine record of 12–5–1. The club used its successes to double its lead in the league from three games, when the homestand began with Parmelee's shutout over the Philadelphia Phillies on August 10.

The team had little time to prepare for its last road swing of the season, beginning the following day in Boston with another six-game square-off rescheduled over four days. The pitching-taxing series was the last chance to make up two games rained out in April.

It was a crucial series for the second-place Braves, who had not been in pennant contention this late in the season in many a moon. Recognizing its importance, the National League assigned a fourth umpire to the series.

(Three arbiters per game was the standard now.) Prior to the game, Terry, who had avoided talking about the pennant all season, allowed himself some practical musings. "If we split the six game series here," he said, "I'll be plenty satisfied. If we divide we'll still be six games ahead of them—and the season that much nearer to the end."[11] Terry had probably crunched the numbers: the 73–47 Giants entered the Braves series with 34 games left to play, while the 69–55 Bostonians had ticked off all but 30 games from their calendar card.

Braves fans came out in droves for the series, including 35,000 for the Thursday afternoon opener, which pitted the team's top winner, Ben Cantwell, against Roy Parmelee. The Braves broke open a tight game with five eighth-inning runs—errors by Johnny Vergez and Parmelee paved the way for four unearned tallies. The Giants plated two runs in the ninth but fell short, losing 7–3.

While only one team claimed victory, both suffered frontline casualties that day. The Braves lost the services of Randy Moore after he was hit on the hand by a Parmelee pitch. One of the Braves' top offensive performers, the right fielder threw out Hughie Critz trying to score in the first inning. Moore was out of action for a two-week span. Later in the day, Vergez underwent an emergency appendectomy and missed the rest of the campaign. The loss of Vergez, who was having a standout season with the bat, was a damaging one for the Giants. His 16 home runs trailed only Mel Ott's 20. The third baseman finished with the second-best slugging percentage—.448—on the team, behind only Ott's .467 year-end total—and ahead of Terry's .423.

The next day, September 1, the largest crowd of the New England baseball season turned out for a doubleheader, with some 48,000 people in attendance. In the opener, Carl Hubbell left the multitude sitting on their hands. On two days' rest, Hubbell stonewalled Boston, 2–0, in ten innings. "[Hubbell's] famous screwball baffled the Braves," wrote *AP* reporter Bill King, "as he chalked up his 20th victory of the season and 10th shutout."[12] The league's first 20-game winner allowed only four hits, walked one and struck out six. He also knocked in the game's first run with a single. The whitewash by Hubbell set a new record for shutouts in a single season by a left-hander, topping Babe Ruth's nine in 1916. (Sandy Koufax established a new mark with 11 in 1963.)

Hubbell had to overcome a lack of timely hitting by his teammates. The Giants loaded the bases in four innings without scoring. Lefty O'Doul grounded out twice and hit into a double play, three times ending serious threats, and Travis Jackson flied out with every base occupied on the other occasion. Seven hits allowed and nine walks—including five to Mel Ott—kept Hubbell's opponent, Fred Frankhouse, in trouble throughout.

7. The Championship Season—Second Half

It took the Braves 17 innings before they gave the capacity-exceeding crowd something significant to cheer. Bill McKechnie's club dented the plate, for the first time on the afternoon, in the bottom of the eighth inning of the second game. Breaking through on starter Freddie Fitzsimmons, the Braves scored three times to tie the contest 3–3. But the Giants responded with a pair of runs in the ninth. Fitzsimmons drove in the go-ahead run with a double. Terry did not allow Fitzsimmons to come out for the last inning, instead sending in Adolfo Luque, who retired the side in order to seal the win. Travis Jackson, who had not played a game in the field since July 11, filled in at third base in both games and went 0-for-8.

On September 2, Schumacher made his third start and fourth appearance in seven days. He gave Terry six effective innings, allowing two runs. Kiddo Davis homered against left-hander Tom Zachary and Ott drove in a pair of runs. The Giants came out on top, 5–3, with Hi Bell hurling the last three innings.

When the six-game clash opened, a record-breaking crowd was expected for the series-concluding Sunday, September 3 doubleheader. The double defeats of September 1 had pared down attendance to around 20,000 for Saturday's single game. The 5–3 Braves loss on that day more than likely prevented the new attendance mark from materializing. Yet on September 3, more than 40,000 patrons put up their hard-earned money in a unified show that they still held out hope for their hometown boys. That hope steadily evaporated, however, throughout what turned into an extended day.

Bill Shores, who had joined the team a few days earlier from the American Association as part of the September roster expansion, opened for the Giants against Boston's Huck Betts. Shores tossed the first six innings and departed with a 3–2 lead. Luque relieved and promptly gave up the tying run. But it was all Luque surrendered, as he summoned forth an effort reminiscent of halcyon days. The game remained tied into the 14th inning, when Luque himself knocked in the go-ahead run with a single to center field. The aged hurler then retired the Braves, in his eighth inning of work, to give the Giants a 4–3, extra-inning victory. Betts went all the way for the Braves in the toilsome loss.

Two hours later, Luque was back on the mound in the day's second contest, started by Roy Parmelee, who was through after six innings. Luque was called in to secure the last out of the eighth inning, extinguishing an uprising by the Braves; the home team had tied the contest at 4–4 against Parmelee's reliever, Glenn Spencer. Luque opened the ninth, but the Sunday Boston curfew law stopped the second game at precisely 6:30 p.m. after two were out. The halted game was declared a tie. Luque pitched nine innings on the day with one run allowed and delivered the game-winning hit in the opener.

Though the series proved disastrous for the Braves' pennant hopes, it was a box office bonanza. The four-day engagement attracted more than 140,000 fans—more than a quarter of owner Emil Fuch's team's 517,803 attendance figure for the year. The rich gate surely moved the Braves' financial ledgers into the black for the year, as they and the Giants were the only NL clubs to post a profit in 1933, according to David George Surdam's researched figures. Incidentally, the Braves carried the second highest team payroll, at $281,928, in the National League, behind the Chicago Cubs' most liberal $343,339. The Giants were third with $271,450 worth of salary commitments.

Pitchers Earl Whitehill, General Crowder and Walter "Lefty" Stewart of the Washington Senators were present for the final games of the series. In town in advance of their first-place Senators team, which was scheduled to begin a series with the Boston Red Sox the next day, the hurlers were scouting the Giants as likely World Series adversaries. The Senators were outdistancing the second-place New York Yankees by 8½ games at the time.

After winning four out of five games in the series, Terry's Giants were most comfortably situated in the National League penthouse by a full eight games. Expectedly dragging after six doubleheaders in ten days, the team headed back to New York to jam in another doubleheader on Labor Day Monday with the second-division Philadelphia Phillies. Meanwhile, Pennsylvania's other major league team, the Pirates, had slipped into second place ahead of the Braves.

Bad weather, as it had through much of the campaign, continued to dog the Giants as both games with the Phillies were washed out. This time, however, the rain must have seemed like a godsend to the overworked starters. The Giants chugged on to Pittsburgh from New York to play five games with the second-place Pirates in four days, beginning Tuesday, September 5. The second of two Polo Grounds rainouts from June forced the Giants to make up the game in Pittsburgh in the teams' last head-to-head meeting of the season. The Pirates were a hot ball club, having won nine of ten games. They had trimmed the Giants' lead to 7½ games entering their first encounter. Carl Hubbell started for the visitors and extended a scoreless innings streak to 24 before the Pirates reached the him for three runs, on five hits, in the third inning. With one out in the fourth, former Giant Freddie Lindstrom doubled home a fourth run and sent Hubbell to the showers, in his shortest start all season. Shores and Jack Salveson, an infrequently used pitcher since his purchase in early June, finished up for Hubbell. The Pirates cruised to a 6–1 victory behind Larry French, who won his 15th game. Five thousand fans witnessed Hubbell's third defeat to the Pirates, more than to any other National League team.

The following day, four times as many locals visited Forbes Field for a twin encounter between the home favorites and the first-place crusaders. Fitzsimmons could not hold an eighth inning, 5–3 lead. Inning-opening triples by Pie Traynor and Arky Vaughan forced Fitzsimmons' removal and a single knotted the game. Hi Bell relieved and quelled any further scoring by the Pirates. But in the bottom of the tenth, Bell surrendered a game-winning single by Pirates reliever Bill Swift. The Giants' lead had been cut to 5½ games.

Whatever pep talk Terry gave to the team between games produced its desired effect. Giants batters jumped on Bucs pitcher Ralph Birkofer for five hits and five runs in the first inning of game two. Given the early cushion, Hal Schumacher had an easy time of it, pitching the distance and registering a 9–1 victory, his 17th on the season.

The next day, September 7, in front of roughly 9,000 fans, the Pirates similarly ambushed Roy Parmelee, knocking out the Giants' starter with a five-run first inning. Following Parmelee, Luque, Clark and Salveson were liberally hit. The Pirates won, 14–2, snipping the lead back to 5½ games. Two other players, along with Bill Shores, had joined the Giants in Boston, as teams were allowed to add to their club's composition over the last month of the season. As promised, outfielder Phil Weintraub was brought up from Birmingham in the Southern Association, and first baseman Joe Malay was obtained from the Scranton Miners of the New York–Pennsylvania League. Bill Terry had played without a back-up since Sam Leslie was dealt to the Dodgers in mid–June. Terry emptied his bench in the blowout loss to Pittsburgh. Weintraub replaced Lefty O'Doul in right field. In his second major league game and first official at-bat, Weintraub homered, his first big league hit. Malay spelled Terry, who had played every inning of every game since he returned to the lineup full-time on June 3. The Brooklyn-born Malay, in his debut game, singled in his initial at-bat.

In the final game of the series, there was little doubt Terry would bring back Hubbell on short rest, especially after his brief previous start. The Dodgers followed the Giants into Pittsburgh, and *Brooklyn Daily Eagle* writer Harold Parrott previewed the scheduled meetings between the teams with a sports lay of the land, which indicated how Hubbell and the Giants fared. "Sampson it was who slew a Biblical army with the jaw bone of an ass," conceptualized Parrott. "Carl Hubbell used a soupbone, but the devastation he wrought was none the less complete. As the doleful Dodgers moved in here to begin a six-game series with the 'hot' Pirates, they found a saddened city, with whispers everywhere of 'What might have been.'"[13] Hubbell disillusioned the Pirates and their followers with a tidy, six-hit, 2–1 victory. Hughie Critz singled in one run and Blondy Ryan plated the other with an outfield fly. The Giants reestablished their 6½-game advantage with only 20 games to play.

On to Cincinnati the team traveled, to play five games with the last-place Reds. The Giants' front office also announced the signing of infielder Charlie Dressen as a back-up for Travis Jackson, who had been manning the hot corner since Vergez's operation. Dressen, nearly 39 years of age, had been the playing manager of the minor league Nashville Volunteers.

Dressen saw his first action in the Redland Field series opener, September 9. The former Reds player substituted for Jackson after the Giants took the lead late in the game. Roy Parmelee (13–7) won for the first time in five starts, 7–2. The Giants swept a doubleheader the next day. Fitzsimmons (15–10) and Hubbell combined for a 6–1 win in the lidlifter. Hubbell pitched the last three innings, retiring all nine batters he faced. In the seventh inning, the left-hander entered the game with the bases loaded and no one out and prevented the Reds from scoring. In the nightcap, Schumacher (18–10) came through with another whale of a game, winning 2–1 in 11 innings. Lefty O'Doul's fly out sent Mel Ott home with the decisive run.

The frontline starters all having been used over the past three days (and Hubbell worked twice), Terry sought an alternate starter for the fourth encounter on September 11. He chose Hi Bell. The versatile bullpen man provided six solid innings, allowing one unearned run. With a 3–1 lead in the bottom of the seventh inning, Bell was pulled when the first batter reached on a base hit. In came the tireless Hubbell, appearing for the third time in four days. Allowing one hit, he secured the final nine outs and registered his second three-inning rescue in two days.

The September 12, fifth game of the series was called off due to threatening weather. With no other meetings scheduled between the clubs and no pressing reason to make up the game, it was the second game the Giants lost on their schedule to the weather.

Terry's club continued westward to Chicago. The Cubs were tied with the Pirates for second place. A few days earlier, September 10, the city and Comiskey Park hosted the first East-West All-Star Game, the Negro Leagues' answer to the initial major league jamboree of two months earlier. The "West" stars defeated their "East" counterparts, 11–7. Pittsburgh Crawfords first baseman Oscar Charleston was the leading vote-getter with 43,793 fan ballots. Hometown slugger from the Chicago American Giants, George "Mule" Suttles, was the offensive star with two long hits and three RBI.

Sitting pretty with a 7½-game lead and less than three weeks to the end of the season, Terry went for the jugular in a scheduled doubleheader at Wrigley Field on September 13. The perhaps overzealous skipper called on

7. The Championship Season—Second Half 161

Hubbell to start the first game. Making his fourth appearance in six days, Hubbell allowed two runs in the first inning. One was unearned, the result of an error by his manager. The game had been delayed by rain and more showers stopped the contest in the third inning. After a stoppage of nearly two hours, Terry did not permit Hubbell to return and placed Bill Shores into the muddy breach. Despite descending temperatures, opposing manager Charlie Grimm stuck his starter, Guy Bush, back out on the mound and he finished a nine-hit shutout, 2–0. The Giants' five-game winning streak was history. Because of deteriorating conditions and the late-concluding first game, management decided to call off the second game. Most of the 18,000 fans stayed until the final announcement.

The postponed second game was rescheduled as part of a doubleheader the next day. But the cold front that had come through and a lingering misty rain from yesterday nixed completion of those plans. The first game, however, was played. Fewer than 3,000 spectators braved the poor conditions, but were rewarded for their loyalty when the Cubs scored twice in the last of the ninth inning to win, 4–3. Gabby Hartnett singled home two runs with the bases loaded against starter and loser Freddie Fitzsimmons. The Giants' lead had dropped to 5½ games over the Cubs.

The weather cleared the following day. The Cubs' performance in the first two games of the series and a Ladies Day complementary admission helped raise attendance to nearly 30,000 for the rescheduled September 15 doubleheader. As he had done in Pittsburgh, Schumacher stepped up and halted the home club's momentum. In the first game, the right-hander delivered his fifth straight win with a six-hit, 5–1 decision. The Giants scored three runs in the ninth inning to ease the way for their pitcher, who won for the 19th time, while registering his 20th complete game. In the nightcap, Roy Parmelee's wildness forced his removal with two outs in the third inning of a scoreless game. Parmelee had walked the bases loaded and had pitched two balls to outfielder Riggs Stephenson. Hi Bell responded to Bill Terry's summons by retiring Stephenson—and the next 15 Cubs he faced before Billy Herman led off the ninth inning with a single. By that time, the Giants had plated four runs. Bell retired the next three batters and closed out the 4–0 victory. Mel Ott homered for one of the runs. It was the Giants' pitching staff's 23rd shutout of the season.

Not giving up hope, a similar crowd to Friday's showed up at Wrigley Field for the Saturday bargain bill series windup. The omnipresent Carl Hubbell took the hill in the opener. He yielded 12 hits but only one run as he defeated the Cubs, 2–1. Ott forced in the deciding run with a base-loaded walk in the top of the eighth inning. Hubbell improved his record to 22–11.

Bill Shores received his second start in the nightcap. Shores had been part of the 1929 and 1930 Philadelphia Athletics' pennant-winning clubs. The pitcher made sure that the Giants could rev up their World Series ticket-printing presses by downing the Cubs, 6–3. He pitched a seven-hitter for his first win of the season. Chuck Dressen, playing third base, drove in two runs with two hits. Gus Mancuso stroked four hits and knocked in a pair of runs for the winners. Mancuso caught both games of the twin bill, as he had the previous day. It was the 18th time this season the industrious backstop had received every pitch of a doubleheader, and the second occasion on back-to-back days.

Holding a fat, 8½-game advantage over the Pittsburgh Pirates with a dozen games to play, the New York Giants rolled into St. Louis to complete a long and gratifyingly successful road excursion that had placed them at the doorstep of the National League's championship mansion.

The Giants won their 15th game of their five-city trip on September 17. They spoiled "Dizzy Dean Day" at Sportsman's Park, and reduced their magic number to clinch the pennant to two in the process. Dean was given an automobile prior to the Sunday afternoon game. The vehicle was a gift from Dean's many fans, 15,000 of whom showed up to view the motor car's delivery on the field. Afterward, taking a turn on the mound and trying for his fifth win of the season against the Giants, the popular pitcher came up short, 4–3, as the New Yorkers clipped Dean for 11 hits. Mel Ott hit a two-run home run, his 22nd, and safeties by Mancuso and Ryan drove in the other runs. Parmelee, the Giants' starter, ran into difficulties in the fifth inning. He permitted a run on a single and double, then filled the bases with a walk and hit batter. Luque relieved him and surrendered a two-run double, but pitched out of the jam. The age-defying veteran was touched for only two more hits the rest of the way, grabbing the victory—his eighth against only two defeats. The Giants opened up their biggest lead of the campaign—nine games—with the win. They also reached a season-high 35 games over .500, at 88–53.

The imminent champions were defeated the following day, as Terry used Hubbell for the 12th time in relief. The overused left-hander suffered the 4–3 loss, allowing two runs over three and two-thirds innings. Hubbell took over for Hi Bell, who had entered the game in the second inning after starter Freddie Fitzsimmons was struck in the neck by a line drive off the bat of Bob O'Farrell. Tex Carleton picked up his 16th win for the Cardinals in a route-going endeavor.

Despite a loss to the Cardinals in the third game of the series, 12–3, the Giants clinched the pennant on September 19, when the second-place Pirates and Phillies divided a pair of games for the second day in a row. "I think we

7. The Championship Season—Second Half

have a great ball club, and when it comes to spirit and fight, there isn't a better one anywhere," hailed a proud but unsatisfied Bill Terry. "I had expected to win the pennant ever since the start of the season, and can only hope to gratify the New York fans by winning the world championship."[14]

The Giants arrived in New York from St. Louis on Wednesday evening, September 20. A large crowd was on hand to greet the squad's train as it arrived at Grand Central Station. The local George Washington High School band and the Grand Central Station Porter's troupe struck up lively medleys, including "Hail, Hail the Gang's All Here." Bill Terry was the first to disembark the hissing Pullman. A long cigar was in his mouth. The first to meet him on the platform was Charles Stoneham. They shook hands. Welcoming Terry next was William A. Dalton, president of the New York Athletic Club, who was serving as special envoy from New York City mayor John O'Brien.

Scheduling happenstance had removed the Giants from their fans for three weeks. The team, coming off a 15–8 road trip, had not only played some of its best ball of the season but had inexorably reaped the glorious reward of the pennant. All without the tangible participation of their faithful followers. Devoted New York fans had not even been able to follow their team's methodical progress over the wireless. But, confoundingly, fans in select other cities had been. "New York permits no broadcasting except to Chicago and Cincinnati stations,"[15] alerted a *Sporting News* story earlier in the season. The medium of radio was experiencing growing pains with baseball, and the Giants (and their fellow New York clubs) were of the opinion that home attendance would suffer by providing "free recreations" of their product to a local audience. The Chicago teams, on the other hand, held a more forward-thinking view and broadcasted all of their games.

The palpable absence of the team, coupled with the euphoria of its victorious return, may have evoked strident emotions too difficult for Giants loyalists to contain. Many undeniably let themselves get caught up in the celebration surrounding their team's triumphant arrival. Attesting to the latter was *AP* sportswriter Edward J. Neil in the following report:

> A turbulent crowd estimated to number at least 20,000 swept like a flood through Grand Central station. They smashed police lines, swamped two bands, tore each others clothing half off, and finally stuffed the ruffled warriors into automobiles that bucked them clear of the mob.... They tossed Terry around like a double play ball. Tiny Hughie Critz was continually coming out from under somebody's elbow. Mel Ott, Lefty O'Doul, Carl Hubbell, Hal Schumacher, Roy Parmelee, Travis Jackson, Blondy Ryan, all fought for their breath as the shouting fans, most of them youngsters, ripped at their clothes, howling, "Atta boy, atta boy!" Freddie Fitzsimmons, caught in the crush with his wife and baby girl, had a terrific time keeping them from getting hurt. Gus Mancuso wound up in the middle of the street, wild eyed, looking like a fugitive from a lynch mob.[16]

The next morning, a caravan of 25 automobiles carrying the first National League pennant-winning club in New York in nine years left the Polo Grounds, accompanied by an entourage of dignitaries, including league president John A. Heydler and John J. McGraw. The caravan arrived at City Hall in lower Manhattan, where the Giants were toasted by Mayor O'Brien.

The mayor, Heydler and McGraw spoke a few words in front of the government building, amid a drizzling rain and blaring refrains from the police and fire department bands. Each service branch deployed uniformed members of their respective baseball teams. Blue-uniformed police personnel, 150 strong, made sure to keep the crowd of 3,000 at bay. "This is the happiest moment of my life,"[17] Bill Terry said, overcoming a slightly embarrassing moment when he addressed the wrong end of the microphone hooked up to

A pennant-acknowledging reception on the steps of City Hall. Bill Terry, light suit, shakes hands with New York City mayor John O'Brien, September 21, 1933. The other dignitaries, left to right: William A. Dalton, president of the New York Athletic League, John McGraw, John H. McCooey, Brooklyn Democratic leader, and John Heydler, president of the National League. Giants team members are intermingled with other invited guests behind the group.

the loud speaker. He introduced each player on his team individually. Every member of the squad walked over to the microphone and chirped, in his own manner, the same greeting—"Hello folks"—before they "retired in a fluster of hand shaking back on the steps."[18]

The rain, a constant companion of the champions all season long, persisted more strongly after the noon hour and canceled the scheduled meeting between the Dodgers and Giants at the Polo Grounds later that afternoon. Two hundred and thirty miles to the south, in the District of Columbia, the Washington Senators sewed up the American League flag with a 2–1 victory over the St. Louis Browns.

The September 21 rainout was the Giants' 27th postponement of the season. Bad weather knocked out 14 of their games in April and May. Nine more were called off over the next three months and four additional dates were canceled in September. (The September 4 Labor Day doubleheader washout against the Phillies was made up in dual fashion on September 27, at the Polo Grounds, an open day for both squads.) The Giants finished the campaign with a 91–61 record. Four tie games which were made up statistically overcompensated for two unplayed ones in the 154-game schedule. The Giants experienced a letdown after clinching, and the Pirates closed the final gap in the standings to five games. Pittsburgh won eight of their final 12 games, while New York was victorious only three times in nine remaining contests. The Cubs were a game further back, and the Braves nine behind in fourth place. The Cardinals, Dodgers, Phillies and Reds brought up the second-division rear.

Terry's champions won the season's series from every team but St. Louis and Boston. The winning club took no fewer than 13 games from each of the other five teams. They posted a record of 48–27 at home and 43–34 away from the Polo Grounds. Accounting for the imbalance in home and away games were two home rainouts against the Chicago Cubs in August, made up at Wrigley Field late in the season. Their record in Chicago was 6–7. In a similar circumstance, the Giants played a 12th game in Pittsburgh to account for a rainout in New York. They gained back a home game on September 24 as the "do over" for the September 3 tie in Boston. The lost games were both road games, versus the Reds (July 15, then the September 12 attempted make-up date) and Phillies (August 14). The Giants engaged both teams in the full complement of 11 home games. The champions had a winning record every month of the season, except in October when they were beaten in their only scheduled game. Perhaps the team's most marked improvement from 1932, and one that had to have warmed Bill Terry's heart, was its 28–18 record in one-run games.

Most responsible for the improvement from 1932's 18–31 record in one-run games, of course, was the pitching. The league's best pitching staff topped their circuit in ERA (2.71) and shutouts (23), and were second in strikeouts (555). The team ERA was the lowest in the National League since 1920. The Giants' "Big Four" accounted for 73 of the team's 91 wins and logged 1,037⅓ of the club's 1,408⅔ innings. Heading the starring quartet was Carl Hubbell, whose final record was 23–12, with 22 complete games and a sensational ERA of 1.66. (Lon Warneke was next best in the NL with an even 2.00 ERA.) Hubbell also led the league in shutouts with ten and innings pitched with 308⅔. He placed second in strikeouts (156) to Dizzy Dean (199). He made 33 starts and 12 other relief appearances. He won 13 games and lost four at the Polo Grounds, including one of the greatest pitching exhibitions in history with his 1–0, 18-inning victory on July 2. Analytically reviewed with new-age numbers, Hubbell's ERA+ computed to 193, his WHIP to 0.98 and his Fielding Independent Pitching to 2.53—all the best in both leagues. Hubbell's WAR calculated to 8.9, well ahead of runner-up Warneke's 7.8 and Triple Crown winner Chuck Klein's 7.5. Only AL Triple Crown champ Jimmie Foxx posted a higher WAR composite at 9.2. (Both leagues boasted players who won the Triple Crown of hitting in 1933, the only time in baseball history that has occurred.) Hubbell was voted the league's Most Valuable Player.

As outstanding as Hubbell was for the Giants, young Hal Schumacher was not that far behind. Schumacher put up numbers that in most years would have easily earned him the title of staff ace. His 19 wins were bettered by only four pitchers in the National League. His 2.16 ERA trailed only Warneke and Hubbell. In 33 starts, he hurled seven shutouts and 21 complete games. Schumacher was the toughest pitcher for hitters to decipher in baseball, allowing only 6.92 hits per nine innings. His WHIP of 1.09 trailed only Hubbell. He posted an ERA+ of 149—bested by only Warneke (165) and Hubbell—and the fourth-highest NL pitching WAR at 5.3. Schumacher's FIP did not make it into the category top ten due to an elevated walk total (84) and low strikeout numbers (96) in 258⅔ innings. More consequentially, Schumacher delivered key road victories for the Giants all season long. He won 11 games and lost only three away from Coogan's Bluff, by far the best percentage among the starters. He was 4–1 on the Giants' pennant-clinching road swing in September. The 22-year-old more than lived up to the faith placed in him by Terry as a regular rotation man—and, not to be forgotten, McGraw as a green conscript.

The same can be said for Roy Parmelee, the other young McGraw discovery. The first-year, full-time Giants pitcher overcame bouts of wildness to record a 13–8 campaign, with a more than respectable 3.17 ERA. The 26-

year-old hurled 218⅓ innings, completed 14 games and threw three shutouts in 32 starts. Parmelee was the only Giants starter that Terry did not use at least once out of the bullpen. He was particularly pleasing to watch for the hometown folks, winning ten of 12 Polo Grounds decisions. He did lead the league in wild pitches and hit batters, with 14 each. The third-best hits-per-nine-innings ratio of 7.87 and second-best strikeouts-per-nine-innings mark of 5.44 helped earn him a top ten FIP placement of 3.38. Though his other analytic pitching computations were not as impressive, Parmelee was indeed a very valuable fourth starter.

Gus Mancuso deserved credit for assisting Schumacher and Parmelee in reaching their higher stations. "Terry told me to go and work on the pitchers when I transferred from St. Louis this year," Mancuso told an interviewer during the dog days of August.

> So I went to work on them. Carl Hubbell and Freddie Fitzsimmons were always good pitchers. I saw right away that both Roy Parmelee and Hal Schumacher had great possibilities. What those two youngsters needed was confidence and the control that comes with it. So I helped them get it by telling them to let me do the signal calling and all they had to do was to throw what I requested. Schumacher has improved his sinker until it is mighty sweet.[19]

The other member of the Giants' starting quartet mentioned by Mancuso, Freddie Fitzsimmons, proved a stalwart from the mound. The veteran pitcher paced the league with 35 starts. Completing 13 of them helped him accumulate 251⅔ innings. He went 16–11, tossed one shutout, and carried more than his own weight, no pun intended, from Opening Day forward. He was the steady, experienced mound presence winning teams usually have. The average age of the Giants, incidentally, was 28.5 years.

Rounding out the main pitching contributions were bullpen men Hi Bell and Adolfo Luque. The relief specialists both finished 22 games on the season for the Giants. In 38 games, seven as a starter, Bell posted a record of 6–5 and saved five games in 105⅓ innings. His ERA was a sharp 2.05. Working strictly in relief, Luque appeared in 35 games; he pitched 80⅓ innings and logged an 8–2 record, including 4–0 at the Polo Grounds. His ERA was 2.69 and he saved four games.

These six pitchers accounted for all but six of the Giants' 91 victories. Watty Clark, Bill Shores and George Uhle combined for the others.

Leading the way with the lumber were Bill Terry, Mel Ott and Johnny Vergez, who missed the last month of the season following an emergency appendectomy. Vergez outslugged Terry .448 to .423, playing in the same number of games, 123, and cranked 16 home runs compared to his manager's six. Hitting .272, the Giants' third baseman drove in 72 runs. Terry hit .322, fourth highest in the league, and knocked home 58 runs. His power stroke, however, like most everyone else's, was significantly diminished. Terry's on-base percentage was a team-best .375, among the regulars. Ott clubbed 23 home runs, the third highest total in the league. (In a year in which home runs dropped significantly in the National League, Chuck Klein's 28 led the circuit.) The outfielder pushed across 103 RBI, surpassed only by Klein's 120 and Wally Berger's 106. Playing in 152 games, most on the club, Ott also led the team in runs (98), hits (164), doubles (36) and slugging (.467). He also paced his circuit in walks with 75. He hit .283 with an OBP of .367.

Other contributors included Ott's fellow outfielder Jo-Jo Moore. Referred to as "Joe" in the newspapers, Moore hit .292 in 524 at-bats, though without a home run. The third outfielder, Kiddo Davis, posted a .258 batting average in 126 games, with seven home runs, fourth-most on the team. Making but three errors in 120 games in center field, Davis outdistanced all other fielders at the position with a .988 fielding average. The swift Davis also stole more bases than anyone on the squad with ten. Lefty O'Doul, a starter in the outfield much of the time after his trade from Brooklyn, hit .306 in 78 games with the Giants. He slugged nine home runs, behind only Ott and Vergez. Fifth outfielder Homer Peel appeared in 84 games and registered a .257 batting mark.

Second baseman Hughie Critz and shortstop Blondy Ryan provided impressive defensive aptitude behind the pitchers. Each headed the league in assists at his respective position. Ryan collected 494 and Critz 541. Critz also had the best fielding percentage among second sackers at .982. After the Giants clinched the pennant, gimpy-kneed Travis Jackson was rested in preparation for the World Series. Jackson hit .246 in 53 games. He could not drive the ball and totaled only five extra base hits all year, all doubles. One of Jackson's fill-ins, utility infielder Bernie James, played every infield position but first base; he swung a weak stick, hitting .224 in 125 at-bats.

Before Vergez went down, from his unique vantage point, Mancuso had offered the following praise for his team's short fielders: "That infield of ours is enough to give confidence to any pitching staff. It's the tightest infield you'll ever see. Terry, Critz, Ryan, and Vergez."[20]

Behind the plate, Mancuso was a workhorse. He caught more games (142) and more innings (1,216), and recorded more putouts (580) than any other backstop in the Senior Circuit. He started 139 games behind the dish and finished 120, both unrivaled totals in either league. He started both games of a doubleheader 25 times, completing both ends on 18 occasions—including back-to-back days *twice* (June 3–4 and September 15–16). In all, he saw combat in both games of 27 of the Giants' 34 double bills on the season. Through it all, he hit .256 with six home runs and 56 RBI.

Mancuso even started a Giants exhibition game held in an unusual setting. With notorious figures like Bonnie and Clyde, John Dillinger and members of the Barker gang gaining national headlines, the place may not have seemed too out of step with the theme of lawlessness that prevailed in some areas of the country that year. On September 25, the Giants jaunted north along the Hudson River to Sing Sing Prison, in Ossining, to play the inmate baseball team. The Giants won, 9–3. Freddie Fitzsimmons started, and Bill Terry had three of 12 hits collected by the Giants.

A day earlier, the Giants voted full World Series shares to 21 players. The group included their starting eight, the six main pitchers, infield reserves Travis Jackson and Bernie James, backup catcher Paul Richards, and outfield sub Homer Peel. Although they had not been with the club the entire season, Lefty O'Doul and Watty Clark were bestowed full shares, perhaps because of their veteran standing or past accomplishments in the game. Glenn Spencer, the only other pitcher besides the primary six to be with the team the entire season, was the final awardee. Sam Leslie, who filled in exceptionally for Terry for a month (he slugged .518), was completely omitted. Half-shares were awarded to third-string catcher Harry Danning, who joined the club at the end of July and had only two at-bats on the season, and to pitcher Jack Salveson, who came up from the minors on June 2. Quarter-shares went to pitcher Bill Shores, who was cut in May and brought back as a September call-up, and to Chuck Dressen, the late-season pick up who filled in at third base for two weeks in late September while Jackson rested his knees.

"It's the easiest crowd of players to handle I ever saw," Terry said around the time of the voting. "I don't believe in hanging around fire escapes to check up on players. But if we had that system of espionage on the Giants there wouldn't be anything to watch. The boys' idea of a wild night is a malted milk and a movie."[21] On the field, of course, it was generally a different story, with the "boys" wreaking havoc on most of the clubs in the league.

Coaches Tommy Clark, Frank Snyder and Al Smith, as well as team trainer Willie Schaeffer and secretary James Tierney, were favorably remembered by the team with full World Series dividends. Groundskeeper Henry Fabian was promised an additional $1,000, while clubhouse man Fred Logan was offered a bonus of $800 and his son and assistant, Ed, $200. Batboy Joe Troy received $500 extra.

Pitching coach Clarence Mitchell was not mentioned as receiving any type of share. He was not listed in the World Series program, and therefore it may be speculated that he left or was dismissed from the team at an undetermined juncture of the season.

Although a manager is usually only as good as his players, Bill Terry deserved special credit for the Giants' capturing the pennant. In less than a year, he overhauled the team and redesigned it into a cohesive mixture of youth and age. He stressed hustling on the field, battling hard until the very end, optimizing all 27 outs—on both offense and defense. Unlike his predecessor, he did not rule with an iron hand, preferring instead to rely on the "honor system."

Terry showed early confidence in Schumacher and Parmelee, and the inexperienced pitchers did not let him down. Every championship team has their ace pitcher, and Terry maximized his good fortune with Hubbell's breakout into superstardom. The manager recognized he had a good thing in the bullpen with Bell and Luque and did not tinker with any changes in regard to those two men.

It is not often that a team wins it all with a rookie shortstop. Terry had the foresight to pick up Blondy Ryan from the International League in exchange for utility infielder Doc Marshall, four months prior to the season, as a back-up to Travis Jackson. Ryan produced an exceptional 3.1 defensive WAR at the most exacting of diamond positions. When Johnny Vergez was going through his ravaging family problems in 1932, Terry put the anguished player's mind at ease by guaranteeing him his job, in advance, for the next year. Vergez responded with his best big league season, despite missing the last month of the campaign with his ill-timed appendicitis. (Vergez missed the World Series to stay with his wife following a miscarriage suffered in September.)

Though Shanty Hogan was no slouch behind the plate, the Giants' skipper sought to bring in a more agile catcher. Terry parted with first-string outfielder Ethan Allen, a nondescript pitcher named Jim Mooney, and two players with their best days behind them, pitcher Bill Walker and catcher Bob O'Farrell, to pry Gus Mancuso (and pitcher Ray Starr) loose from St. Louis in a post–1932 season trade. Mancuso earned his salary behind the plate. To some degree, the blossoming of Schumacher and Parmelee should be recognized as occurring under Mancuso's tutelage.

Boss Terry also upgraded the outfield. He brought Jo-Jo Moore back from the minors shortly after taking over as manager in 1932, and obtained Kiddo Davis in the Freddie Lindstrom trade. Terry utilized Sam Leslie, at the peak of his tradable value, to acquire proven commodities Lefty O'Doul and Watty Clark. While Clark continued to underperform from the mound, O'Doul became Terry's second biggest offensive threat, behind Ott, in the outfield pasture.

As a handler of pitchers, Terry may have been cited for wastefully misusing Hubbell in relief on more than one occasion. But Hubbell did not seem

7. The Championship Season—Second Half 171

to be hurt by the meaningless appearances. Terry pitched Hubbell often on short rest, and the pitcher rarely did not respond. It was an age in which top-of-the-line pitchers carried the extra work load with regularity. Hubbell was simply a shining thoroughbred, and Terry may have drawn criticism if he had *not* used him as much as he did. Throughout the campaign, consistent, first-rate performances from the rest of the staff overcame any other questionable decisions Terry himself may have later preferred to reassess. The only unsuccessful moves Terry made were purchasing George Uhle from the Detroit Tigers in April, and the unfruitful free agent pickup of Waite Hoyt the prior year. He had expunged Hoyt ahead of the 1933 season and released Uhle mid-season. These minor, failed transactions only cost the Giants money. The team more than made up for those financial losses not only in wins on the diamond, but in what Bill Terry gave the Giants as both an adroit field general and stellar player.

While the Giants' pennant victory was not widely expected in most knowledgeable circles, with some prognosticators even predicting a second-division finish again, one astute baseball man ran contrary to the pundit majority shortly before spring training. "The dark horse is New York," Branch Rickey said in February. "Bill Terry will have a hustling team. If a couple of his young pitchers come through he may run the league ragged."[22]

Proving that Terry's team did not defy all odds, by any means, Missouri sportswriter Ed Lawson wrote the following in his syndicated column around the same time as Rickey's declarations: "If Joe Cronin, Washington's new manager, and Bill Terry, field boss of the New York Giants, steer their teams to the pennant—as many experts believe they may—the number of playing managers who have won pennants will have increased to 16."[23]

Seven and a half months after the column was printed, Lawson's words seemed to have been tapped from clairvoyant sources.

All that remained to be seen now was whether Cronin or Terry emerged as the 12th playing manager to win the World Series.

8

The World Series: The Terrymen versus the Croninites

Game One

The New York Giants' American League opponents in the World Series were the Washington Senators, managed by young Joe Cronin. The 26-year-old Cronin had been the Senators' starting shortstop since 1929. This was his first season at the helm of the team. He led his club to an exceptional 99–53 record (eight games better than the Giants), winning the AL pennant by seven lengths over the reigning world champion New York Yankees. Cronin had become a standout player at his position, as evidenced by his selection as the only shortstop for the American League in the All-Star exhibition game this past July. He was one of the best hitters on his team. He was young, handsome, successful, talented and single. He was considered one of the most eligible bachelors in one of the most high-profile cities in America (though he was dating one of team owner Clark Griffith's nieces). No single participant in the 1933 World Series had more of the world on a string than Joseph Edward Cronin.

The rookie manager hit .309 with an on-base percentage of nearly .400 (.398). Although he hit only five home runs, Cronin led his club in RBI with 118. He was one of four regulars to hit over .300 on his squad, with two others batting .295 or higher. Not surprisingly, the Senators had the league's best team batting at .287. The club finished third in the circuit in runs scored with 851 (compared to the Giants' 636).

Playing in a much bigger ballpark, only the Yankees outdrew the Senators in home attendance in the American League, 728,014 to 437,533. Washington was the only team in the American League to turn a pre-tax profit during the year, based on net operating income (gross operating income minus gross operating expenses). This without the potential benefit of beer revenues. Washington was one of the teams that had decided to remain "dry" within their ballpark's perimeter.

Cronin handled a top-quality pitching staff that allowed the fewest runs (665) and posted the loop's second-best ERA at 3.82. The pitching was led by 24-game winner General Crowder and 22-game victor Earl Whitehill. Lefty Stewart (15–6) and Monte Weaver (10–5) rounded out the frontliners. The mound corps received a great contribution, as well, from bullpen man Jack Russell, who went 12–6, with a retroactively estimated league-leading 13 saves, in 50 appearances.

Cronin would be vying with Bill Terry to become the first playing manager since Rogers Hornsby in 1926 to win the World Series. Comparisons of Cronin and Terry were inevitably plastered on sports pages around the country, leading up to the fall showcase. One writer offered the following perspective: "Memphis Bill and Joe are the new type of managers. Each asks of his players to give him 100 percent on the field, the rest of the 24 hours belongs to them. Terry comes in often to consult with his pitcher, surrounded by his infield. He listens to everybody and then makes his decision. Cronin is more apt to jump and look afterward. Each is quick to yank a pitcher with a big lead."[1]

It was pointed out that Terry had not levied a fine on a player all year long, while Cronin had docked pay from Goose Goslin, for not hustling sufficiently in the outfield, and General Crowder, for not leaving the pitching mound quickly enough following his removal from a game.

On Tuesday, October 3, nine days before Joe Cronin's 27th birthday, the 1933 World Series began in New York. Hosting the first two games was the well-known entity in the city's most well-known borough.

The Polo Grounds was located along 8th Avenue and 155th Street in upper Manhattan. It was nestled within a flattened roll of hilly terrain buttressing the Harlem River, beneath a rocky overhang called Coogan's Bluff. One of several parks of the same name, the final steel and concrete version was constructed in 1911, following a fire that leveled most of the previous all-wooden structure. The land on which the stadium was built was part of the real estate holdings of James J. Coogan, a former Manhattan borough president.

In the early 1920s, work began on extending the second deck out over the lower outfield grandstands. In left field, the upper deck hung out several feet over the field. Eventually, the top decks nearly enclosed the ballpark except for center field, where executive offices and clubhouses were erected. The expansion produced a unique horseshoe configuration as seen from an overhead view. The open end of the horseshoe faced the Harlem River. Across the waterway, to the southeast, Yankee Stadium lay easily within sight. As with Yankee Stadium, the sun slanted harshest in center and left fields.

Bill Terry spoke about this biospheric occurrence prior to the Fall Classic, while also stating a decision to abandon a platoon system he had put in place after the acquisition of Lefty O'Doul. "We have the worst sun field in the world at the Polo Grounds," said Terry. "We also have the best sun fielder in the world at the Polo Grounds. His name is Joe Moore. Moore will play every game for me. In fact, I won't use an alternating outfield against left and right-handers, but will stick with Moore, Davis and Ott. O'Doul will be used as a pinch-hitter."[2]

Terry was obviously anticipating a low-scoring Series and preferred the Giants as a pitching- and defense-centric club for their battle with the Senators. "As for Lefty Clark," he added. "I'm not planning on using him at all. We have the pitchers and that ought to swing the final results. It always does."[3] The manager said he would use Hubbell, Schumacher and Fitzsimmons, in that order, as his World Series starters. Parmelee would not receive a start. With no off-days scheduled in the seven-day conflict, the starters would be burdened with pitching on short rest.

Terry also addressed the Johnny Vergez issue. The player's non-playing status for October had been confirmed. "Jackson's knees are all right now, even though he's still a bit lame, and he will start for us at third," said the Giants' leader. "The only trouble with 'Jax' since he returned to the lineup is a charley horse and he will work himself out of that. He will come through on defense and he will hit."[4] Terry may not have been altogether honest in his assessment of Jackson's physical condition, but Jackson answered the bell for every game of the Series and performed admirably. (A charley horse was usually a reference to a leg pull.)

Jackson was one of five Giants who had previously played in the World Series. The others were Terry, Mancuso, Luque and Bell. Heading to the ballpark on the morning of October 3, neither Jackson nor his teammates knew whom they were going to face on the opposing hill. Cronin had kept hidden the identity of his Game One starter, while Terry had announced Hubbell more than a week earlier.

A crowd estimated at 6,000 was on line early in the morning to buy 5,000 available bleacher seat tickets, priced at $1.10, which went on sale at 8:00 a.m.—an hour before the Polo Grounds' gates opened. Some fans were injured in a rush forward when the windows opened. All 4,000 box seats, with a price tag of $6.50, had been sold out in advance. Reserve seating, which encompassed 20,000 grandstand seats ($5.50) and 20,000 upper deck

8. The World Series: The Terrymen versus the Croninites

reserve seats ($3.30), could not be sold in the usual block of games. Demand was not sufficient at the $5.50 price. Therefore, the Giants' sales office agreed to sell the tickets on a per-game basis. (The Washington Senators adopted the same measure with their non-box seat ticket offerings. New York Yankees officials had implemented the same sales technique for 1932's Fall Classic when World Series games did not sell out for the first time at Yankee Stadium.)

The "tip off" on Washington's starter did not come until Lefty Stewart took pre-game batting practice swings with the other regulars. During batting practice, an autogyro circled the Polo Grounds, pulling an advertising sign for beer. With his decision to use Stewart, Cronin appeared to be stating that he did not want to spend his biggest winner, Crowder, against Hubbell, and that he was hoping to steal one from Hubbell or the Giants, with Stewart nullifying the left-handed swings of Terry, Ott and Moore. If this was the case, Cronin's choice of not using his best available southpaw (Whitehill) gave the outward appearance that he was conceding the game. All of Cronin's starters were sufficiently rested, as were Terry's. In a few days, Clark Griffith would say that Whitehill was Cronin's intended starter for Game One, but that the left-hander had developed a sore arm/elbow in an outing on September 29 against the Yankees.

Under sunny skies and temperatures in the mid-60s, Dennis J. Mahon, president of the New York Board of Aldermen, threw out the ceremonial first pitch. This occurred shortly after a band played the national anthem and the raising of the flag on the center field flagpole. Honus Wagner, Walter Johnson, Jimmie Foxx, Connie Mack and John McGraw were among the baseball celebrities present. Babe Ruth was also on hand, having contracted a newspaper gig to cover the Series, with the assistance of a "ghost writer." "The crowd," it was written, "gave the Baltimore Orphan as big a reception as the whole Giant team."[5] Commissioner Landis was also dutifully in attendance. A newspaper note explained that the game's first pitch, slated for 1:30 p.m., was delayed until cameramen left the field, at the behest of the umpires.

The first pitch of the game was fouled off by leadoff hitter Buddy Myer. Four pitches later, he struck out, as did the next two batters to face Hubbell—Goose Goslin and Heinie Manush. Hubbell was cheered loudly as he walked off the mound and back to his home first-base dugout. In the lower half of the inning, Cronin's pitching strategy absorbed a disquieting jolt. In his first World Series at-bat, clean-up hitter Ott homered into the lower right field stands. A man was on base thanks to an error by second baseman Myer. It was all the scoring in the inning and both runs were unearned.

Hubbell tamed the Senators over the next two innings, allowing one hit

Posing for the camera prior to World Series Game One at the Polo Grounds: Left to right, Washington coach Nick Altrock, Babe Ruth, Joe Cronin, Christy Walsh, Bill Terry and an overweight John McGraw.

(to Cronin), while the Giants plated two more in runs in their half of the third. After a Hughie Critz safety, Terry signaled for the hit-and-run with the next batter—himself. He singled to right, moving Critz to third. Ott singled to right field, Critz scored and Terry raced to third. Cronin replaced Stewart, who had allowed six hits. Jack Russell, who had been throwing in the bullpen, came in. Russell struck out Davis, and retired Jackson on a hot shot that hit off first baseman Joe Kuhel and was fielded by Myer, who threw to Russell covering first base. Terry scored the Giants' fourth run on the play. The next hitter, Mancuso, flied out to end the inning. Mancuso was participating in his third World Series in four years—his first as a starter.

An error in the top of the fourth by Critz permitted the Senators to get on the board. Myer opened things with a base hit. Goslin grounded to Terry, who took it himself for the unassisted putout. Meyer moved up to second. Critz fumbled a roller by Heinie Manush. Pitching to Cronin with runners at the corners, Hubbell's first offering was fouled back behind the plate. Either

Mancuso was crossed up, or did not like the pitch's location, for he called time to go out and visit with Hubbell. Blondy Ryan joined them. Two pitches later, Cronin grounded to Jackson at third. He forced the runner at second, with Myer crossing the plate. The next man, Fred Schulte, reached on an infield single off Hubbell's glove. But Hubbell retired Joe Kuhel on a ground-out to stonewall any further scoring.

Including the last out of Kuhel in the fourth, Hubbell retired 11 batters in a row, until Senators catcher Luke Sewell walked with one out in the eighth inning. During this period, the Senators' premier reliever also shut down the Giants. Russell hurled five innings, yielding four hits, no walks and no runs.

In the eighth inning, Hubbell walked two consecutive batters, his bases on balls total for the game. The second free pass was to Dave Harris, pinch-hitting for Russell. Bill Terry walked over from his first base position to speak to Hubbell, with the rest of the infield huddling around their pitcher and Mancuso. Adolfo Luque was warming up in the Giants' bullpen. After the conference broke up, Hubbell dug in and coaxed leadoff batter Myer into a force out (shortstop Ryan juggled the ball before gaining control and shoveling to Critz at second base). Harris was out and Sewell reached third. The ace pitcher then retired Goslin on a line drive to Terry at first base. An *AP* description of the inning's final out indicated that Terry was not employing the modern game's late-inning, "guard the line" positioning, which made the play possible. "Goslin belted one pitch into the lower right field stands, but it was foul," read the report. "He was looking very dangerous. Finally he caught an outside pitch on the nose and smashed it toward right field, about fifteen feet inside the foul line. But Terry nailed the ball with his glove hand as it was sailing by, and the uprising was over."[6] The Senators left two men on base. The Giants did not score in the lower half of the inning.

Hubbell had struck out nine batters through eight innings. In the ninth, holding on to his 4–1 lead, he had to work out of more difficulties to pick up his first World Series win. The difficulties were not all his doing. Manush opened the inning by reaching on an error by Blondy Ryan, the Giants' second of the game. The infield sparkplug let an easy grounder go through his legs. The second hitter, Cronin, singled, putting runners on first and second. Terry requested a game stoppage again to confer with Hubbell. Luque was still throwing in the pen. Terry left Hubbell in. The next batter, Fred Schulte, hit a hard grounder at Jackson, who could not field the ball cleanly. It was ruled a hit, loading the bases with no one out.

Kuhel, the Senators' leading home run hitter with 11, stepped into the batter's box. Terry stayed with Hubbell. On a 2–1 pitch, the left-handed-hitting Kuhel grounded to Ryan, who made a nifty throw to first to record the out. Manush scored on the play, with the other runners moving into scoring position. Third baseman Ossie Bluege was next. Bluege struck out on three pitches, swinging at a slow curve for the second out. Luke Sewell was the Senators' last hope. The Giants' infield once more conferred on the mound and then dispersed. With the tying runs on second and third, Hubbell quickly got ahead of Sewell, 0–2, before the catcher bounced the third offering to third. Jackson fielded it and threw to Terry for the final out. The run by the

World Series Game One starters Carl Hubbell and Lefty Stewart shake hands. Hubbell obtained the better of Stewart in the Fall Classic opener.

Senators was unearned, as was their first score. Hubbell allowed only five hits and struck out ten. After the game he was asked to describe his outing. "Oh, I was throwing them a little bit of everything," he said. "Fast balls, hooks and the old screwball in the pinches. They've got a mighty good ball club and I was in some tight spots, but managed to work out of them. It's a great thing to get off to a four-run lead in the third inning."[7] Hubbell explained that he experienced a bit of a chill in the ninth, which may have affected his pitching. Hubbell may have sweated through the black, long-sleeved undershirt he was wearing.

One of Gus Mancuso's post-game comments indicated that Hubbell had his signature pitch working to perfection. "That dipsydoo [screwball] pitch had me digging in the dirt all day," the catcher declared, "and if I had to dig for it, I don't see how they figured to hit it."[8]

As he gulped from a bottle of beer in the clubhouse, a pleased-as-punch Terry said, "Oh, boy—what a kick. You get the feeling out there that you're playing for the whole league, and for all the fans of the league, not just one club."[9]

The game's hitting star, Mel Ott, who went 4-for-4 with three RBI, stated that his home run was the greatest thrill of his life. Travis Jackson, hitless in the game, called this edition of the Senators "a much more powerful club"[10] than the 1924 version. He had no complaints about his knees and said his charley horse was improving. He also indicated he was prepared to play all seven games, if needed. The Senators, on several occasions, tried to test Jackson's knees with bunt attempts in his direction. But none of those who squared up were able to put the ball in play where they wanted against Hubbell's pitches, and Jackson was not tested.

From the other bench, Cronin lamented, "It was a mighty close game and anybody's game up until the last out." The boy manager vowed his team would bounce back. "We've just begun to fight. I'm telling you we'll win this series. Hubbell can't beat us again."[11]

GAME ONE HEROES: Hubbell and Ott. GOAT: Buddy Myer (3 Errors).
ATTENDANCE: 46,672
TIME OF GAME: 2:07
UMPIRES: HP–Charlie Moran (NL); 1B–George Moriarty (AL); 2B–Cy Pfirman (NL); 3B–Red Ormsby (AL).

Game Two

Jack Salveson pitched batting practice to Terry's men as he had done prior to the opener. Mel Ott received the loudest cheer from the early arrivals of any player to step on the field. Bill Terry was "greeted with a roar when he trotted in from the centerfield exit of the clubhouse." Terry also hit the longest drive in BP, the ball reaching the "entrance opening in the farthest section of the lower right field stands."[12]

At the start of the game, ominous dark clouds settled over the Polo Grounds. But they quickly moved off or dissipated, and the game was played under ideal conditions for a second day in a row. "Baseball could not have ordered to specifications a more perfect day," wrote one of the more than 500 newspaper reporters covering the Series, including three from Tokyo, Japan. "The sun poured down as it did yesterday, and a light breeze was just enough to cool mildly perspiring brows and flap the flags that encircled the roof of the covered stands stretching almost completely around the field."[13]

Away from the diamond, gambling remained prominent in the mainstream media. Much less discreetly than today, newspapers touted World Series betting lines, with multi-paragraph articles using prime column space. Across the country, the Senators had opened 7-to-10 favorites to win baseball's blue ribbon classic, although the Giants, with Hubbell on the mound, were the smart money bet to win the opener. The first-game victory by the Giants shifted the betting odds to 6-to-5 toward the National League champions to win it all. In the Empire State, it was a different story, with New York bookmakers compelled to set the Giants as favorites from the start, the result of the hometown sympathy. After Game Two concluded, it might have been difficult to find a Senators backer outside of the Beltway.

Cronin kept no one in the dark about his Game Two starter, announcing after the first game loss that he would give the ball to his top right-hander, General Crowder. Terry countered with his second-biggest winner, as he had stated he would.

Al Schacht, Senators coach and historically known as one of baseball's "clown princes," entertained the crowd before the 1:30 p.m. start time with a "burlesque routine" at the third base bag. He wore a high hat and coat tails. There were noticeable pockets of unoccupied seats at game time in the left and right field upper deck sections of the Polo Grounds.

Hal Schumacher walked leadoff hitter Buddy Myer on five pitches to open the game. After Schumacher fell behind two balls on the second-place hitter, Goose Goslin, Terry signaled for Hi Bell to start warming up in the bullpen. Getting his obvious jitters out of the way, young Schumacher retired the next three batters. On a 2–1 pitch, Goslin bounced to Ryan, who threw out the Senators' right fielder at first. Heinie Manush flied to Moore in center. Schumacher struck out Cronin, the only regular besides Sewell not to whiff yesterday against Hubbell, for the third out. Myer was left stranded at second base, and Bell sat down.

8. The World Series: The Terrymen versus the Croninites

The first three Giants went down in order. In the second inning, Schumacher issued a two-out walk, in an otherwise uneventful half-inning of work in which he faced four batters. Mel Ott received a fine hand from the spectators, leading off the second. When he walked, the crowd booed. Davis followed with a single to center, Ott moving up a base. Jackson sacrificed the runners to second and third. Mancuso grounded out to third base, with Ott unable to score. Ryan rolled out to Joe Kuhel at first base for the third out. The ball struck Ryan's bat in his attempt to move away from a high hard one.

In the top of the third inning, Goslin smashed a two-out offering from Schumacher into the upper deck in right field to give the Senators their first lead in the Series. No one was on base. Manush flied out harmlessly to Moore in left to end the inning. Crowder set down the first two batters in the lower half of the frame. On a 3–2 pitch culminating a ten-pitch at-bat, he walked Hughie Critz. Crowder walked half way in from the mound to register a protest with the ball-four call by home plate umpire George Moriarty. Bill Terry swung under a Crowder pitch and lofted it into center field for the inning's third out.

Leading off the fourth, Cronin took two balls from Schumacher and hit Schumacher's 2–0 delivery to Ott in short right field. Schumacher retired the next two batters, Schulte and Kuhel, on infield outs. In the bottom half of the inning, the Giants went down timidly against Crowder. Cleanup hitter Ott allowed no build-up of expectations by swinging at the first pitch, popping up to Kuhel at first base. Kuhel recorded the next out also, settling under a high pop off the bat of Kiddo Davis, about halfway from the first base line to the Giants' dugout. Jackson, the sixth-place hitter, was retired on a hard-hit grounder to Cronin at short.

Ossie Bluege was the first batter of the Senators' fifth. Two pitches after fouling a ball off his foot that left him gingerly walking off the sudden pain, Bluege sent a pitch deep to left field which Moore, on his horse, hauled in. Sewell grounded out to Ryan. Crowder batted and was given hearty applause for his effort so far from the appreciative crowd. Crowder singled, Washington's second hit of the contest. Myer grounded to Critz, who relayed to Ryan at second base, forcing Crowder.

Looking for his first hit of the Series, Mancuso opened the Giants' half of the fifth inning. He hit a hard smash to third. Bluege fielded and threw poorly to first, pulling Kuhel off the bag, but Kuhel had time to tag Mancuso before the catcher reached the base. Ryan singled to center. Crowder quickly threw two strikes to Schumacher, then fell behind with three straight balls. After taking a moment with the resin bag, Crowder's next pitch was hit by Schumacher to Cronin, who started a 6–4–3 double play.

Precariously ahead 1–0, the Senators looked to score again in their sixth turn at bat. Goslin led off with a hit to center field. Manush walked on four pitches. Terry came over to try and settle his young pitcher down. Hi Bell began warming up again. At the game's most critical juncture for Schumacher, he bore down and retired Joe Cronin on a popup to Mancuso in foul ground. Facing Fred Schulte, Schumacher threw a wild pitch, allowing the runners to move up a base. The next pitch was a ball. Schulte swung at the next offering and grounded to Jackson. The third baseman threw home to cut down Goslin in a rundown (5–3–5). Schulte reached on the fielder's choice, with Manush scurrying to third. Pitching carefully to the left-handed-swinging Kuhel, Schumacher issued his second walk of the inning. "It wasn't exactly an intentional pass," confided Terry afterwards. "But we just didn't give Kuhel a good ball to hit to get to the next man in the order. Unless we could get him to chase a bad ball, we figured it was better to walk him."[14] With the bases loaded, Schumacher escaped harm by striking out "the next man in the order," Ossie Bluege, swinging. The strikeout brought the cheering crowd to its feet.

Holding the tentative lead, Crowder ran into trouble of the bottom of the sixth inning. Jo-Jo Moore singled. Critz forced Moore at second base after an improperly executed bunt attempt. Terry followed with a double to the opposite field, sending Critz to third. After Mel Ott was intentionally walked, Terry motioned from second base; he was pinch-hitting for Kiddo Davis, who was 3-for-6 in the two games so far. Intuitively sensing a chance at a big breakthrough, Terry called upon the left-handed-swinging power threat of Lefty O'Doul to bat in place of the right-handed Davis. Cronin ordered Tommy Thomas to begin warming up. After throwing a ball on the first pitch, Crowder worked O'Doul to his advantage in the count, 1–2. The second strike was fouled directly back into the netting behind the plate. Cronin halted the proceedings for a brief chat with Crowder. The next pitch was called a ball, followed by a foul into the dirt. On the sixth pitch, O'Doul smacked a clean single to center, plating two runs. The crowd roared.

Following O'Doul, Travis Jackson picked an opportune time for his first hit of the Series. His base hit into center scored Ott from second and permitted O'Doul to reach third. Terry then boldly called for the "squeeze play," with Mancuso batting and the count 1–1. The unexpected move caught the Washington defense so thoroughly on their heels that the slow-footed Mancuso was able to beat out his bunt down the third base line. O'Doul raced in to score from third and Jackson moved up to second. The Giants now led, 4–1. Ryan looked at a third strike for the second out, but Schumacher did himself a great service with a base hit to left field, sending Jackson home with the Giants' fifth run. Batting for the second time in the frame, Moore singled again, this time up the middle; Mancuso scored from second, with Schumacher occupying the same bag in his advance from first base. Unlike Terry, Cronin seemed to be managing his pitcher as if it were a regular season game. Sticking too long with his ace, Cronin finally replaced Crowder with Thomas, a hittable pitcher on the season for the Senators. Critz greeted Thomas with an infield hit to short which the Senators manager could not make a play on. Schumacher made it to third and Moore to second. With the bases loaded, Terry grounded to Myer, who elected to toss to Cronin at second, forcing Critz. The Giants, on eight hits and a walk, had cracked open the game, 6–1.

As a renewed Schumacher took the mound, several policemen were needed to help Lefty O'Doul reach the Giants' clubhouse in center field. The closest bleacherites feverishly pawed at O'Doul's uniform as he climbed the clubhouse steps to exit the field. Once the inning started, Schumacher retired Sewell on a fly ball to right, but gave up a hit to pinch-hitter Sam Rice, batting in the ninth spot for Thomas. Recording all three putouts in the inning, Mel Ott hauled down consecutive long drives up against the right field wall hit by Myer and Goslin.

Ott made the first out of the seventh for the Giants. He was followed by Homer Peel, who had come into the game to play center in place of Moore. Peel grounded out, and so did Jackson for the third out.

Hoping to start a rally, Manush singled off Schumacher to start the eighth. But that greatest of rally killers materialized when Cronin hit into an around-the-horn double play. Schulte popped up to Mancuso behind the plate. The Giants went down in order again in the lower half of the inning.

Schumacher had yielded five hits and four walks. He had struck out only two, but the second one had victimized Ossie Bluege to end the sixth inning with the bases loaded. In the ninth, he coasted home. He set down all three hitters, and the Giants were victorious, 6–1.

"My whole family was up there in the stands watching me," said the pitcher of the hour shortly afterward. "I had to make good. They all came down from Dolgeville to see the game—Pa and Ma, my three brothers and two sisters. With a rooting section like that behind me I had to come through…. Oh—I was throwing fast sinkers most of the time. They had me in a couple of bad holes and I was lucky to get out of them. I got a bigger kick out of winning this World Series game in my first season in the big leagues than when I got my diploma."[15]

"The ball I hit was a curve," said Lefty O'Doul. "Say, and did I feel good when I saw it sailing away."[16]

Bill Terry was indisputably on top of his managerial game in this contest.

He was ready to replace Schumacher in the first inning, if necessary. Playing the percentages, he "intentionally" walked Kuhel to fill the bases with two outs in the sixth, to have Schumacher pitch to the right-handed-hitting Bluege, who fanned. Terry played a hunch with O'Doul. Not saving him for later, he used his prime pinch-hitter in the sixth inning with the bases loaded and obtained positive results. "I figured the squeeze would take them by surprise and it did," Terry said about another laudable decision. "Gus executed it perfectly."[17] (This was an era in which every man in the lineup was expected to be able to execute the fundamentals of the game.)

Terry also rather bluntly made mention of one of his opposite number's moves—or lack thereof. "He likes to leave his pitcher in there," he said, referring to Cronin's late call to the bullpen. "I'd never fool around with any pitcher as long as he did with Crowder."[18] As the Senators departed up the visiting clubhouse steps, fans in the bleachers serenaded Cronin and company with, "We Made Chowder Out of Crowder! We Made Chowder Out of Crowder!"[19] The boy pilot was naturally second-guessed by the press over his reluctance to remove his starting pitcher as the Giants batted around in the sixth. His explanation: "With Jack Russell nursing an injured thumb from yesterday's game, I had no one to send in who I thought could do any better than Crowder."[20]

Despite the shortfall in games, Cronin maintained a staunch attitude. "We'll send Earl Whitehill against them [tomorrow]. Just remember this is a seven game series, and we'll win it yet. Mark my words."[21]

GAME TWO HERO: Hal Schumacher GOAT: General Crowder
ATTENDANCE: 35,461
TIME OF GAME: 2:09
UMPIRES: HP–Moriarty; 1B–Pfirman; 2B–Ormsby; 3B—Moran.

Game Three

While Cronin tried to keep a positive approach, the rest of the team and their fans were having a more difficult time of it, according to this report of the club's arrival in D.C. from New York: "Only a small group of faithful rooters greeted the grim-faced group of Senators as they derailed last night after two disastrous days spent in almost vain swinging against the offerings of Carl Hubbell and Hal Schumacher."[22]

A cloudy day dawned over the nation's capital on Thursday, October 5, and intermittent showers started to fall over Griffith Stadium an hour before game time. The light rain forced the players off the field and brought out the tarpaulin, which was not removed from the infield until 1:15 p.m., only 15 minutes prior to the scheduled game time. The showers dampened the act of the Senators' traveling comedian and third base coach to some degree. "Al Schacht," read one of the various *news and notes* of the game addendums, "waited until the rain stopped before downing a battered top hat and leading one of the bands in 'It Ain't Gonna Rain No More' and 'How Dry I Am.' It promptly rained again."[23]

The rain had subsided to a drizzle when Washington owner Clark Griffith ordered the tarpaulin's removal in anticipation of a special guest's arrival. Minutes after the scheduled game time, the President of the United States, Franklin D. Roosevelt, arrived in a presidential limousine and was taken to honorary boxes reserved for him at the park. The president shook hands with Griffith and Judge Landis, and then Cronin and Terry. He hammed it up for newsreel footage and posed for flash photographs.

The ball players stood at attention, caps over their chests, as the "smartly uniformed" United States Army Band played "Hail to the Chief" and "The Star Spangled Banner." The Stars and Stripes was run up the flagpole in back of center field. The flag was then lowered to half-staff, in memoriam to William L. Veeck. The president of the Chicago Cubs had passed away from complications of influenza early that morning. The 67-year-old Veeck had been in critical condition for more than a week. (His death did not interrupt the 20th "City Series" between the Cubs and White Sox. The second game of the series was conducted at Wrigley Field as Game Three of the World Series was being played. Eight thousand-plus fans showed up in less than ideal weather conditions in Chicago to see their rival teams play.)

President Roosevelt threw out the ceremonial first ball. It was an American League ball, as would be used for the games in Washington, following usage of the National League's "brand" at the Polo Grounds. The president stayed for the entire game, in the company of several members of his cabinet. Keeping with a Washington tradition whereby members of the Senators jockeyed with one another, hoping to be on the receiving end of the presidential pitch, Heinie Manush turned out to be the lucky recipient of the "first toss" from the nation's chief executive. As a native New Yorker, the president had to be employing his best form of bipartisan diplomacy.

The skies cleared prior to Earl Whitehill's first delivery to leadoff batter Jo-Jo Moore. Some cheers for Moore from a contingent of New York fans who had made the trip to Washington could be distinguished in the crowd. Moore flied to short right field. Critz stretched the count to 3–2 before he was retired on a grounder to Bluege at third base. Terry swung at the first pitch and bounced to second baseman Myer, who completed the play with the toss to first.

The Senators, in their home white pinstripe uniforms with rigid "W" emblem on each sleeve, came out swinging against Giants starter Freddie Fitzsimmons. On a 2–2 pitch, Myer singled in between Ryan and Jackson. On the first pitch, Goose Goslin clubbed a double against the right field fence, Myer scooting around to third. Terry and Jackson had a quick get-together with Fitzsimmons. Manush popped up to Ryan in short left, the runners holding. Hi Bell began to warm up, on Terry's orders. Cleanup hitter Cronin stepped in. The skipper chopped a pitch to the left side, which Fitzsimmons cut off. Myer broke for home, but Fitzsimmons slipped and lost a play at the plate. The pitcher smartly opted for the out at first. Schulte, next up, sliced an opposite-field double to right. He barely beat Ott's throw into second. Bluege, who was on third base, sauntered home with the Senators' second run. Schulte became too aggressive on the base paths when sixth-place hitter Joe Kuhel bounced to Jackson at third base. Schulte was caught too far off second base and was tagged out after a brief rundown, Jackson to Critz, for the inning-ending putout.

The Giants put two men on base in the second frame, a one-out single by Kiddo Davis and walk to Travis Jackson. But Gus Mancuso grounded into a 6–4–3 double play to end the threat. Manush, in left, had made a fine play near the line, retiring Ott for the first out of the inning.

The Senators kept up the offensive pressure in the home half-inning. Bluege ripped the third double of the game already for the home team, just inside the third base foul line. With the pitcher on deck, Cronin let Luke Sewell hit away, and the catcher rapped to Critz at second, Bluege moving easily to third. Whitehill stepped up to the plate. He looked at a ball, and on the second pitch, Cronin called for the squeeze; Whitehill fouled the pitch into the dirt. A pitch later, in a good bunting count again, 2–1, Cronin tried to cross up the visitors. His pitcher swung away and missed. Then Whitehill hit a comebacker. Fitzsimmons tried to catch Bluege off third base, but his throw was late. Whitehill reached first on the fielder's choice. Myer came up with runners on the corners and stroked the fourth Washington double in ten batters, scoring Bluege and sending Whitehill prancing to third. Terry asked for time to speak to Fitzsimmons again, once more joined by Jackson. After the conference ended, Goslin lofted a fly to left. Moore pegged perfectly to Mancuso at home plate to nab Whitehill, who had tagged up. The double play ended the inning, with the Senators having to settle for the one run and a 3–0 lead.

Fitzsimmons and second-place hitter Critz both singled in the third inning. But outs by each of the batters preceding them quashed any real scoring chance. Blondy Ryan, hitting in front of Fitzsimmons, was robbed of a hit by second baseman Buddy Myer's leaping stab of his looping liner. On a groundout, leadoff hitter Moore forced Fitzsimmons at second. Terry then left two men on base, Moore and Critz, when he bounced out to first base. In the bottom half of the frame, Schulte recorded his second hit and the Senators' sixth. But there were two outs and nothing more came from it.

In the fourth inning, Jackson cracked a two-out double. He was left marooned at second by the next hitter, Mancuso, who flied out to center field. The Senators were retired in order over the next two innings and were held scoreless again in the sixth in spite of a leadoff single.

Following Mancuso's fly out to end the fourth, ten Giants hitters were dispatched without interruption until a one-out single in the eighth inning by Homer Peel, pinch-hitting for Fitzsimmons. The Giants were trailing, 4–0, at this point, with the Senators having plated another run on a Buddy Myer RBI single in the seventh. After Peel's hit, Moore rapped a grounder to Cronin, who booted it, with both runners safe. Critz tapped back to Whitehill, who threw Critz out at first. Terry batted with runners at second and third and two outs. The Giants first baseman popped one straight up, which Sewell caught right in front of the plate.

Replacing Fitzsimmons, Hi Bell pitched the bottom of the eighth without incident. Ott opened the ninth with a walk and got as far as third base before Whitehill registered the final out and shutout, 4–0. The left-hander, whose start was in question as late as a few minutes prior to game time because of the previously publicized sore elbow, had pitched the Senators back into the Series.

"Whitehill looked superb,"[24] crowed Cronin after the game. And who could argue? The 22-game winner allowed only five hits, one extra-base hit (Jackson's double) and two walks. The southpaw, who led the American League in starts with 37, struck out two, Mel Ott both times. "Whitehill was just too good for us today,"[25] admitted Terry. "Fitzsimmons was pitching well enough to win an ordinary ball game, but Whitehill was having a big day."

"Earl has been a mighty fine pitcher for us all year," his catcher, Luke Sewell, said the following day, "but I've never seen him with better control than was his fortune yesterday."[26]

Whitehill, for his part, revealed that he was getting stronger as the game wore on, the classic yardstick of a commanding performance by a pitcher. "I felt better as I went along. I was feeling great toward the end."[27]

GAME THREE HERO: Whitehill, GOAT: Fitzsimmons
ATTENDANCE: 25,727
TIME OF GAME: 1:55
UMPIRES: HP—Pfirman; 1B—Ormsby; 2B—Moran; 3B—Moriarty.

Game Four

"You can tell those Senators they'll see plenty more of Hubbell," Bill Terry had proclaimed after Hubbell's brilliant Game One performance. "I'm going to pitch him just as often as I can."²⁸ But after the Giants won Game Two, Terry had publicly toyed with the notion of using Roy Parmelee as his Game Four starter—*if* the Giants won the first game in Washington, or if, for some reason, Hubbell did not feel up to pitching on short rest. Following Whitehill's victory, that alternative was trashed. Terry announced Hubbell as his starter in the fourth game, without giving the ace left-hander much of a say, as it turned out.

The day after Hubbell's first-game victory, John McGraw had compared him to the pitcher he considered the greatest of them all. "They have qualities in common," the former Giants manager said. "Hubbell has Matty's coolness. He didn't become flustered when things went against him in the last two innings yesterday. He is unquestionably a very great pitcher and gives the Giants a big advantage in a short series."²⁹

McGraw's closing words were no more greatly reinforced than by Hubbell's own repeat virtuoso performance against the Senators on October 6. "It was the greatest ball game I ever played in,"³⁰ Terry said at the conclusion of Hubbell's and the Giants' 2–1 victory in 11 innings.

"I can't express what kind of game Hubbell pitched," raved the man who caught all of Hubbell's pitches throughout the extra-inning contest. "He was greater than he was in the opener. Can you imagine that, on two day's rest?" Gus Mancuso asked. "He's got the heart of a damn lion. The scoring chances we missed would break the spirit of four out of five pitchers, but Hubbell, he's the king of everything."³¹

"King Carl" did not allow an earned run in the game, outdueling Monte Weaver, the number four pitcher on the Washington staff. The Commander-in-Chief was not in attendance due to prior White House commitments.

The game began under sunny skies. A bigger turnout than yesterday was expected but never materialized. The 27-year-old Weaver walked Jo-Jo Moore on five pitches, leading off the encounter. Following Moore out of the third base visiting dugout, Critz hit a liner to Myer at second, doubling off Moore at first. Terry bounced a single to second, the ball skipping off Myer's glove. But Ott popped to Bluege at third base. Mr. Hubbell retired the first ten Washington batters.

Weaver seemed to find an early groove, putting the Giants down in order in the second and third innings. He retired Hughie Critz, leading off the fourth inning, as the eighth consecutive batter set down since Terry's hit.

Dead Ball Era great Honus Wagner is warmly received by opposing World Series managers Cronin and Terry, prior to Game Four in Washington.

Batting for the second time, Terry ended the string by driving a Weaver pitch deep to center field and into the temporary bleacher section that had been erected there (and in left field) to increase the park's seating capacity. Perhaps a bit flustered by the blast, Weaver walked Ott. Kiddo Davis beat out a dribbler down third to further perturb Washington's pitcher. Weaver induced a pop-up from Travis Jackson for the second out, but walked Mancuso on four pitches to fill the bases. Weaver collected himself and struck out Blondy Ryan—but not before Cronin had gestured for Jack Russell and Lefty Stewart to start throwing in the Senators' bullpen.

Trailing 1–0 in the home half of the fourth, Myer tried to bunt himself on. Falling to the ground, Hubbell made a fine play to come up with the ball. Lying on his side, he threw to first to barely nip the swift runner. With one out, Goslin recorded the home team's first hit, a single. Hubbell issued his first walk, on four pitches, to Heinie Manush. Cronin flied to Ott, with Goslin advancing to third. Schulte grounded to short; Critz made an athletic play to catch Ryan's off-line throw and force Manush at second base.

In the Giants' next turn, Hubbell led off with a line drive that Cronin caught. Moore reached base for the second time with a single to left field. Critz was retired on a pop-up to his second base counterpart, Myer. Terry flied deep to center. Hubbell came out in the lower half of the fifth inning and struck out Joe Kuhel swinging. Moore sprinted into left-center to haul down a drive hit by Ossie Bluege. Sewell stroked a pitch into right for a hit. Weaver fanned.

As the sixth inning's first batter, Ott registered his first hit since his 4-for-4 showing in the Series opener. (He had been 0-for-6, but with four walks.) Davis bunted Ott to second. Myer camped under a pop-up off the bat of Jackson in short right for the second out, Ott holding at second. Preferring to pitch to Ryan, Cronin ordered Mancuso intentionally passed. The strategy worked, as Ryan tapped back to the box for the third out.

The Senators put the leadoff man on base for the first time in the game when Myer opened the sixth inning with a base hit. He was duly sacrificed to second by Goslin. Manush was called out on a close play at first, after grounding to Critz, with Hubbell covering. Manush began walking back to the bag, thinking he was safe. When he was advised otherwise, he engaged in a hot dispute with first base umpire Charlie Moran, who ejected the Senators outfielder. The crowd loudly voiced their displeasure at the umpire's call. A pop bottle rained down from the second-deck right field stands, settling close to Moran. (While this was occurring, Adolfo Luque began warming up in the bullpen. Hubbell was due to lead off the next inning.) Play was finally resumed with Myer on third and two outs. Cronin, who was the on-deck hitter and had considerably argued the call on Manush's behalf, had to collect himself in order to hit. He swung through a 2–2 pitch and struck out.

In the next inning, right fielder Goslin shifted over to left field to replace Manush, while back-up Dave Harris took over Goslin's spot in the right field

8. The World Series: The Terrymen versus the Croninites 191

pasture. In an apparent defiant gesture, Manush took his regular defensive position at the start of the inning. The ejected player's reluctant removal was recorded by one of the wire services.

> Manush stood like a statue in the left field position. [Umpire] Ormsby waved Manush to the dugout. But Heinie just waved right back at him. Manager Cronin ordered Harris to play. Manush was wild with anger as he walked from the field. Cronin and Myer and Bluege escorted him to the dugout. [Umpire] Moriarty came up to Manush and put his arm around him as he walked the few last sad steps.[32]

When play commenced, Hubbell batted and grounded out to Cronin. Moore doubled into the left-center field gap. Critz bounced to Cronin and was thrown out. Moore was able to advance to third on the play. On the first pitch thrown to him, Terry hit a soft pop-up to Weaver. The multitude in attendance emitted extended jeers at Moran.

In the bottom of the seventh, still holding the 1–0 lead, Hubbell coerced Schulte to pop up to Terry for the inning's initial out. Kuhel bunted ineffectively back to Hubbell, but the pitcher bobbled the ball and lost a chance for an easy out. Playing for the tie, Cronin had Bluege bunt Kuhel over to second, with Hubbell fielding it and Terry recording the putout. Sewell singled to center field, scoring Kuhel with the tying run. Weaver popped to Critz for the final out.

Leading the top of the eighth, Ott stroked his second hit of the game, to Cronin at short, who could not make the play. Davis whiffed. Jackson hit a hard shot to Myer, who had to take the out at first (Cronin was late covering second). With Ott in scoring position, Mancuso tapped a 3–2 offering back to Weaver.

In the home half of the eighth, Myer led off an inning for the third time and walked, Hubbell's second free pass of the game. Luque began loosening up again. Goslin's bunt attempt was fielded by Hubbell, who wheeled and threw to second to force Myer. Dave Harris bounced to second but not hard enough for the Giants to turn two. Cronin dropped a base hit in front of Mel Ott, and Harris sped to third. Terry and Jackson met with Hubbell. The pitcher remained focused. With the go-ahead run 90 feet away, he prodded Schulte to swing under a pitch and pop it to Critz, who squeezed it for the inning-ending out.

The Giants threatened in the ninth. Ryan led off with a single. He was sacrificed to second by Hubbell and moved to third on Moore's soft comebacker to Weaver, but was stranded there when Critz lined out to Harris in right field. The crowd began its natural ninth-inning motivational cheering, but Hubbell systematically stifled the collective whooping by registering his first 1-2-3 inning since the fifth. The 1–1 game moved into extra frames.

The hometown rooters gained back some inspirational wind after Weaver set down the Giants' three, four and five hitters, in order, in the top of the tenth inning. The pitcher's spot was due to lead off the bottom of the stanza for the Senators. Cronin did not send in a pinch-hitter. Weaver struck out. The next batter, Myer, singled. Goslin bounced out, but Myer was able to advance to second. Hubbell briefly lost his command and walked Harris on four pitches. Regrouping, the left-hander threw a first-pitch strike past Cronin. After a ball, Cronin swung and missed the third pitch. On the 1–2 offering, Hubbell retired the dangerous hitter on a force out, short to second. It was the third time in the game Cronin had made an out with a runner in scoring position.

Jackson started the Giants' 11th inning promisingly with a single against Weaver, who had not pitched past the ninth inning in any of his 21 starts on the season. Jackson reached second on Mancuso's successful sacrifice. Then Blondy Ryan came through with his biggest hit of the season—and career—a single to left field. Jackson, bad knees and all, was able to score. Hubbell followed with another single, prompting Cronin to make a pitching change. The top bullpen man in the league, Jack Russell, entered the game. Stranding runners on first and second, Russell struck out Moore and retired Critz on a fly out to Schulte.

Protecting the slim lead, Hubbell immediately ran into trouble in the home team's last at-bat. Schulte led off with a hard single to left. The boisterous crowd cheered. On the first pitch, Kuhel laid down a well-placed bunt along the first base line. The ball, appearing to be rolling foul, kicked back and stayed fair when it apparently struck an undetected bit of hardened earth. Terry hopped in the air in dismay. Kuhel was safe at first. The fans roared. Bluege bunted, moving the runners into scoring position. All five of the Giants' inner defensive players converged around Hubbell. "I guess you saw us huddle," Terry candidly told reporters after the game. "Well, I didn't know what to do. But Ryan and Critz knew. 'Walk Sewell, Bill,' they suggested all in the same breath and 'we'll get that next guy to hit into a double play.'"[33]

Sewell was passed intentionally, loading the bases. The "next guy" was pinch-hitter Cliff Bolton, batting for Russell. Bolton, a back-up catcher, had been Cronin's most productive emergency hitter throughout the season. He was also a left-handed swinger. Cronin had right-handed batters available on the bench, though not as many as usual. One of them, Dave Harris had been called to duty earlier in place of the ejected Manush. Cronin went with Bolton based on the player's performance off the bench that season (9-for-22) and perhaps also from a gained insight in Hubbell's greater effectiveness on right-handed batters with his screwball. Cronin may have been tempted to use left-handed-hitting Sam Rice. At 43 years of age, the longtime Washington star had hit .294 in 73 games as a pinch-hitter and part-time outfielder. He also singled as an emergency batter in Game Two. Bolton had pinch-hit unsuccessfully in Game Two. All things considered, the choice of Bolton seemed more defensible than not.

Washington right-hander Tommy Thomas was loosening up in case the game was extended. With a Senators player occupying every base, Bolton stepped in and Hubbell's first pitch sailed high. Bolton swung over the next pitch without making contact, frustrating the anxiously excited spectators. Hubbell missed with his next pitch and the decibel excitement increased again. The unflappable Hubbell delivered; Bolton swung and hit into a tailor-made double play—Ryan to Critz to Terry. The Giants were victorious, 2-1. "I think Hubbell and Weaver both pitched magnificent ball," said the dejected Cronin in his locker room comments. "Of course Carl has done it before. But Monte was almost as great this afternoon. He lived his greatest World Series day, and I'm only sorry we couldn't score more runs for him."[34]

Bill Terry's 15-year-old son and wife were in attendance. The teenager was let into the Giants' clubhouse after the nail-biter. "How's mother?"[35] the drained Terry asked him.

"She had to have smelling salts,"[36] Bill Jr. grinned.

GAME FOUR HEROES: Hubbell and Ryan; GOAT: Cronin (as player and manager)
ATTENDANCE: 26,762
TIME OF GAME: 2:59
UMPIRES: HP—Ormsby; 1B—Moran; 2B—Moriarty; 3B—Pfirman

Game Five

Hal Schumacher was a physically worn pitcher. A photo of him taken prior to the second game of the World Series with the Senators' General Crowder showed him as a gaunt young man with markedly sunken cheekbones. The rigors of the season, his first as a regular starter, had taken their toll. Ahead as he was in the Series, Terry had no reason to bring Schumacher back, on two days' rest, to pitch Game Five. Schumacher had simply been too good in Game Two, and the performance conceivably swayed Terry's better judgment. Parmelee would have been the better choice for the final game in Washington, holding back Schumacher for Game Six, with Hubbell for the deciding game, if needed.

Cronin came back with his ace, Crowder, on short rest, and the October 7 autumn confrontation opened with a Game Two rematch on the mound.

General Crowder delivered the first pitch of the game, under sunny skies, to Jo-Jo Moore. The Giants left fielder promptly smacked it past third baseman Ossie Bluege into left field for a hit. With one out, Terry singled, sending Moore to third. Ott came up, and Jack Russell began warming up. Catcher Sewell trotted out to speak to his pitcher. In an early test, Crowder reached back and struck out Ott. The fifth batter, Davis, grounded into a force play, wrapping up the half-inning. Washington rooters enthusiastically applauded Crowder as he walked to the dugout.

The applause built up again as Buddy Myer stepped in as the first batter against Schumacher. Myer lofted a ball to Moore in left-center for the first out. Goslin obtained the Senators' first hit, a single. Manush, who had been ejected yesterday, hit one on the nose but right at Jackson, who fired to first to double off Goslin.

A leadoff single by Jackson and a walk to Mancuso put the Giants back in business at the start of the second. Eighth-place hitter Ryan was coming up with the pitcher to follow. Although Ryan was coming off a two-hit game, including the game-winner, he was called on to bunt. He did so successfully. Schumacher, a .214 hitter on the year, came through with a bloop hit over the second base bag, scoring Jackson and Mancuso. The next two hitters, Moore and Critz, made outs to right fielder Goslin.

Ott came running in to pull off a nifty catch of Joe Cronin's dying quail for the first out of the Senators' second at-bat. Schulte bounced out and Kuhel hit a lazy fly that Moore camped under near the left field line.

For the third inning in a row, the Giants' leadoff man reached base. Terry slapped a hanging curve into right field for his second hit. Crowder's curve was more effective on Ott, who, with two strikes, swung and missed the breaking pitch. Davis popped up to Cronin in short left field, and Crowder fanned Jackson on an offspeed pitch. In the bottom of the inning, Ryan, at shortstop, made all three outs on Washington's 7, 8 and 9 hitters. In the fourth, each team put a man on base but did not score.

Crowder retired the Giants in order in the fifth, including Terry and Ott. Schumacher did not have such an easy time of it with Crowder's teammates. Schulte beat out a slow dribbler to third baseman Jackson for the Senators' second hit of the game. Kuhel stroked a hit to left field, getting the crowd even more loudly into the game. The Giants' infield conferred on the mound. Bluege attempted to bunt on three consecutive pitches and was unsuccessful, fouling off the third strike. Catcher Sewell hit one on the button to Moore in left, who caught the ball running back. With Crowder batting, Schumacher uncorked a wild pitch. Schulte advanced to third but Kuhel held at first. Crowder grounded to short.

The Senators and their fans regretted the missed scoring opportunity

8. The World Series: The Terrymen versus the Croninites 195

even more in the subsequent half-inning. Davis doubled barely inside the foul line in left field. Jackson moved him up on a bunt. Mancuso was due up with one out. The Senators' infielders crowded around Crowder in the center of the diamond. When they returned to their positions, Mancuso doubled into left-center, easily plating Davis. Cronin yanked Crowder. Russell came in and whiffed Ryan and Schumacher.

The Giants led, 3–0, with Schumacher needing 12 more outs. He recorded only two—the first two batters of the sixth inning. Schumacher set down Myer and Goslin before the home squad mounted a two-out rally. Manush singled. The Senators received a break when Cronin bailed away from a pitch, which somehow struck his bat. The ball caromed all the way into short left-center field. The "excuse me" hit left runners at first and third. Schulte then laid into one and clubbed the Senators' second home run of the Series, tying the game. As the screaming fans rose to their feet, Terry and his men gathered around Schumacher. Adolfo Luque had gotten up in the Giants' bullpen. After the players had manned their positions again, Kuhel ripped a single past Critz, and Terry visited his pitcher again. Terry went back to first. The seventh batter of the inning, Bluege, hit a hot one down to Jackson, who made a diving stop. His throw to first was in the dirt, bouncing off Terry's chest. The errant throw allowed Kuhel to race to third. Bluege was awarded a hit—the Senators' fifth in a row—and a throwing error was charged to Jackson for permitting Kuhel the extra base. Schumacher, who had yielded only three hits and one walk entering the sixth, had run out of gas. Terry, from first base, called for Luque.

Mancuso came out to the mound to meet Luque and say something to the veteran hurler. His first pitch to Sewell was a sweeping curve that skipped in front of the plate, temporarily escaping Mancuso but not far enough for Kuhel to attempt to score from third base. The Giants catcher went back out to confer with his pitcher, and he was joined by Ryan and Terry. Luque had crossed up Mancuso, who had signaled for a fastball. The pitcher, Russell, was on deck, but Terry decided to let Luque go after Sewell. Cronin would have faced a dilemma if Terry had forced his hand by intentionally walking Sewell (and thereby putting another runner in scoring position). Would Cronin have permitted Russell, who had just entered the game and who was far and way his best reliever, to bat, or would he have pulled him and used Bolton again, or Sam Rice this time, as a pinch hitter? Terry decided against inviting that scenario. The second pitch to Sewell was another ball. Sewell swung at the "cripple pitch" offering and fouled it off. Luque kept Sewell waiting a bit as he tossed over to first base, keeping the baserunner honest. Kuhel, at third, and Bluege, at first, took their leads. Luque delivered. Sewell grounded to Critz, who tossed it to Terry for the final out.

Luque escaped the jam, but it was a brand new ballgame, 3–3, much to the delight of the majority in attendance. Six batters came up to the plate in the seventh inning and all were sent back to the bench in orderly fashion; Luque struck out the side.

In the Giants' eighth frame, Davis cracked a one-out single, but Jackson hit into a twin killing. The Senators similarly tried to prosper with a one-out hit by Cronin in their turn. The situation was made more exciting as the home run hero from a prior inning followed Cronin. Schulte gave the clapping fans an ever-so brief thrill when he flied deep to left-center field, Davis ranging back to pull in the ball. Luque retired Kuhel on a bouncer to Jackson.

Mancuso popped up to start the Giants' ninth. Ryan followed with a single to right field; Goslin failed on a shoestring catch attempt. The shortstop unwisely tried to stretch the hit into a double but was gunned down at second base by Goslin. Luque singled to right center field, becoming the first Latin American player to hit safely in the World Series. Moore chased a pitch outside of the strike zone for strike three.

Luque put down the first two batters to face him in the sudden-death ninth inning. He whiffed Bluege and had Sewell top one to Ryan on the left side of the infield. Covering the game, legendary sportswriter Grantland Rice provided this overview of Luque and his developing performance: "Short and now chunky, almost fat, the Cuban, with a fast, jerky motion … had a low, fast breaking curve ball that had the Senators hitters helpless all down the stretch."[37] But with two outs, the aged pitcher lost his concentration with Jack Russell and walked his mound opponent. Russell was forced at second by Myer, who bounced to Critz, who flipped to Ryan at second for the force. For the second straight day, the World Series extended into extra innings.

In the tenth, Russell began his fifth inning of work in relief. In quick succession, Critz flied out and Terry grounded out. That brought up Mel Ott. The slugger took two balls and a called strike. Ott put a tremendous scare into Russell and the vocal majority on the next pitch when he whacked a screaming liner into the right field stands on the wrong side of the foul pole. He fouled Russell's fifth pitch back into the screen. After getting even in the count, Russell clearly meant to retire Ott, rather than continue pitching carefully to him and face a far less menacing Kiddo Davis, on deck. Russell's sixth pitch was met squarely by the home run hitter, who drove the offering into left-center field. The ball sailed high and deep and descended into the bleachers, just out of the reach of center fielder Fred Schulte. The ball apparently glanced off Schulte's glove, as he fell over the short wall into the non-permanent stands. For some reason, second base umpire Cy Pfirman decreed a ground rule double, then reversed himself after consulting with his three

8. The World Series: The Terrymen versus the Croninites 197

umpiring associates, correctly ruling a home run. The final ruling sat well with very few in the ballpark. Cronin and several other Senators surrounded Pfirman to voice their stern objections. Umpiring crew chief George Moriarty tried to calm Cronin down. Later, Cronin would concede the issue of Ott's home run. "My contention was that Schulte butted the ball over the rail off his knee," he would say. "But I guess it went in on the fly all right."[38] Fans continued to boo as play resumed and as Russell corralled a Kiddo Davis bouncer to the box to close the half-inning.

The crowd was still booing when Luque began *his* fifth inning of work. The all-important first out was secured on a fine play by Terry, who scooped up a difficult grounder and tossed to his pitcher covering the bag. Manush lined to Critz, and things appeared grim for the American League champions. But Cronin garnered his third straight hit, a single, which breathed life back into the crowd. Schulte stepped to the plate and Luque pitched cautiously to him. Too cautiously—he walked the Senators' center fielder, pushing the tying run to second base. Schulte had hurt his leg in the bleacher dive for Ott's home run and was limping. Cronin inserted John Kerr as a running substitute for the banged-up outfielder.

"The crowd began screaming for Kuhel to bat in the tying run," recorded one writer, "but Luque speaks very little English anyway and didn't understand what they were saying to frighten him."[39] Luque's first pitch was a called strike. Kuhel swung and missed the second pitch, putting him in the hole. Damon Runyon, writing for the Hearst syndicate, described Luque's "first two pitches [as] curves that would have done Mae West credit."[40] On the third pitch, Luque threw his million-dollar curve. Kuhel waved at it and missed, to the collective groan of the frenzied Washington supporters.

"When the last ball thudded into Mancuso's mitt," documented another scribe, "the Giant catcher leaped far off the ground, waving both arms in the air and letting out a victory whoop that could be heard above the noise of the crowd. Then he ran to throw his arm around Luque, holding out the victory ball to him when the pitcher asked for it."[41]

GAME FIVE HEROES: Luque and Ott; GOAT: Jack Russell
ATTENDANCE: 28,454
TIME OF GAME: 2:39
UMPIRES: HP–Moran; 1B—Moriarty; 2B–Pfirman ; 3B—Ormsby.

Hubbell was voted MVP of the World Series. He hurled 20 innings and did not give up an earned run. Ott, who homered his first and last times up in the Series and who led all hitters with batting and slugging marks of .389 and .722, came in second. Blondy Ryan, who had the winning hit in Game Four, placed third. The Giants outscored their opponents, 16–11. Jack Russell was the Washington team's standout performer. Pitching in three games, Russell allowed only one run (Ott's second home run), posting a 0.87 ERA in 10⅓ innings.

The full players' share came to roughly $4,600 for the winning Giants and $3,400 for the runner-up Senators, taken from a cash-paying clientele of 164,076 and gate receipts of $679,365. The Giants had to give back to the public at large a hefty gate from tickets sold for the unplayed Game Six. The attendance for the five games was disappointing but consistent with the reduced patronage seen in big league ballparks throughout the year. Total attendance fell under three million in the American League in 1933, a steep decline, especially if compared to the over five million league gate in 1925, the last time the Senators participated in a World Series, and the 4.6 million cumulative audiences throughout the Junior Circuit as recently as 1930. It was a similar turnstile story in the elder league, with 3,162,821 fans showing up for games during the season compared to the 5.4 million peak in 1930. None of the World Series games sold out, although the first game in New York came close. The additional bleacher seating Clark Griffith installed was not needed.

Griffith made his way to the Giants' clubhouse to congratulate Bill Terry personally after the final pitch. "The Giants played great ball and deserved their victory,"[42] the gracious owner of the Senators acknowledged.

In the Series, Terry outgeneraled Cronin in all phases, from starting pitching selections to in-game moves. Terry's choice of bringing back Schumacher on short rest to pitch the fifth game was questionable, but things worked out due to the stellar relief pitching of Luque and home run swing of Ott. The choice of bringing in the second-oldest player in the National League was thought out. "I sent Luque in because I figured his low breaking curve would be just the thing to follow Schumacher's speed," the Giants manager advised. "Luque is 43 years old. Yet he had as much stuff today for three or four innings as he ever has—and I can say that's plenty."[43]

In the losing clubhouse, a dejected Cronin all but conceded losing to the better team. "Terry's got a fine club," he said, "and they hustled hard. They've got great pitching. Boost them to the skies. They deserve it."[44] Employing unadulterated praise for the man who succeeded him, John McGraw summarized the Series for the team that sat on top of the sports world.

> It's full time to realize that Bill Terry has done one of the greatest jobs in baseball. I haven't seen a team that pulled together any better, that showed more winning spirit on the field or that had more consistently resourceful pitching. In a short series, pitching is fully 75 percent of the issue and the marvelous work of Hubbell and Schumacher and the veteran Adolfo Luque turned the scales in favor of the Giants.[45]

Postscript

The encore season for the world champion Giants culminated in a crashing collapse at the worst possible time. Losing six out of their final seven games—including the last five in a row—the Giants squandered a three-game, first place lead and lost out on the pennant by two games. Sorely compounding the matter, the defending champions were beaten the last two games of the 1934 campaign by the second-division Brooklyn Dodgers. Prior to the season, Terry had made an off-the-cuff reply to the press about his team's hated rival's chances at competing for the NL flag. "I was just wondering," asked Terry, "whether they [Brooklyn] were still in the league?" The sardonically-spinned remark came back to bite Terry and his club and ingrained itself in the long-standing acerbic history between the two long gone but not forgotten New York clubs. (Terry, for the remainder of his playing career, would be booed louder than any other Giants player visiting Ebbets Field. He was also jeered at the Polo Grounds whenever a large contingent of Dodger fans showed up, which was often, when the Giants and Brooklyn squared off. Terry was booed not only when he batted, but when he traipsed over to the pitcher's mound to consult with his hurler. He became caustically referred to as "Vinegar Bill" by Dodgers' fans.)

The Giants steadfastly won 91 games in 1935 but finished well behind the 100-win, pennant-grabbing Chicago Cubs. In 1936 and '37, Terry led his team back to the World Series. Both times, the Giants were defeated by Joe McCarthy's New York Yankees. Though Terry's Giants failed to beat the American League champions in back-to-back years, his teams were the only ones to win any Fall Classic games against the fearsome Yankees during their seven World Series appearances from 1927 to 1939.

Charles Stoneham was not around to enjoy the Giants' subsequent pennant captures. He died from Bright's disease, January 6, 1936. His 32-year-old son Horace assumed control of the Giants, becoming the youngest team owner in baseball history.

Appendix: New York Giants 1933 Team Statistics

POS	No.	Player	G	AB	R	H	2B	3B	HR	RBI	SB	BB	SO	AVG	OBP	SLG
C	8	Gus Mancuso	144	481	39	127	17	2	6	56	0	48	21	.264	.331	.345
1B	3	Bill Terry	123	475	68	153	20	5	6	58	3	40	23	[.322]	.375	.423
2B	6	Hughie Critz	133	558	68	137	18	5	2	33	4	23	24	.246	.279	.306
3B	7	Johnny Vergez	123	458	57	124	21	[6]	16	72	1	39	[66]	.271	.332	.448
SS	23	Blondy Ryan	146	525	47	125	10	5	3	48	0	15	62	.238	.259	.293
LF	1	Jo-Jo Moore	132	524	56	153	16	5	0	42	4	21	27	.292	.323	.342
CF	2	Kiddo Davis	126	434	61	112	20	4	7	37	[10]	25	30	.258	.298	.371
RF	4	Mel Ott	[152]	[580]	[98]	[164]	[36]	1	[23]	[103]	1	**75**	48	.283	.367	.467
C	9	Paul Richards	51	87	4	17	3	0	0	10	0	3	12	.195	.222	.230
C	28	Harry Danning	3	2	0	0	0	0	0	0	0	1	0	.000	.333	.000
1B	22	Sam Leslie	40	137	21	44	12	3	3	27	0	12	9	.321	.380	[.518]
1B	27	Joe Malay	8	24	0	3	0	0	0	2	0	0	0	.125	.125	.125
IF	24	Bernie James	60	125	22	28	2	1	1	10	5	8	12	.224	.271	.280
IF	5	Travis Jackson	53	122	11	30	5	0	0	12	2	8	11	.246	.292	.287
3B	7	Chuck Dressen	16	45	3	10	4	0	0	3	0	1	4	.222	.239	.311
OF	16	Lefty O'Doul	78	229	31	70	9	1	9	35	1	29	17	.306	[.388]	.472
OF	26	Homer Peel	84	148	16	38	1	1	1	12	0	14	10	.257	.325	.297
OF	14	Phil Weintraub	8	15	3	3	0	0	1	1	0	3	2	.200	.333	.400
OF	27	Hank Leiber	6	10	1	2	0	0	0	0	0	0	2	.200	.200	.200

Team leader in brackets. League leader in **bold**.

POS	No.	Player	G	GS	CG	SHO	GF	SV	IP	H	HR	R	ER	BB	SO	W	L	ERA
P	11	Carl Hubbell	[45]	33	[22]	**10**	11	[5]	**308.2**	[256]	6	69	57	47	[156]	**23**	[12]	**1.66**
P	17	H. Schumacher	35	33	21	7	1	1	258.2	199	9	71	62	84	96	19	[12]	2.16
P	12	F. Fitzsimmons	36	**35**	13	1	1	0	251.2	243	[14]	[106]	[81]	72	65	14	11	2.90
P	18	Roy Parmelee	32	32	14	3	0	0	218.1	191	9	94	77	77	132	13	8	3.17
P	15	Hi Bell	38	7	1	1	[22]	[5]	105.1	100	4	31	24	20	24	6	5	2.05
P	20	Adolfo Luque	35	0	0	0	[22]	4	80.1	75	4	27	24	19	23	8	2	2.69
P	19	Glenn Spencer	17	3	1	0	5	0	47.1	52	3	33	27	26	14	0	2	5.13
P	10	Watty Clark	16	5	0	0	5	0	44	58	3	25	23	11	11	3	4	4.70
P	22	Bill Shores	8	3	1	0	3	0	36.2	41	4	18	16	14	20	2	1	3.93
P	25	Jack Salveson	8	2	2	0	4	0	30.2	30	4	17	13	14	8	0	2	3.82
P	28	George Uhle	6	1	0	0	4	0	13.2	16	1	12	12	6	4	1	1	7.90
P	16	Ray Starr	6	2	0	0	3	0	13.1	19	0	11	8	10	2	0	1	5.40
Total			282	156	75	22	81	15	1408.2	1280	61	514	424	400	555	91	61	**2.71**

Team leader in brackets. League leader in **bold**.

World Series Line Scores

Tuesday, October 3, Polo Grounds

	1	2	3	4	5	6	7	8	9	R	H	E
Washington Senators	0	0	0	1	0	0	0	0	1	2	5	3
New York Giants	2	0	2	0	0	0	0	0	x	4	10	2

WSH—Stewart, Russell (3), Thomas (8) and Sewell
NYG—Hubbell and Mancuso
WP—Carl Hubbell
LP—Lefty Stewart
SAVE—none
HOME RUNS: WSH—none
NYG—Ott

Wednesday, October 4, Polo Grounds

	1	2	3	4	5	6	7	8	9	R	H	E
Washington Senators	0	0	1	0	0	0	0	0	0	1	5	0
New York Giants	0	0	0	0	0	6	0	0	x	6	10	0

WSH—Crowder, Thomas (6), McColl (7) and Sewell
NYG—Schumacher and Mancuso
WP—Hal Schumacher
LP—General Crowder
SAVE—none
HOME RUNS: WSH—Goslin
NYG—none

Thursday, October 5, Griffith Stadium

	1	2	3	4	5	6	7	8	9	R	H	E
New York Giants	0	0	0	0	0	0	0	0	0	0	5	0
Washington Senators	2	1	0	0	0	0	1	0	x	4	9	1

NYG—Fitzsimmons, Bell (8) and Mancuso
WSH—Whitehill and Sewell
WP—Earl Whitehill
LP—Freddie Fitzsimmons
SAVE—none
HOME RUNS: NYG—none
WSH—none

Friday, October 6, Griffith Stadium

	1	2	3	4	5	6	7	8	9	10	11	R	H	E
New York Giants	0	0	0	1	0	0	0	0	0	0	1	2	11	1
Washington Senators	0	0	0	0	0	1	0	0	0	0	0	1	8	0

NYG—Hubbell and Mancuso
WSH—Weaver, Russell (11) and Sewell

New York Giants 1933 Team Statistics

WP—Carl Hubbell
LP—Monte Weaver
SAVE—none
HOME RUNS: NYG—Terry
WSH—none

Saturday, October 7, Griffith Stadium

	1	2	3	4	5	6	7	8	9	10	R	H	E
New York Giants	0	2	0	0	0	1	0	0	0	1	4	11	1
Washington Senators	0	0	0	0	0	3	0	0	0	0	3	10	0

NYG—Schumacher, Luque (6) and Mancuso
WSH—Crowder, Russell (6) and Sewell
WP—Dolf Luque
LP—Jack Russell
SAVE—none
HOME RUNS: NYG—Ott (2)
WSH—Schulte

source: baseball-reference.com

World Series Batting and Pitching Records (New York Giants)

	POS	G	AB	R	H	2B	3B	HR	RBI	BB	IBB	SO	HBP	SH	SB	CS	AVG	OBP	SLG
Gus Mancuso	C	5	17	2	2	1	0	0	2	3	1	0	0	1	0	0	.118	.250	.176
Bill Terry	1B	5	22	3	6	1	0	1	1	0	0	0	0	0	0	0	.273	.273	.455
Hughie Critz	2B	5	22	2	3	0	0	0	0	1	0	0	0	0	0	0	.136	.174	.136
Travis Jackson	3B	5	18	3	4	1	0	0	2	1	0	3	0	2	0	0	.222	.263	.278
Blondy Ryan	SS	5	18	0	5	0	0	0	1	1	0	5	0	1	0	0	.278	.316	.278
Jo-Jo Moore	LF	5	22	1	5	1	0	0	1	1	0	3	0	0	0	0	.227	.261	.273
Kiddo Davis	CF	5	19	1	7	1	0	0	0	0	0	3	0	0	0	0	.368	.368	.421
Mel Ott	RF	5	18	3	7	0	0	2	4	4	1	4	0	0	0	1	.389	.500	.722
Homer Peel	OF	2	2	0	1	0	0	0	0	0	0	0	0	1	0	0	.500	.500	.500
Lefty O'Doul		1	1	1	1	0	0	0	2	0	0	0	0	0	0	0	1.000	1.000	1.000
Carl Hubbell	P	2	7	0	2	0	0	0	0	0	0	0	0	1	0	0	.286	.286	.286
Hal Schumacher	P	2	7	0	2	0	0	0	3	0	0	3	0	0	0	0	.286	.286	.286
F Fitzsimmons	P	1	0	1	0	0	0	0	0	0	0	0	0	0	0	0	.500	.500	.500
Adolfo Luque	P	1	1	0	1	0	0	0	0	0	0	0	0	0	0	0	1.000	1.000	1.000
Hi Bell	P	1	0	0	0	0	0	0	0	0	0	0	0	0	0	0	—	—	—
Total		50	176	16	47	5	0	3	16	11	2	21	0	3	0	1	.267	.310	.347

	POS	G	GS	CG	SHO	GF	SV	IP	H	HR	R	ER	BB	IB	SO	WP	HBP	W	L	ERA
Carl Hubbell	P	2	2	2	0	0	0	20	13	0	3	0	6	1	15	0	0	2	0	0.00
Hal Schumacher	P	2	2	1	0	0	0	14.2	13	2	4	4	5	0	3	2	0	1	0	2.45
F Fitzsimmons	P	1	1	0	0	0	0	7	9	0	4	4	0	0	2	0	0	0	1	5.14
Adolfo Luque	P	1	0	0	0	1	0	4.1	2	0	0	0	2	0	5	0	0	1	0	0.00
Hi Bell	P	1	0	0	0	1	0	1	0	0	0	0	0	0	0	0	0	0	0	0.00
Total		7	5	3	0	2	0	47	37	2	11	8	13	1	25	2	0	4	1	1.53

World Series Batting and Pitching Records (Washington Senators)

	POS	G	AB	R	H	2B	3B	HR	RBI	BB	IBB	SO	HBP	SH	SB	CS	AVG	OBP	SLG
Luke Sewell	C	5	17	1	3	0	0	0	1	2	1	0	0	0	1	0	.176	.263	.176
Joe Kuhel	1B	5	20	1	3	0	0	0	1	1	0	4	0	0	0	1	.150	.190	.150
Buddy Meyer	2B	5	20	2	6	1	0	0	2	2	0	3	0	0	0	0	.300	.364	.350
Ossie Bluege	3B	5	16	1	2	1	0	0	0	1	0	6	0	2	0	0	.125	.176	.188
Joe Cronin	SS	5	22	1	7	0	0	0	2	0	0	2	0	0	0	0	.318	.318	.318
Heine Manush	LF	5	18	2	2	0	0	0	0	2	0	1	0	0	0	1	.111	.200	.111
Fred Schulte	CF	5	21	1	7	1	0	1	4	1	0	1	0	0	0	0	.333	.364	.524
Goose Goslin	RF	5	20	2	5	1	0	1	1	1	0	3	0	1	0	0	.250	.286	.450
Dave Harris	OF	3	2	0	0	0	0	0	0	2	0	0	0	0	0	0	.000	.500	.000
Cliff Bolton		2	2	0	0	0	0	0	0	0	0	0	0	0	0	0	.000	.000	.000
Sam Rice		1	1	0	1	0	0	0	0	0	0	0	0	0	0	0	1.000	1.000	1.000
John Kerr		1	0	0	0	0	0	0	0	0	0	0	0	0	0	0	—	—	—
General Crowder	P	2	4	0	1	0	0	0	0	0	0	0	0	0	0	0	.250	.250	.250
Monte Weaver	P	1	4	0	0	0	0	0	0	0	0	2	0	0	0	0	.000	.000	.000
Earl Whitehill	P	1	3	0	0	0	0	0	0	0	0	0	0	0	0	0	.000	.000	.000
Jack Russell	P	3	2	0	0	0	0	0	0	1	0	2	0	0	0	0	.000	.333	.000
Lefty Stewart	P	1	1	0	0	0	0	0	0	0	0	1	0	0	0	0	.000	.000	.000
Alex McColl	P	1	0	0	0	0	0	0	0	0	0	0	0	0	0	0	—	—	—
Tommy Thomas	P	2	0	0	0	0	0	0	0	0	0	0	0	0	0	0	—	—	—
Total		58	173	11	37	4	0	2	11	13	1	25	0	3	1	0	.214	.269	.272

	POS	G	GS	CG	SHO	GF	SV	IP	H	HR	R	ER	BB	IB	SO	WP	HBP	W	L	ERA
General Crowder	P	2	2	0	0	0	0	11	16	0	9	9	5	1	7	1	0	0	1	7.36
Jack Russell	P	3	0	0	0	2	0	10.1	8	1	1	1	0	0	7	0	0	0	1	0.87
Monte Weaver	P	1	1	0	0	0	0	10.1	11	1	2	2	4	1	3	0	0	0	1	1.74
Earl Whitehill	P	1	1	1	1	0	0	9	5	0	0	0	2	0	2	1	0	1	0	0.00
Lefty Stewart	P	1	1	0	0	0	0	2	6	1	4	2	0	0	0	0	0	0	1	9.00
Alex McColl	P	1	0	0	0	1	0	2	0	0	0	0	0	0	0	0	0	0	0	0.00
Tommy Thomas	P	2	0	0	0	1	0	1.1	1	0	0	0	0	0	2	0	0	0	0	0.00
Total		11	5	1	1	4	0	46	47	3	16	14	11	2	21	2	0	1	4	2.74

source: retrosheet.org

Chapter Notes

Introduction

1. David George Surdam, *Wins, Losses, & Empty Seats: How Baseball Outlasted The Great Depression* (Lincoln: University of Nebraska Press, 2011), 10.

Chapter 1

1. A variant to Terry's face-to-face words of acceptance to McGraw's offer was "I accept." Both Blanche McGraw and Peter Williams wrote, in their books, "I'll take it" as what Terry said. Presumably, the response used by Blanche came from McGraw himself. Williams' interview with Terry was conducted many years later.
2. Harold C. Burr, "Terry Extracts Pledge from McGraw Before He Accepts New Post," *Brooklyn Daily Eagle*, June 4, 1932.
3. Frank Graham, *McGraw of the Giants: An Informal Biography* (New York: G. P. Putnam's Sons), 261.
4. "Terry Battles to Rally Giants When M'Graw Suddenly Quits," *The Sporting News*, June 9, 1932.
5. Peter Williams, *When Giants Were Giants* (Chapel Hill, NC: Algonquin Books, 1994), 123.
6. "McGraw's Resignation Ends Thirty Year Reign as Giants' Boss," *San Bernardino County Sun*, June 4, 1932.
7. Quentin Reynolds, "Giants Go on Field Without McGraw First in Thirty Years," *Kane (PA) Republican*, June 4, 1932.
8. "Giants to Get New Freedom," *San Bernardino County Sun*, June 4, 1932.
9. Ibid. Single games usually started around 3:00 p.m.
10. "McGraw Comment," *Scranton Republican*, June 4, 1932.
11. Ibid.
12. Harold C. Burr, "Terry Extracts Pledge from McGraw Before He Accepts New Post," *Brooklyn Daily Eagle*, June 4, 1932.
13. Ibid.
14. "Terry, Giants' Star, Signs His Contract," *New York Times*, February 20, 1932.
15. Ibid.
16. Peter Williams, *When Giants Were Giants* (Chapel Hill, NC: Algonquin Books, 1994), 126.
17. Ernest J. Lanigan, "M'Graw Insisted on Bill Terry No. 2 First Baseing," *Brooklyn Daily Eagle*, January 13, 1924. The Bridegroom's William H. Terry, better known as "Adonis" Terry, was the pitcher who surrendered Ed Delahanty's four home runs in one game on July 16, 1896.
18. "Giants Retain Terry as Deal is Abandoned," *Evening News*, December 12, 1924.
19. "Pilot of Giants Likes His Team," *Lincoln (NE) Star*, December 23, 1925. The 1925 off-season potential trades involving Terry were from *Times Recorder*, December 27, 1925.
20. "Infield Stars May Go in Big Deal in Making," *Journal News*, December 31, 1924.
21. "Trade Rumor Names Terry," *Evening Review*, April 1, 1926.
22. Henry L. Farrell, "M'Graw Is the Biggest Reason," *Daily Republican*, March 17, 1926.
23. Alan Gould, "Sport Slants," *Daily Free Press*, June 16, 1930.
24. Tommy Holmes, "Inhospitable West Won't Offer Brooklyn Many Chances to Stretch Lead," *Brooklyn Daily Eagle*, August 6, 1930.
25. Joe Vila, "Terry Rated Ahead of Chase by McGraw," *The Sporting News*, December 4, 1930.
26. "Giants Down Phillies to Hold Third Place," *Brooklyn Daily Eagle*, September 28, 1930.
27. Joe Vila, "Terry Rated Ahead of Chase by McGraw" *The Sporting News*, December 4, 1930.
28. Bill Dixon, "Terry is Still Holdout," *Times Herald*, February 14, 1931.
29. "Giant Slugger Still Holdout; Slashes Terms," *Scranton Republican*, March 11, 1931.

30. "Terry is Ready to Join New York," March 12, 1931; *Ogden Standard-Examiner*, March 12, 1931. In 1930, attendance in the National League peaked at 5,446,532, with every team but the Cincinnati Reds posting an after income tax profit, according to David George Surdam's figures from the post-World War II owners' opening of their books before Congress. With 868,714 fans passing through the Polo Grounds turnstile gates, New York's free and clear revenues—described as real net income—were $151,000. Awash in money were the league's top-drawing teams, the Brooklyn Dodgers and Chicago Cubs, who drew 1,097,329 and 1,463,624 fans, respectively. The Dodgers' ledgers showed a $427,000 after-tax gain, while the Cubs were $524,000 in the black after the same expenditures. (Adjusting for inflation, $100,000 in 1930 would be equal to roughly $1,365,000 in 2015, according to dollartimes.com.)
31. "Terry Comes to Giants' Terms," *Evening News*, March 13, 1931.
32. "Mel Ott May Yet Show Those Proud Yankees How to Hit Home Runs," *Brooklyn Daily Eagle*, September 21, 1932.
33. Ibid.
34. Alan Gould, "Sport Slants," *Corsicana Daily Sun*, October 28, 1930.
35. "Vergez Looks For Big Year," *Altoona (PA) Tribune*, December 19, 1931.
36. Jack Cuddy, "Reason Behind John Vergez 1932 Slump," (Lincoln, NE) *Evening State Journal*, January 25, 1933.
37. "Travis Jackson is Remarkable Player," *Daily Republican*, November 6, 1923.
38. "M'Graw Puzzles Fans About His 1924 Giants," *The News*, December 11, 1923.
39. "Faith Justified in Jackson," *Delaware County Daily Times*, October 3, 1924.
40. "Link Names of Frisch and Luque in Baseball Deal," *Bridgeport Telegram*, November 3, 1925.
41. "Travis Jackson of Giants Marries Hometown Girl," *Brooklyn Daily Eagle*, January 24, 1928.
42. "Travis Jackson Will Be Offered Giants Captaincy," *The Oil City Derrick*, February 20, 1928.
43. "Travis Jackson to Captain N.Y. Giants This Year," *News-Herald*, February 21, 1928.
44. "McGraw Declares War on Holdouts," *Index-Journal*, March 15, 1930.
45. "Jackson Favors His Team," *Daily Mail*, April 2, 1931.
46. Bryan Bell, "On The Sidelines," *Amarillo Globe*, March 3, 1931.
47. Harold C. Burr, "Giant-Yank Trial Game Cleared the Air of Many Wrong Baseball Notions," *Brooklyn Daily Eagle*, September 10, 1931.
48. "Travis Jackson's Legs Patched Up 'as Good as New,'" *Abilene Morning News*, October 22, 1932.
49. "Critz's Father Advised Player Against Football," *Brooklyn Daily Eagle*, July 10, 1930.
50. "Critz Uses 'Sixth Sense' in Fielding Batted Balls," *Coshocton Tribune*, May 29, 1930.
51. "Cincy Fans Demand Critz Back in the Fold," *Evening Standard*, April 15, 1927.
52. Harold C. Burr, "Critz Won His Chance by Making Batters Think He Was Smart Fielder," *Brooklyn Daily Eagle*, May 24, 1931.
53. Ibid.
54. "Critz Uses 'Sixth Sense' in Fielding Batted Balls," *Indiana Gazette*, May 29, 1930.
55. Hank Casserly, "Hank Casserly Says," *Capital Times*, May 29, 1930.

Chapter 2

1. Cullen Cain, "Ott, Wonder Boy of Baseball, Joined Giants at 16–And Stuck," *Brooklyn Daily Eagle*, January 4, 1931. Ott's father and uncle, George Miller, played semi-pro ball. The uncle, on his mother's side, tossed a 1–0 victory over the Cleveland Indians in a 1921 exhibition game.
2. Billy Evans, "Billy Evans Says," *Reading Times*, July 3, 1926.
3. Cain, Cullen, "Ott, Wonder Boy of Baseball, Joined Giants at 16–And Stuck," *Brooklyn Daily Eagle*, January 4, 1931. In this mention of McGraw, Ott does not refer to him as "Mr.," as was his usual reference. Ott was about to turn 22 at the time, and the informality would seem not to be in character.
4. Ibid.
5. Fred Stein, *Mel Ott: The Little Giant of Baseball*. (Jefferson, NC: McFarland, 1999), 19.
6. Harold C. Burr, "'It's Land of Forgotten Men for Us,' Dan Howley Moans of Second Base," *Brooklyn Daily Eagle*, June 8, 1932.
7. Cullen Cain, "Ott, Wonder Boy of Baseball, Joined Giants at 16–And Stuck," *Brooklyn Daily Eagle*, January 4, 1931.
8. Fred Stein, *Mel Ott: The Little Giant of Baseball*. (Jefferson, NC: McFarland, 1999), 19.
9. "Giants Suffer Double Defeat Against the Braves," *Brooklyn Daily Eagle*, May 17, 1929.
10. Tommy Holmes, "Brooklyn's Joke Scouting System Will Never Catch a Mel Ott," *Brooklyn Daily Eagle*, May 23, 1929.
11. "Two Phils Set Marks," *Kansas City Star*, October 6, 1929.

12. Fred Stein, *Mel Ott: The Little Giant of Baseball* (Jefferson, NC: McFarland, 1999), 35.
13. Tommy Holmes, "Mel Ott Contradicts Moan That Youngsters Cannot Play." *Brooklyn Daily Eagle*, January 6, 1930.
14. "News from the Training Camps," *Kingsport Times*, April 2, 1930.
15. Harold C. Burr, "Giants Dump Cards, 9–7, on Ott's Homer's," *Brooklyn Daily Eagle*, June 8, 1930.
16. "Mel Ott Works Double Steal," *Daily Plainsman*, November 19, 1930. While several newspapers published September 30 as Ott's wedding day, biographer Fred Stein stated that it took place October 2.
17. Fred Stein, *Mel Ott: The Little Giant of Baseball*. Jefferson, NC: McFarland, 1999, 42.
18. "Melvin Ott Joins Terry in Refusing Salary Cut," *Reading Times*, January 13, 1932. Baseball owners may not have *all* been cheapskate ogres, and they did absorb losses during the Depression they could have avoided with sterner tactics, based on this explanation by David George Surdam: "Although owners possessed bargaining strength due to the reserve clause, they did not cut salaries sufficiently to stave off revenue losses between 1931 and 1935. The decrease in real revenues was not met by any widespread decrease in real salaries until possibly 1934." From Surdam, *Wins, Losses & Empty Seats: How Baseball Outlasted the Great Depression*. (Lincoln: University of Nebraska Press, 2011), 91. Real revenues were net revenues and real salaries were players, managers and coaches' salaries. It must be added that owners cut the 25-man roster limit to 23 in 1932.
19. Harold C. Burr, "Giants Dump Cards, 9–7, on Ott's Homer's," *Brooklyn Daily Eagle*, June 8, 1930.
20. Harold Parrott, "George 'Kiddo' Davis Commits 'Burglaries' with Trusty Bludgeon," *Brooklyn Daily Eagle*, April 7, 1936.
21. *Ibid*.
22. "He doesn't look like a runner…," Tommy Holmes, "George Davis Didn't Look Impressive but He Poisoned Dodgers," *Brooklyn Daily Eagle*, December 1, 1932.
23. *Ibid*. The writer's description is reminiscent of a modern-day Hunter Pence.

Chapter 3

1. Alan Gould, "Carl Hubbell, Oklahoma Youth Hurls Giants to Victory Over Cardinals," *Joplin Globe*, September 23, 1928.
2. Fritz A. Buckallew, *A Pitcher's Moment: Carl Hubbell and the Quest for Baseball Immortality* (Oklahoma City: Forty-Sixth Star Press, 2010), 25.
3. *Ibid*.
4. *Ibid.*, 11.
5. Jack Sords, "Sords Points," *Oxnard Daily-Courier*, April 23, 1929.
6. Jack Sords, "Says Little; Pitches a Lot," *Decatur Evening Herald*, May 16, 1929.
7. "Carl Hubbell Puts 'Fast One' Across Plate." *Morning Herald*, February 13, 1930. Hubbell biographer Fritz A. Buckallew noted that Lucille Herrington was born in Sparks, Oklahoma. She was two years younger than Hubbell.
8. Harold C. Burr, "Pirates Are Perfect Gentlemen in Losing That Hard Luck Game," *Brooklyn Daily Eagle*, July 25, 1930.
9. Les Conklin, "New York Giants Having Trouble with Holdouts," *New Castle News*, February 25, 1931.
10. Eric H. Allen, *1931: The Year of the Great Worldwide Financial Crash*. Self-published, 2011, 135.
11. Tommy Holmes, "Nebraska Has Produced Another Budding Mound Ace," *Brooklyn Daily Eagle*, August 28, 1928.
12. "Screw-Ball Has 'Em Guessing," *The Sporting News*, May 4, 1933.
13. Fritz A. Buckallew, *A Pitcher's Moment: Carl Hubbell and the Quest for Baseball Immortality*. (Oklahoma City: Forty-Sixth Star Press, 2010), 20.
14. "Mel Ott and Carl Hubbell: New York Giant Outfielder and Pitcher Sign Contracts," *Jacksonville Daily Journal*, January 17, 1932. The only years the Giants lost money, based on real net income after income taxes, during the 1930s were in 1931 and 1932. The Giants made more money during the decade than any other National League team. Only the New York Yankees and Detroit Tigers earned greater after-tax profits in the ten-year span.
15. "One of McGraw's Pitchers Visits a Bit in Amarillo," *Amarillo Globe-Times*, February 17, 1932.
16. "Koenecke Gets Once-Over by Mgr. McGraw," *Brooklyn Daily Eagle*, February 29, 1932. McGraw, it was told, came across Koenecke on a scouting trip to Louisville to see big league prospect Billy Herman. The Giants were in nearby Cincinnati at the time. The Chicago Cubs beat McGraw to the "signing punch" with Herman, and Koenecke never panned out. Although the former American Association star did hit .320 with Brooklyn in 1934, Koenecke met with an untimely and strange death the following year, at the age of 31.

17. "Rookies Are Unusually Prominent in Ball Camps," *Pampa (TX) Daily News*, February 29, 1932.
18. Harry T. Brundidge, "Ambition to Learn What Made Pitched Balls Curve Induced Fitzsimmons to Develop into a Hurler," *The Sporting News*, February 19, 1931.
19. Peter J. DeKever, *Freddie Fitzsimmons: A Baseball Life* (Bloomington, IN: AuthorHouse), 16.
20. Harry T. Brundidge, "Ambition to Learn What Made Pitched Balls Curve Induced Fitzsimmons to Develop Into a Hurler," *The Sporting News*, February 19, 1931.
21. Peter J. DeKever, *Freddie Fitzsimmons: A Baseball Life* (Bloomington, IN: AuthorHouse), 21.
22. "Roush and Luque Too Old Says McGraw, Rejecting Deal," *Brooklyn Daily Eagle*, December 23, 1925.
23. Harry T. Brundidge, "Ambition to Learn What Made Pitched Balls Curve Induced Fitzsimmons to Develop into a Hurler," *The Sporting News*, February 19, 1931.
24. "Giants Open Before 40,000 at Home to Beat Phils, 5–1," *Reading Times*, April 21, 1927.
25. Tommy Holmes, "Petty Loses Pitching Duel With Fitzsimmons; Solitary Run Decides," *Brooklyn Daily Eagle*, September 2, 1928. Fitzsimmons' biographer, Peter J. DeKever, wrote that Fitzsimmons' "alliterative sobriquet" was part of the pitcher's descriptive persona since at least 1927, although no origin for it was given.
26. "Long, looping drive..." "'Twas the Clout of Memphis Bill," *Brooklyn Daily Eagle*, September, 19, 1928.
27. "[All] Fat Fred Fitzsimmons of the Giants..." "Red Whitewasher," *Lebanon Daily News*, August 23, 1929.
28. William Hennigan, "29,000 Fans Jam Way into Flatbush Park, 15,000 Are Turned Away as Giants Register Seventh Straight Victory by a 10–4 Count," *Reading Times*, April 28, 1930.
29. William Brauchner, "Night Baseball Grows—So Grandmas Now Get But One Burial." *Daily Mail*, August 2, 1930. When the National League voted to allow night baseball, at its winter meeting in December 1934, Charles Stoneham vowed his team would never participate. "I am against night baseball," he said, "and have no intentions of allowing the Giants to play it, no matter how alluring the financial prospect may be. With pitchers like Dizzy Dean, Roy Parmelee and Van Mungo throwing at night, we may have serious injuries to batsmen. It costs about $40,000 to install a good lighting system. What do you think it costs to keep those lights burning? It seems to me that any club that has that much money to spend might better put it into a good few ball players." Dan Daniel, "Night Ball Dangers Steer Giants Away," *The Sporting News*, December 27, 1934.
30. Ibid.
31. Tommy Holmes, "Robins Are in a Dismal Batting Slump as Series with Giants Ends," *Brooklyn Daily Eagle*, August 5, 1930.
32. Peter J. DeKever. *Freddie Fitzsimmons: A Baseball Life* (Bloomington, IN: AuthorHouse), 107.
33. Ibid., 108.
34. "Yankees Holdouts Have Best Chance Get Better Wages," *Corsicana Daily Sun*, January 19, 1932.
35. "Fitzsimmons Puts in Twelve Innings," *Brownsville Herald*, February 26, 1932.
36. "Klem's Pride is Target of McGraw's Ire," *Brooklyn Daily Eagle*, May 17, 1932.
37. Harold Burr, "Parmelee, as Kid in Toledo, Rooted Hard for Future Giants," *Brooklyn Daily Eagle*, April 30, 1930.
38. Tommy Holmes, "Babe Phelps Finds National League a Great Place for Hitting," *Brooklyn Daily Eagle*, April 30, 1930.
39. "McGraw Brings Giants Along in Easy Steps," *Brooklyn Daily Eagle*, March 1, 1931.
40. Fred Hayes, "Pitching Boosts Columbus," *The Sporting News*, May 28, 1931. According to Parmelee, there existed a well-known softball pitcher based in Toledo by the name of Bud Parmelee. His nickname was automatically applied to "Leroy" as well.
41. Joe Vila, "Sterling Pitching Puts Giants Back in National League Pennant Race," *The Sporting News*, September 10, 1931.
42. W. E. Gould, "Bill's Blarney," *Santa Cruz Sentinel*, March 30, 1932.
43. Frank Graham, *McGraw of the Giants: An Informal Biography* (New York: G. P. Putnam's Sons), 1944, page 254.
44. "Giants Training in California," *Greely Daily Tribune*, February 19, 1932.
45. "Youngsters Steal Show Second Week Major Loop Games," *Lincoln Evening Journal*, April 18, 1932.
46. Daniel, Dan, "Pitching: Staple and Fancy," *The Sporting News*, April 12, 1934.

Chapter 4

1. "Farrell Protests Sale of Two Cuban Stars," *Washington Times*, August 8, 1913.
2. "Louisville Players Register," *Huntington Press*, May 30, 1917.

3. "Cuban Pitches a Great Game," *Cincinnati Enquirer*, August 9, 1918.
4. *Boston Globe*, August 1, 1919.
5. Thomas S. Rice, "Luque Holds First Place as Ready Relief Pitcher," *Brooklyn Daily Eagle*, May 23, 1920.
6. "St. Louis in Second Place," *Durham Morning Herald*, June 27, 1920.
7. Jack Ryder, "Fortune Favors Frisky Cubs," *Cincinnati Enquirer*, July 2, 1920.
8. Jack Ryder, "Havana is Still Cheering," *Cincinnati Enquirer*, July 19, 1920. It would not be until 1952 that the major leagues would adopt a four-man umpiring crew for regular season games.
9. "Stengel's Homer Defeats Redlegs," *New York Times*, June 12, 1922.
10. "Luque's No Fluque," *Fort Wayne Sentinel*, July 17, 1923.
11. "Grist From the Box Scores," *Brooklyn Daily Eagle*, August 8, 1923. John McGraw stated afterward that it was Bill Cunningham, and not Stengel, who shouted the name(s) to which Luque objected. And that he, McGraw, was sitting close to Stengel on the bench. (This seems unlikely.) Luque was adamant in postgame comments that it was Stengel, attesting that he was familiar with Stengel's voice. McGraw may have been trying to shield his player, who had been in the doghouse with the league, stemming from two recent "indiscretions." Stengel had been disciplined for being involved in a fight with Phillies pitcher Lefty Weinert. The future celeb manager had also been fined by the league for making denigrating comments about Barney Dreyfuss, over the Pittsburgh Pirates owner's stingy salary-paying methods. The remarks were purposely made by Stengel before a game within earshot of the box seat-sitting executive. Klem, who was umpiring behind the dish, said he did not hear "Stengel say anything out of the way," but added that he ejected Stengel from the game on "general principles."
12. Jack Ryder, "Rough House Scrap Mars Final Game of New York Series," *Cincinnati Enquirer*, August 8, 1923.
13. Jack Ryder, "Eight of McGraw's Hurlers Walloped," *Cincinnati Enquirer*, August 16, 1923. That year, construction of the outfield second deck began at the Polo Grounds, and continued during the season. Extending from the foul poles, the decks eventually curved out and over the left and right field bleachers.
14. Jack Ryder, "Notes of the Game," *Cincinnati Enquirer*, September 26, 1923.
15. Tom Swope, "Reds Admittedly Not at Their Best." *The Sporting News*, April 22, 1926.
16. "$25,000 Offered Cincy for Luque," *Santa Ana Register*, March 4, 1927. On a personal note, Luque's marriage to Mae had been on the rocks for some time. He had returned as usual to Cuba in the off-season—but without his bride of a few months. The *Brooklyn Eagle* of March 4, 1927, reported that Mrs. Luque charged her husband with "gross neglect and failure to provide" and that she had requested a legal writ "preventing the transfer of any of the purchase price to Luque," in the purported Cincinnati-Giants deal. A Cincinnati judge refused to grant the latter injunction request. The couple briefly reconciled, but in October of 1927, Mrs. Luque was granted a divorce from her Cuban husband on the grounds of extreme cruelty. Mrs. Luque implied that she was subjected to physical abuse. Luque was ordered to provide her with a $2,500 flat alimony settlement.
17. Tom Swope, "Reds Leader Pays a Tribute to Luque," *The Sporting News*, April 5, 1928, 2.
18. Tommy Holmes, "Vance Has Great Hook Ball, But the Craftiest Curveball Pitcher is Luque." *Brooklyn Daily Eagle*, January 19, 1929.
19. "Gives up Hope of Securing Luque," *Delaware County Daily Times*, January 14, 1929.
20. Eric H. Allen, *1931: The Year of the Great Worldwide Financial Crash*. Self-published, 2011, 135.
21. William Brauchner, "Hooks and Slides," *Hope Star*, June 26, 1930.
22. Brian Bell, "On the Sidelines," *Scranton Republican*, April 16, 1930.
23. Tommy Holmes, "Inhospitable West Won't Offer Brooklyn Many Chances to Stretch the Lead," *Brooklyn Daily Eagle*, August 6, 1930.
24. Ibid.
25. "Interesting Squibs of Different Kinds of Sports," *Fayette County Leader*, November 20, 1930.
26. "Training Camp Baseball Shots," *Journal News*, March 6, 1930.
27. Leo H. Peterson, "Veteran Cuban Hurler is Near End of His Career," *Courier News*, January 30, 1932.
28. William Braucher, "Hooks And Slides," *News-Herald*, February 19, 1932.
29. "Lowly Cardinals Cut Some Capers," *The Sporting News*, July 24, 1924. Johnny Stuart had thrown doubleheader complete game victories for the Cardinals the prior season, with Rickey as manager. The pitching exertions were pointed to as having had an adverse effect on the 24-year-old pitcher's career, which ended in 1925, after three big league seasons.

30. "Holm And Bell Doing Well in Spring Training," *Lake Park News*, April 7, 1927.
31. Eric H. Allen, *1931: The Year of the Great Worldwide Financial Crash*. Self-published, 2011, 1.
32. *Ibid.*, 91.
33. *Ibid.*
34. David George Surdam, *Wins, Losses & Empty Seats: How Baseball Outlasted the Great Depression* (Lincoln: University of Nebraska Press, 2011), 16.
35. "Herman Bell Latest to Sign Giants Papers," *Brooklyn Daily Eagle*, February 19, 1932.

Chapter 5

1. Fred Stein, *Mel Ott: The Little Giant of Baseball*. (Jefferson, NC: McFarland, 1999), 45.
2. Tommy Holmes, "Giants Beat Dodgers, 5–3, in 12th," *Brooklyn Daily Eagle*, September 4, 1932.
3. George H. Beale, "Today's Sports Parade." *The San Mateo Times*, February 25, 1933.
4. Jack Cuddy. "Terry Predicts Race Between Giants, Cubs and Pittsburgh Club," *Fresno Bee-Republican*, February 6, 1933.
5. Alan Gould, "McGraw Honored at Banquet at Baseball Writer's Club, Which Laments His Departure," *Miami Daily News-Record*, February 6, 1933.
6. "John McGraw Guest of Honor," *Brooklyn Daily Eagle*, February 6, 1933.
7. "Piping 'Em Off," *Santa Ana Register*, February 25, 1933.
8. "Bill Terry Grooms Ryan as Sub for Jackson," *Scranton Republican*, March 18, 1933.
9. "Travis Jackson Hops on 'New' Knees and There's Rejoicing in Giants' Camp," *Lubbock Morning Avalanche*, February 25, 1933.
10. "Chatter from the Diamond," *Brownsville Herald*, March 1, 1933.
11. Brian Bell, "Bill Terry's Men Rather Upset, But Will Get Over It." *Waco News-Tribune*, March 15, 1933.
12. "Terry Hits Home Run," *Emporia Gazette*, March 13, 1933.
13. "Al Smith Is the Pitcher Giants May Need," *Dunkirk Evening Observer*, March 14, 1933.
14. Harold C. Burr, "Never Again $80,000 Ball Player Like Ruth, Says Yankee Official," *Brooklyn Daily Eagle*, March 25, 1933. Burr wrote that Ruth, with this most recent salary capitulation, had accumulated $800,000 in pay during his baseball career, plus another $40,000 in World Series shares.
15. Harold C. Burr, "Here Ye, Here Ye You Giant Cubs and Boss Terry Come to Trial," *Brooklyn Daily Eagle*, April 20, 1933.
16. "Giant Rookies Fear for Jobs," *Brooklyn Daily Eagle*, April 5, 1933.
17. Harold C. Burr, "Jobs Are Scarce So Carl Doesn't Mind Overworking for Boss Bill," *Brooklyn Daily Eagle*, April 21, 1933.
18. Harold C. Burr, "The Dodgers Might Blame It on Overconfidence but Not on Southpaws," *Brooklyn Daily Eagle*, April 26, 1933.
19. "Sport Tips," *Daily News*, May 2, 1933. In a future interview, Parmelee would state that Jimmy Powers was the New York writer responsible for tagging him with the "Tarzan" label.
20. "Braves Twice Flog Giants," *Altoona Tribune*, May 1, 1933.
21. "Sign of the Times," *The Sporting News*, May 4, 1933.
22. "Between Innings," *Sedalia Democrat*, May 10, 1933.
23. Harold C. Burr, "Roy's Satisfied, Even if Finn Did Mar Classic–He'll Stick This Time," *Brooklyn Daily Eagle*, April 27, 1933.
24. "Giants Cut Deeply Into Buccos' Lead," *Salt Lake Tribune*, May 27, 1933.
25. Harold C. Burr, "Terry's Pleased," *Brooklyn Daily Eagle*, June 1, 1933.
26. "Mancuso has been a great player for me…," "Baseball Siftings," *Taylor Daily Press*, June 6, 1933.
27. "Major Leaguer Gets Degree During Season," *Montana Butte Standard*, June 13, 1933.
28. "Terry's Men Blank Cards in Both Ends of Twin Bill," *Scranton Republican*, July 3, 1933.
29. Fritz A. Buckallew, *A Pitcher's Moment: Carl Hubbell and the Quest for Baseball Immortality* (Oklahoma City: Forty-Sixth Star Press, 2010), 51.
30. Bob Broeg, "King Carl Superb Mound Craftsman," *The Sporting News*, May 2, 1970, 14–16.

Chapter 6

1. Cheryl A. Ganz, *The 1933 Chicago's World Fair: A Century of Progress* (Chicago: University of Illinois Press, 2008), photo caption from unnumbered page.
2. "Fans' Dream of Greatest Game Comes True at Chicago July 6," *The Sporting News*, July 6, 1933.
3. George Kirksey, "Almost 50,000 Will See New Inter-League Contest," *Oshkosh Daily Northwestern*, July 6, 1933.
4. Ed Kelly, "Kel-e-graphs," *Scranton Republican*, July 7, 1933.

5. Charles Dunkley, "McGraw Sees Better Days," *Salt Lake Tribune*, July 7, 1933.
6. Ibid.

Chapter 7

1. Edward J. Neil, "Great Showing of New York Giants Surprises Fans," *Modesto News-Herald*, June 16, 1933.
2. Ibid.
3. "Blondy's Welcome," *Brooklyn Daily Eagle*, July 13, 1933.
4. George Kirksey, "Chicago Cubs Continue as Menace for National Lead," *San Bernardino County Sun*, July 13, 1933.
5. "Pirates Take Second as Cubs Are Beaten," *Brownsville Herald*, July 30, 1933.
6. "Giants Still Trying to Land Jewish Star," *Rushville Republican*, July 31, 1933.
7. "Scribes Called in to Eat with Bill Terry," *Lincoln (NE) Star*, August 15, 1933.
8. Harold C Burr, "Bill Terry's Giants Not Worrying But Not Talking Pennant Either," *Brooklyn Daily Eagle*, August 16, 1933.
9. "Giants Must Forget Big Lead," *Daily Mail*, August 22, 1933.
10. Harold C. Burr, "Pirates Break Winning Streak of Terry Clan," *Brooklyn Daily Eagle*, August 27, 1933.
11. Harold C. Burr, "Terry Needs Only to Split in Boston to Raise His Pennant Hopes," *Brooklyn Daily Eagle*, August 31, 1933.
12. Bill King, "Hubbell and Fitzsimmons Hurl Brilliantly; Opening Contest Goes 10 Frames," *Sandusky Register*, September 2, 1933.
13. Harold Parrott, "Pirates' Trips May Kill All Their Chances," *Brooklyn Daily Eagle*, September 9, 1933.
14. "Fans To Greet Flag Winning Giants Today," *Brooklyn Daily Eagle*, September 20, 1933.
15. "Where They Broadcast," *The Sporting News*, May 4, 1933. It was not until 1939 that the Giants began broadcasting their home games over the radio, although not on the traditionally big-drawing Sundays.
16. Edward J. Neil, "Turbulent Crowd of 20,000 Fans Turns Out for Giant Homecoming," (Bloomington, IL) *Daily Pantagraph*, September 21, 1933.
17. "New Yorkers Formally Greet National Champs," *Morning Herald*, September 22, 1933.
18. Ibid.
19. Jack Cuddy, "Confidence Back of Giants' Mark," *San Bernardino County Sun*, August 22, 1933.
20. Harold C. Burr, "Simplicity of Giant Outlook Big Asset for Giants in Series With Senators," *Brooklyn Daily Eagle*, September 24, 1933.
21. Ibid.
22. Edward J. Neil, "Charlie Gelbert Definitely Out of Cards' Lineup This Year," *Scranton Republican*, February 7, 1933.
23. Ed Lawson, "Speaking of Sports," *Sedalia Democrat*, February 16, 1933.

Chapter 8

1. Harold C. Burr, "The Series Parade—The Managerial Strategy," *Brooklyn Daily Eagle*, October 2, 1933.
2. Davis J. Walsh, "Terry Keen for Giant Pitchers," *Lincoln (NE) Star*, September 23, 1933.
3. Ibid.
4. "Infield Situation Finds Giants Relying on Jackson to Hold Down Third Base Duties," *Kansas City Star*, September 23, 1933.
5. Harold C. Burr, "Just Chatter," *Brooklyn Daily Eagle*, October 4, 1933.
6. "Carl Hubbell Triumphs in World Series Opener," *Fitchburg Sentinel*, October 4, 1933.
7. "Confidence in Hubbell Bourne Out in Victory, Says Terry," *Evening News*, October 4, 1933.
8. Pat Robinson, "The Giants In Four Straight–If–Schumacher's Right," *Indiana Gazette*, October 4, 933.
9. "Confidence in Hubbell Bourne Out in Victory, Says Terry," *Evening News*, October 4, 1933.
10. Ibid.
11. Ibid.
12. Edward J. Neil, "New York Crowds Pour into Polo Grounds," *Corsicana Daily Sun*, October 4, 1933.
13. Ibid.
14. Harold Parrott, "Fitz To Start Against Nats in Third Game," *Brooklyn Daily Eagle*, October 5, 1933.
15. "Schumacher, O'Doul Heroes As N.Y. Beats Washington Again," *Scranton Republican*, October 5, 1933.
16. Walsh J. Davis, "American Leaguers Back Among Friends," *Indiana Gazette*, October 5, 1933.
17. "Master-minding By Terry Upsets Senators in Second," *Evening News*, October 5, 1933.
18. Ibid.
19. Ibid.
20. "Schumacher, O'Doul Heroes As N.Y. Beats Washington Again," *Scranton Republican*, October 5, 1933.

21. "Master-minding By Terry Upsets Senators in Second," *Evening News*, October 5, 1933.
22. "Giants Knock General Crowder From the Box in the Sixth to Give New Yorkers Second Game, 6 to 1." *Bee*, October 5, 1933.
23. John F. Chester, "World Series Notes," *Scranton Republican*, October 6, 1933.
24. Ted Vosburgh, "Hurlers Seen As Big Factor in Ball Series," *Sandusky Register*, October 6, 1933.
25. *Ibid*.
26. "Sewell Sagacious," *Indiana Gazette*, October 6, 1933.
27. "We're on Our Way! Jubilant Nats Cry after Victory," *Sandusky Register*, October 6, 1933.
28. "Giants Gloat Over 2 Plays That Won 1st," *Brooklyn Daily Eagle*, October 4, 1933.
29. Alan Gould, "Carl Hubbell Continues To Be Topic of World Series Gossip," *Daily Plainsman*, October 4, 1933.
30. "Cronin Holds Aching Head While Players Argue with Umpires," *Winnipeg Tribune*, October 7, 1933.
31. "Hubbell's Pitching and Bats of Terry and Ryan Spell Victory," *Bakersfield Californian*, October 6, 1933.
32. "Cronin Holds Aching Head While Players Argue with Umpires," *Winnipeg Tribune*, October 7, 1933.
33. "Hubbell's Pitching and Bats of Terry and Ryan Spell Victory," *Bakersfield Californian*, October 6, 1933.
34. Harold C. Burr, "Singing Blues Away," *Brooklyn Daily Eagle*, October 7, 1933.
35. Ted Vosburgh, "Giants Call Thriller Greatest Game They Ever Played," *Sandusky Register*, October 7, 1933.
36. *Ibid*.
37. Grantland Rice, "Mel Ott Does Repeat Homer to Send NY to Title," *Winnipeg Tribune*, October 9, 1933.
38. "Giants Capture Series, Winning Fifth Game, 4–3," *Brooklyn Daily Eagle*, October 8, 1933. The home run by Ott, incidentally, was voted "greatest athletic thrill of 1933"—in more modern terms, "greatest sports moment of the year." In a tabulation of 176 sportswriters across the country, the majority picked Ott's blast. In second place was Notre Dame's blocked punt for a touchdown, with one minute left in the game, that provided its victory margin over undefeated Army.
39. *Ibid*.
40. Damon Runyon, "New York Giants, Who Nobody Thought Could Do It, Take Series," *Lincoln (NE) Star*, October 8, 1933.
41. John F. Chester, "Series Gossip," *Salt Lake Tribune*, October 8, 1933.
42. "Clark Griffith One of the First To Hail Giants," *Winnipeg Tribune*, October 9, 1933.
43. "Terry Believes Difference in Ball Fooled Experts on Hitting Power," *Winnipeg Tribune*, October 9, 1933.
44. "Clark Griffith One of the First To Hail Giants," *Winnipeg Tribune*, October 9, 1933.
45. Alan Gould, "Giants Sitting on Top of the Baseball World for the First Time Since 1922," *Reading Times*, October 9, 1933.

Bibliography

Alexander, Charles C. *Breaking the Slump Baseball in the Depression Era*. New York: Columbia University Press, 2002.

Alexander, Charles C. *John McGraw*. Lincoln: University of Nebraska Press, 1988.

Allen, Eric H. *1931: The Year of the Great Worldwide Financial Crash*. Self-published, 2011.

Buckallew, Fritz A. *A Pitcher's Moment Carl Hubbell and the Quest for Baseball Immortality*. Oklahoma City: Forty-Sixth Star Press, 2010.

Burtt, Robert, and Bill Main, and Debbie Main. *1933 Commemorative Yearbook*. Champlain Publishing Services, 1999.

DeKever, Peter J. *Freddie Fitzsimmons A Baseball Life*. Bloomington, IN: AuthorHouse, 2013.

Figueredo, Jorge S. *Cuban Baseball a Statistical History 1878-1961*. Jefferson, NC: McFarland, 2003.

Freedman, Lew. *The Day All the Stars Came Out*. Jefferson, NC: McFarland, 2010.

Ganz, Cheryl A. *The 1933 Chicago's World Fair: A Century of Progress*. Chicago: University of Illinois Press, 2008.

González Echevarría, Roberto. *The Pride of Havana: A History of Cuban Baseball*. New York: Oxford University Press, 1999.

Graham, Frank. *McGraw of the Giants: An Informal Biography*. New York: G.P. Putnam's Sons, 1944.

McGraw, Blanche, edited by Arthur Mann. *The Real McGraw*. New York: David McKay, 1953.

McGraw, John J. *My Thirty Years in Baseball*. Lincoln: Bison Books, University of Nebraska, 1995.

Sarnoff, Gary. *The Wrecking Crew of '33: The Washington Senators' Last Pennant*. Jefferson, NC: McFarland, 2009.

Skipper, John C. *A Biographical Dictionary of Major League Baseball Managers*. Jefferson, NC: McFarland, 2003.

Spatz, Lyle. *The SABR Baseball List & Record Book*. New York: Scribner, 2007.

Stein, Fred. *Mel Ott: The Little Giant of Baseball*. Jefferson, NC: McFarland, 1999.

Surdam, David George. *Wins, Loses & Empty Seats: How Baseball Outlasted the Great Depression*. Lincoln: University of Nebraska Press, 2011.

Vincent, David. *Home Run: The Definitive History of Baseball's Ultimate Weapon*. Herndon, VA: Potomac Books, 2009.

Williams, Peter. *When Giants Were Giants*. Chapel Hill, NC: Algonquin Books, 1994.

Articles

Bradley, Michael. "Aligning the Stars." *MLB Insiders Club Magazine* 7, No. 4 (2014).

Web Articles

1933 East-West Game. baseball-reference.com.

Renner, James. "Coogan's Bluff and the Polo Grounds." hhoc.org.

Documentaries

A Nation of Hypocrites. PBS. Original air date, October 4, 2011.

The Roosevelts. PBS. Original air date, September 14, 2014.

Websites

Baseball-almanac.com.
Baseballencyclopedia/new yorkgiants.com.
Baseballlibrary.com.
Baseball-reference.com.
Britannica.com/johnmcgraw.
Centerfieldmaz.com.
Christy Mathewson entry at wikipedia.com.
Elysianfielders.com.
Findagrave.com.
newyorkgiantspreservationsociety.com.
nfl.com.
Nyhistory.org/bill-slocum.
Sportsattic.com/araig/nflruleshistory.htm
Wrigley Field (Los Angeles) entry at wikipedia.com.

SABR Bioprojects

Corbett, Warren. Gus Mancuso at bioproject.sabr.org.
Erion, Greg. Travis Jackson at bioproject.sabr.org.
Green, John F. Homer Peel at bioproject.abr.org.
Harrison, Don. Kiddo Davis at bioproject.sabr.org.
Jensen, Don. John McGraw at bioproject.sabr.org.
McKenna, Brian. Lefty O'Doul at bioproject.sabr.org.
Melin, Roger. Hal Schumacher at bioproject.sabr.org.
Sandoval, Jim. Jake Daubert at bioproject.sabr.org.
Stein, Fred. Bill Terry at bioproject.sabr.org.
Stein, Fred. Carl Hubbell at bioproject.sabr.org.
Stein, Fred. Frankie Frisch at bioproject.sabr.org.
Stein, Fred. Freddie Lindstrom at bioproject.sabr.org.
Stein, Fred. Mel Ott at bioproject.sabr.org.

Index

Numbers in ***bold italics*** indicate pages with photographs.

Adams, Sparky 71
Aldridge, Vic 71
Alexander, Grover Cleveland "Pete" 33, 55, 58, 62, 64, 69–70, 97, 99–100, 102, 106, 112
Allen, Eric H. 60, 113
Allen, Ethan 48, 116, 135, 170
Allen, Nick 96
Altrock, Nick ***176***
American Association 41, 50, 62, 82, 84, 91, 93, 112, 116, 128–129, 138, 157
American League 31, 77, 90, 138–139, 172, 185, 187, 198, 199
Aragón, Angel 90
Atlanta Crackers 11
Averill, Earl 141, 142

Baker Bowl 15, 19, 39, 43, 46, 59, 67, 69–70, 76, 85, 88, 96, 98, 130, 149, 151
Bancroft, Dave 8, 26–27, 30, 47, 59, 63, 73, 86, 109, 121
Barker gang 169
Barnes, Jesse 13, 56, 99
Barnes, Virgil 67, 69
Barrow, Ed 121
Barry, Jack 119
Bartell, Dick 129, 140, 142
Beale, George H. 117
Beaumont club 54
Beck, Walter "Boom-Boom" 130
Bell, Emma (Goebel) 113
Bell, Herman "Hi" 88, 109–110, ***111***, 112–114, 122, 125, 127, 129, 130–133, 135–136, 147, 152, 154, 157, 159, 160–162, 167, 174, 180, 182, 186, 187
Bell, Mattie 109
Bell, Nathan 109
Belmont Park 45
Bender, Charles "Chief" 82
Benge, Ray 150
Benton, Larry 30, 35, 55–58, 69–72, 74, 101
Berg, Moe 108
Berger, Wally 140, 142, 168
Betts, Walter "Huck" 148, 157
Birkofer, Ralph 159
Birmingham Barons 151, 159

Bissonette, Del 75
Bluege, Oswald "Ossie" 178, 181, 183, 185–186, 188, 190–191, 194–196
Bohne, Sam 33, 100
Bolton, Cliff 192, 193, 195
Bonnie and Clyde 169
Boston Braves 7, 9, 13, 16, 23, 25, 27, 34, 36–37, 43, 45, 57, 60, 63, 67, 69, 79, 83, 88, 90–92, 94, 95, 97, 110, 114, 117, 123, 125, 132–133, 136, 148–150, 153, 155–158, 165
Boston Daily Globe 94
Boston Red Sox 140, 158
Bottomley, Jim 22, 70
Bowman, Joe 116
Brannick, Eddie 83, 114
Braves Field 17, 20, 42, 63, 81, 83, 92, 100, 114, 125
Bresnahan, Roger 12–13
Bressler, Raymond "Rube" 95, 105
Bridgeport Bears 51, 85–86
Brooklyn Daily Eagle 13, 20, 41, 45, 71, 123, 159
Brooklyn Dodgers 7–9, 23, 27, 52, 63, 68, 122, 125–126, 129–133, 147, 150, 159, 165, 199
Brooklyn Robins 16, 18, 27, 59, 62, 68, 70–71, 73–77, 81, 91, 93, 97, 100, 102, 104–108
Broun, Heywood 118
Brown, Joe E. 62
Buckeye, Garland 50
Buffalo Bisons 113, 116, 148
Burns, George 51
Burr, Harold C. 41, 45, 49
Bush, Donie 29
Bush, Guy 144, 161

Cadore, Leon 97
Cantwell, Ben 136, 156
Carey, Max 130, 139
Carleton, James "Tex" 126, 134–136, 145, 162
Casserly, Hank 36
Central League 65
Chaplin, James "Tiny" 59
Chapman, Ben 140, 142
Charleston, Oscar 160
Chase, Hal 19
Chicago American Giants 160

Chicago Cubs 18–19, 23, 29–30, 32, 34–36, 57, 62–63, 70–72, 74, 76–77, 83, 85–86, 93, 95–97, 100, 105–107, 110, 118–120, 125–126, 128–129, 133–134, 140–142, 144, 148–150, 152–153, 158, 160–161, 165, 185
Chicago Daily Tribune 137
Chicago White Sox 32, 65, 73, 76, 94, 119, 140, 185
Cincinnati Enquirer 97
Cincinnati Reds 14–15, 19, 26, 30, 33–35, 39, 46, 48, 51, 55, 61, 63–64, 67, 72, 74, 77–79, 92–109, 126, 128, 134, 146, 149, 151–152, 160, 165
Clark, William "Watty" 63, 133–134, 144, 146, 149, 153–154, 159, 167, 169–170, 174
Clarke, Tommy 84, 86, 121, 154, 169
Clarkson, Bill 81
Cleveland Indians 42, 50, 141
Clymer, Bill 92
Cobb, Ty 54, 149
Cochrane, Mickey 18
Cocreham, Gene 91
Cohen, Andy 35, 41, 45
Coleman Rangers 51
Collins, Phil 150
Columbus Red Birds 82, 84
Combs, Earl 50, 107
Comiskey Park 32, 94, 138, 160
Community Park 84
Coogan, James J. 173
Cooney, Johnny 110
Cooper, Wilbur 98
Cornwallis, Gen. Charles 64
Cotton State League 35
Couch, Johnny 99
Crawford, Pat 128
Crawford, Sam "Wahoo" 62
Critz, Hugh, Sr. 32
Critz, Hughie 32, **33**, 34–37, 51, 74, 76, 78, 119, 122–123, 130–131, 134–135, 150, 156, 159, 163, 168, 176, 181–186, 188, 190–191, 193–197
Critz, Julia Gillespie 32
Critz, Julia Moon 32
Critz, Wiley Gillespie 32
Cronin, Joe 18, 139, 141, 171–175, **176**, 177–187, **189**, 190–198
Crowder, Alvin "General" 141–142, 158, 173, 175, 180–182, 184, 187, 193–195
Cuban Winter League 95
Cubs Park 13, 96
Cuccinello, Tony 130, 142
Cueto, Johnny 75
Cueto, Manuel 93
Cuyler, Hazen "Kiki" 34, 68

Dallas Steers 130
Dalton, William A. 163, 164
Danning, Harry 148, 169
Daubert, Jake 14
Davis, Bessie Rutter (James) 50
Davis, George "Kiddo" **49**, 50–51, 116, 118, 121–123, 125, 135, 147, 150, 157, 168, 170, 174, 176, 181–182, 186, 189, 190, 194–197
Davis, George, Sr. 50
Dawson, Joe 16
Dean, Dizzy 126, 128, 134, 136, 145, 154–155, 162, 166
DeKever, Peter J. 65, 77
Delker, Eddie 123
Denver Bears 57
Detroit Tigers 14, 54, 88, 121, 140, 171
Dillinger, John 169
Dinneen, Bill 138
Donahey, A. Victor 105
Donohue, Pete 14, 99–101, 103–104
Dothan club 11
Doyle, Larry 20, 92
Dressen, Charlie 160, 162, 169
Dunn Field 50
Durocher, Leo 126, 130
Durst, Cedric 50
Dyer, Eddie 112
Dykes, Jimmy 139–142

Eastern League 51, 85
Ebbets Field 16, 36, 58, 73, 75, 78, 97, 104, 107, 122, 125, 129–131, 147, 150, 153, 199
Edward L. Grant Memorial (Captain) 23, 48
Elberfeld, Norman "Kid" 12, 26
Eller, Horace "Hod" 94
Elliot, James "Jumbo" 70
English, Gil 32, 88, 116

Fabian, Henry 169
Fairbanks, Douglas 138
Farrell, Edward "Doc" 69
Farrell, Frank J. 90
Faulkner, Jim 55
Fe B.B.C. 89
Fenway Park 91
Ferrell, Rick 140, 142
Ferrell, Wes 18
Finney, Hal 153
Fisher, Ray 94, 97
Fitzsimmons, Freddie 14, 16, 22, 46, 55, 57–60, 64–65, **66**, 67–80, 86, 104, 109, 115, 120, 122–136, 145–146, 148–152, 153–155, 157, 159–163, 167, 169, 174, 186, 187
Fitzsimmons, Gordon 66
Fitzsimmons, Helen (Borger) **66**, 68, 163
Fitzsimmons, Helen Louise 73, 163
Fitzsimmons, Margaret Ellen 64
Fitzsimmons, Mary Louise 64
Fitzsimmons, Richard 64, 66
Fitzsimmons, Thomas 64
Flagstead, Ira 17
Florida-Alabama-Georgia-League 11
Flowers, Jake 75
Fonseca, Lew 140
Forbes Field 29, 67, 82, 90, 110, 159
Ford, Horace "Hod" 34
Fordham Rams 122

Index

Foxx, Jimmie 141, 166, 175
Frankenhouse, Fred 156
Frazee, Harry 106
Frederick, Johnny 73
French, Larry 127, 146–147, 158
Frisch, Frankie 14–16, 22, 27–28, 36, 69, 98, 103–104, 126, 129, 140–141, 146, 154
Fuchs, Emil 158
Fullis, Charles "Chick" 46, 48, 56, 116, 118

Gallant Fox 45
The Gay Divorcee 115
Gehrig, Lou 9, 18, 22, 50, 107, 140–142, 152
Gehringer, Charlie 18, 140, 142
Gelbert, Charlie 130
Genewich, Joe 55, 72, 86, 105
George Washington High School Band 163
Georgia-Alabama League 11
Gibson, Sam 114
Gilbert, Wally 73
Goebel, Peter (mayor) 113
Gómez, Lefty 77, 139, 140
González, Miguel Angel "Mike" 93, 98
Goslin, Leon "Goose" 173, 175, 177, 180, 182–183, 186, 190, 192, 194–196
Gould, Alan 24, 53
Graham, Frank 84
Grand Central Station Porter's band 163
Grantham, George 18
Greenfield, Kent 69
Griffith, Clark 172, 175, 185, 198
Griffith Stadium 184
Grimes, Burleigh 14, 47, 55, 69–71, 99–100
Grimm, Charlie 71, 134, 140, 152, 161
Groh, Heine 26, 96, 98
Grove, Lefty 18, 142

Hafey, Charles "Chick" 10, 22, 140–143
Haines, Jesse 136
Hallahan, "Wild Bill" 45, 128, 139–141, 145, 155
Hargrave, Eugene "Bubbles" 104
Harper, George 40, 41
Harris, Bill 33
Harris, Dave 177, 190, 192
Hartnett, Charles "Gabby" 62, 141, 161
Healy, Francis *91*, 108
Heimach, Fred 77
Hemsley, Rollie 146
Hendricks, Jack 14, 35, 105
Henline, Walter "Butch" 14
Hennigan, William 73
Herman, Babe 16, 19–20, 22, 75
Herman, Billy 161
Hernández, Félix 147
Hernández Henriquez, Antonio 89–90
Herrington, John 72
Herrmann, August "Garry" 15, 33–34, 94, 99
Heving, Joe 59
Heydler, John 79, 96–97, 102, *164*
Higgins, Michael "Pinky" 140
Hogan, Francis "Hefty" 60, 71

Hogan, James "Shanty" 84, 108, 117–118, 170
Hollywood Stars 119–120
Holm, Roscoe "Wattie" 110
Holmes, Tommy 18, 43, 61, 71, 75, 105
Hornsby, Rogers 16, 28–29, 31, 34–36, 41, 62, 69–70, 106, 112, 173
Houston Buffaloes 54–55
Hoyt, Waite 115–116, 171
Hubbell, Carl 16, 22, 42, 43, 53–55, *56*, 57–64, 72, 75–76, 81, 83, 106, 109, 114, 120–123, 125–129, 131–136, 139, 142, 144–148, 150–156, 158, 159–161, 163, 166–167, 170–171, 174, *178*, 179–180, 184, 188, 190–193, 197–198
Hubbell, George 54
Hubbell, Lucille (Herrington) 58
Hubbell, Margaret 54
Huggins, Miller 106
Hunnefield, Bill 37
Hurst, Don 150

Indianapolis Indians 65, 66, 67
International League 85, 113, 116, 170

Jackson, Mary (Blackman) 28
Jackson, Travis 16, 18, 26–32, 36, 46, 49, 56, 105, 116, 119, 122, 125–127, 135, 144–145, 163, 168–170, 174, 176, 178–179, 181–182, 186–187, 190–192, 194–196
James, Bernie 116, 122, 130, 145, 147, 150, 156–157, 160, 168–169
James, Bill 115
Jennings, Hughie 26
Jersey City Skeeters 37, 51, 74, 90, 127
Johnson, Ban 93
Johnson, Floyd 41
Johnson, Walter 75, 175
Jones, Edward 83
Jurges, Billy 126

Kansas City Blues 129
Keaton, Buster 62
Kelly, Ed (mayor) 139
Kelly, George "High Pockets" 13–15, 19, 27, 39, 63, 68, 98, 104
Kerr, John 197
King, Bill 156
Kinney, Al 85
Kinsella, Dick 54
Klem, Bill, 1, 63, 79, 96, 97, 138
Klein, Chuck 18, 19, 22, 43–44, 47–48, 57, 59, 62, 73, 129, 140–142, 166, 168
Koenecke, Len 48, 51, 62, 79, 115, 118
Koenig, Mark 107
Kopf, Larry 98
Koufax, Sandy 156
Krichell, Paul 50
Kuhel, Joe 176–177, 181, 184, 186, 190, 192, 194–195, 197

Landis, Kenesaw Mountain 10, 105, 139, 175, 185

Index

Lanigan, Ernest J. 13
Lawrence Larries 132
Lawson, Ed 171
Leach, Freddy 18, 46, 48, 58, 60, 78- 79
Leiber, Hank 121–122, 127
Leslie, Sam 109, 122, 124–126, 129, 133, 159, 169, 170
Lewis, George "Duffy" 95
Lindbergh, Charles, Jr. 26
Lindstrom, Freddie 8, 13, 18, 24, 30, 36, 37, 42, 46, 49, 51, 58–59, 61, 68, 71, 76, 78, 86, 105, 108, 116, 118, 158, 170
Little Rock Travelers 12, 26
Logan, Ed 169
Logan, Fred 169
Long Branch Cubans 89, 90
López Al 63, 108
Los Angeles Angels 119, 120
Louisville Colonels 91, 92
Lucas, Charles "Red" 146
Luque, Adolfo 14, 18, 26, 34, 36, 68, 81, 89–90, *91*, 92–109, 122–123, 125, 128, 132, 144, 146–147, 150, 153, 157, 159, 162, 167, 174, 177, 190, 195–198
Luque, Eugenia (Valdés) 104
Luque, Mae (Dennison) 104
Luque, Olga 104

Macía, Carlos 89
Mack, Connie 9, 106, 138–139, 141, 143, 175
Mahon, Dennis J. 175
Malay, Joe 159
Malone, Pat 29
Mancuso, Gus 64, 116–117, 119, 121, 122, 125, 129–131, 134–136, 144, 148, 162–163, 167, 168, 170, 174, 176, 177, 179, 181–184, 186–188, 190, 194–195, 197
Manush, Heine 175–176, 180–183, 185, 190, 191, 192, 194, 195
Maranville, Walter "Rabbit" 90
Marianao club 66
Marquard, Rube 56
Marshall, Eddie "Doc" 24, 32, 51, 116–118, 170
Martin Pepper 139–140, 155
Mathewson, Christy 75, 188
McBride, George 54
McCarthy, Joe 9, 199
McCooey, John H. *164*
McCurdy, Harry 123
McGowen, Bill 138
McGraw, Blanche 83
McGraw, John J.: All-Star manager 130, 133, 138–143; Frisch incident 28; hitting advice to Terry 22; illnesses and absences 16, 21, 24, 31, 43, 57, 70, 80, 106, 114; miscellaneous 13–14, 18, 19, 24, 29, 51, 53, 55–56, 60, 63, 68, 72–74, 81–84, 86, 88–89, 96, 99, 101, 104, 105, 118, 123, *164*, 166, 175, *176*, 187, 198; Ott relationship 42, 45; player salary disputes 9–10, 22, 30, 58, 75, 79; resignation 7–8, 24, 37; signs Hubbell 53, 55; signs Ott 38, 44;
signs Terry 12; trades and acquisitions 16, 27, 35, 37, 48, 57, 58, 62, 67, 69, 74, 85, 108
McGrew, Ted 154
McInnis, John "Stuffy" 111
McKechnie, Bill 132, 139, 157
McManus, Marty 140
McQuillan, Hugh 69, 101
McWeeny, Doug "Buzz" 106
Medwick, Joe "Ducky" 126, 134, 135
Memphis Chicks 58, 121
Meusel, Bob 50
Meusel, Emil "Irish" 13, 39
Minneapolis Millers 33, 34, 116
Mitchell, Clarence 59, 60, 76, 108, 109, 115, 169
Molina Agustín "Tinti" 89
Montreal Royals 113
Mooney, Jim 78, 109, 116, 170
Moore, Charles 51
Moore, Eddie 116
Moore, Jewel (Ely) 52
Moore, Jo-Jo 51–52, 84, *117*, 118–119, 122, 135, 144, 147, 149, 152, 155, 168, 170, 174–175, 180, 182–183, 185–188, 190, 194, 196
Moore, Maude Rowena 51
Moore, Randy 156
Moran, Charlie 92, 179, 184, 187, 190, 191, 193, 197
Moran, Pat 93, 95–98, 101–103
Moriarty, George 54, 179, 181, 184, 187, 191, 193, 197
Mueller, Clarence "Heinie" 40–41
Mungo, Van 117, 130, 133
Muskegon Muskies 65
Myer, Charles "Buddy" 175–177, 179, 180, 183, 185–188, 191–192, 194–195

Nashville Volunteers 160
National League 31–34, 37, 61, 77–78, 81, 86, 90, 93, 98, 103, 108, 109, 115, 129–130, 133, 138–139, 148, 150, 153, 155, 158, 162, 185, 198
Navin Field 88
Nehf, Art 71
Neil, Edward J. 163
New England League 81
New York Athletic Club 163
New York Daily News 118
New York Herald-Tribune 84
New York Highlanders 90
New York–New Jersey League 89
New York–Pennsylvania League 159
New York Sun 8, 126
New York World-Telegram 73
New York Yankees 27, 31, 50, 77, 90, 95, 107, 112, 121, 139, 158, 172, 175, 199
Newark Bears 51, 82
Newnan Cowetas 11
Niehof, Bert 72

Oakland Oaks 24, 25, 74
O'Brien, John (mayor) 123, 163, *164*
O'Day, Hank 98

Index

O'Doul, Lefty 20, 41, 48, 58, 63, 79, *117*, 118, 129, 133, 141, 144, 148–150, 152, 155–156, 159, 160, 163, 168–170, 174, 182–183, 184
Oeschger, Joe 97
O'Farrell, Bob 30, 41, 58, 86, 116, 154, 162, 170
Ogden, Warren "Curly" 56
Ogden Gunners 24
Oklahoma City Indians 54
Oklahoma State League 54
Olson, Ivan "Ivy" 2, 121
Ormsby, Emmet "Red" 179, 184, 187, 191, 193, 197
Ott, Caroline 39
Ott, Charles, Jr. 39
Ott, Charles, Sr. 38
Ott, Margaret 47
Ott, Marguerite 39
Ott, Mel 8, 15, 22, 23, 30, 31, 38–39, *40*, 41–49, 51, 57, 61, 64, 74, 109, *117*, 119, 122, 124, 128, 131, 146–149, 152–154, 156–157, 160–163, 167–168, 174–175, 179, 181–183, 186–188, 190, 194, 196–198
Ott, Mildred (Wattigny) 46

Pacific Coast League 24, 41, 116, 119
Padgett, Ernie 110
Padrón, Luis 90
Parmelee, Roy "Bud" "Tarzan" 58, 73, 78, *80*, 81–84, 86, 108, 116, 119, 122, 124, 125, 127–134, 136, 144, 146–147, 150–157, 159–163, 166–167, 170, 174, 188, 193
Parrott, Harold 159
Paschal, Ben 50
Peel, Homer 116, 122, 131, 168, 169, 183, 187
Pennock, Herb 31, 118
Pfirman, Charles "Cy" 179, 184, 187, 193, 196, 197
Phelps, Ray 18
Philadelphia Athletics 36, 82, 106, 113–114, 141
Philadelphia Phillies 7, 9, 14, 17, 19–20, 23, 30–32, 35–36, 43–44, 46, 48, 50, 55, 58–62, 69–70, 73–74, 76, 83–85, 88, 96, 98, 107, 109–110, 123–124, 130–132, 149, 150–151, 155, 158, 162, 165
Pickerling, Urbane 24
Pickford, Mary 138
Piedmont League 120, 131
Pittsburgh Crawfords 160
Pittsburgh Pirates 14, 16, 26–29, 41, 55–56, 59, 67–68, 70–72, 74, 76, 83, 90, 96–98, 102, 110, 112, 121, 127–129, 134, 146, 152–153, 158–160, 162, 165
Polo Grounds 1, 18–23, 29, 30, 36, 38, 40–41, 45–46, 48, 50, 53, 55–56, 58, 61–62, 64, 68–69, 71, 74, 76–77, 81–82, 84, 88, 98–100, 105, 109, 112, 122–123, 126, 130–131, 133, 148, 150, 152, 154, 158, 165–167, 173–176, 180, 185
Ponce de Leon Park 11
Porter, Cole 115
Portland Beavers 116
Pruett, Hubert "Hub" 69, 73

Rand, Sally 137
Rath, Morrie 98
Redland Field 26, 34–35, 63, 72, 77, 79, 93–94, 96–105, 128–129, 160
Reese, Andy 35
Rennie, Rud 84
Reynolds, Quentin 8
Rice, Grantland 8, 196
Rice, Sam 183, 192, 195
Rice, Thomas S. 95
Richards, Paul 116, 122, 149, 169
Rickey, Branch 110, 118, 171
Rigler, Cy 89, 92, 138
Ring, Jimmy 16, 68, 94, 98
Rixley, Eppa 14, 99, 101, 103–105, 134
Robinson, Wilbert 102, 105–107
Rochester Red Wings 85, 113–114
Roosevelt, Franklin D. 118, 185
Root, Charlie 62, 70, 105, 133
Roush, Edd 15, 29–30, 39, 41, 58, 68, 70, 98, 104
Rudolph, Dick 147
Ruether, Walter "Dutch" 94, 97, 98
Runyon, Damon 197
Ruppert, Jacob 22, 121
Russell, Jack 173, 176–177, 184, 190, 192, 194–198
Ruth, Babe 10, 16, 18, 20, 31–32, 50, 77, 95, 103, 107, 112, 121, 138, 140–143, 156, 175, *176*
Ryan, John "Blondy" 116–118, 122, 125–127, 129, 130, 131, 135–136, 145, 160, 162–163, 168, 170, 177, 180–182, 186, 190–193, 195–197

Sacramento Senators 74
St. Louis Cardinals 16, 20, 22–24, 28–31, 35–37, 45, 47, 53, 63–64, 71, 75–78, 83, 86, 93, 96, 99–100, 104–105, 109–110, 112–115, 126–128, 131, 134–136, 149–150, 152, 154–155, 165
St. Paul Saints 50
Salem Witches 81
Sallee, Harry "Slim" 94, 96–97
Salveson, Jack 130, 149, 158, 159, 169, 179
San Antonio Indians 51
San Francisco Mission Reds 86
San Francisco Seals 84
Santa Cruz Sentinel 83
Schacht, Al 185
Schaeffer, Willie 169
Schalk, Ray 72
Schneider, Pete 92
Schulte, Fred 177, 182, 183, 186, 190, 191, 194, 196
Schumacher, Andrew 84, 152
Schumacher, Hal 25, 60, 78, 84–86, *87*, 88, 108–109, 116, 119, 121–127, 131–136, 144, 146–147, 149–151, 154–155, 157, 160–161, 163, 166–167, 170, 174, 180–184, 193, 195, 198
Schumacher, Joseph 84–85
Schumacher, Margaret 84
Scott, Everett 152
Scranton Miners 159

Index

Seals Stadium 86
Seattle Indians 83, 120
Segris, George 109
Sewell, Luke 177, 180–181, 183, 186, 191, 192, 194–196
Shaute, Joe 122, 124
Shibe Park 9
Shores, Bill 121–122, 129, 157, 158–159, 161–162, 167, 169
Shotton, Burt 44, 123
Shreveport Gassers 11
Simmons, Al 18, 22, 138, 140–141
Sing Sing Prison 169
Sioux City Packers 109
Smith, Al 120, 122, 131, 169
Smith, Al (Villanova) 130
Snyder, Frank 121, 169
Soldier Field 138
Southern Association 11–12, 159
Southworth, Billy 28, 121
Speaker, Tris 62
Spencer, Glenn 50, 116, 122, 125–128, 133, 149, 157, 169
Spencer, Vern 98
The Sporting News 19, 68, 82, 126, 138, 163
Sportsman's Park 16, 20, 39, 47, 55, 63, 69, 110, 112, 146, 162
Stallings, George 91
Standard Oil Polarines 12
Starr, Ray 64, 116, 122–124, 128, 133, 170
Stein, Fred 43, 115
Stengel, Casey 26, 50, 81, 99, 101, 102
Stephenson, Jackson "Riggs" 35, 161
Stewart, Walter "Lefty" 158, 173, 175, **178**, 190
Stoneham, Charles A. 7–9, 16, 21, 69, 130, 133, 153, 163, 199
Stoneham, Horace C. 199
Street, Gabby 47, 136, 145–146
Stripp, Joe 125
Surdam, David George 114, 158
Suttles, George "Mule" 160
Swanton, Fred 83
Swift, Bill 159

Taylor, Danny 22, 77
Terrell Terrors 24
Terry, Bertha (Blackman) 11
Terry, Bill: appointed Giants manager 7–9, 23; as Giants player 12–36, 37, 45, 70–71, 77, 103, 105, 107, 109; as Giants player-manager 32, 48, 49, 51, 63, 80, 84, 88, 115–116, **117**, 118–163, **164**, 165–175, **176**, 177–188, **189**, 190–199; hitting .400 17–21; as minor league player 11–13; 1924 World Series 13–14; off-season jobs 12, 21; position change 13; salary disputes 9–10, 21–22, 30, 47, 58, 62, 78; signs with Giants 12; trade proposals 14–15
Terry, Elvena (Sneed) 11, 193
Terry, Kenn 16
Terry, Marjorie 14
Terry, William H. "Adonis" 13
Terry, William, Jr. 12, 193
Terry, William T. 11
Texas League 11, 51, 116, 130
Thomas, Tommy 182, 183, 193
Thompson, Lafayette "Fresco" 35
Thurston, Hollis "Sloppy" 23
Tierney, James 16, 44, 55, 61, 79, 83, 86, 169
Tierney, James "Cotton" 110
Tinning, Lyle "Bud" 145
Todd, Al 123
Toledo Mud Hens 12–13, 41, 81
Toronto Maple Leafs 91
Travis, William Barrett 26
Traynor, Harold "Pie" 62, 129, 159
Tri-State League 109
Troy, Joe 169
Tuero, Oscar 93
Tyson, Ty 39, 40

Uhle, George 124, 125, 129, 144, 148–149, 167, 171
Utah-Idaho League 24

Vance, Dazzy 16, 22, 105, 106
Vaughan, Joseph "Arky" 129, 159
Veeck, William L. 185
Vergez, Gabriel 24
Vergez, Helen Fay (Porterfield) 24, 25
Vergez, Jean Louis "Johnny" 24, **25**, 79, 88, 109, 122, 124, 126, 132, 134, 136, 144–147, 152–153, 156, 160, 167, 170, 174
Vergez, John Louis 25
Vergez, Theresa (Bordenave) 24
Vila, Joe 8, 20, 83
Vincent, David 95

Waco Cubs 51
Wagner, Honus 64, 175, **189**
Walker, Bill 36, 56, 58–59, 61–62, 64, 72, 75–76, 78, 109, 116, 155, 170
Walker, Frank 67
Walker, Jimmy (mayor) 69
Walsh, Christy **176**
Walsh, William J. 32
Waner, Lloyd "Little Poison" 57
Waner, Paul "Big Poison" 57, 71, 129, 142
Ward, Arch 137
Warneke, Lon 64, 83, 88, 129, 133, 139, 141–142, 145, 166
Washington Senators 13, 141, 158, 165, 172, 175–198
Waters, Ethel 152
Watson, John "Mule" 103
Weaver, Monte 188–189, 191–192
Weeghman Park 93
Weintraub, Phil 151, 159
Welsh, Jimmy 41
West, Mae 197
West, Sam 141
West Texas League 51
Western League 54

Wheeler, Floyd "Rip" 13
White, Guy Harris "Doc" 65
Whitehill, Earl 158, 173, 175, 184–187
Whitted, George "Possum" 13
Williams, Harry 38
Williams, Peter 13, 120
Williams, Ted 20
Wills, Helen 106
Wilson, Hack 13, 18–19, 41, 59
Wilson, Jimmie 140–141

Wingo, Ivey 96–97
Wright, Glenn 75
Wrigley Field 35, 70–71, 74, 86, 138, 152, 160–161, 165, 185
Wrigley Field (Los Angeles) 62, 74, 119

Yankee Stadium 31, 77, 107, 174
Youngs, Ross 14, 27, 39–40, 98, 102

Zachary, Tom 157

www.ingramcontent.com/pod-product-compliance
Ingram Content Group UK Ltd.
Pitfield, Milton Keynes, MK11 3LW, UK
UKHW041947140426
5217IPUK00014B/688